T0288227

Writing Baseball

THE SOUTHERN ILLINOIS UNIVERSITY PRESS SERIES

The Baltimore Orioles

In 1943, G. P. Putnam's Sons began a series of major league team histories with the publication of Frank Graham's history of the New York Yankees. From 1943 to 1954, Putnam published histories for fifteen of the sixteen major league teams. The Philadelphia Athletics ball club was the only one not included in the series, though Putnam did publish a biography of Connie Mack in 1945.

Thirteen of the fifteen team histories in the Putnam series were contributed by sportswriters who were eventually honored by the Hall of Fame with the J. G. Taylor Spink Award "for meritorious contributions to baseball writing." Three Spink recipients actually wrote eleven of the team histories for the series. The famed New York columnist Frank Graham, after launching the series with the Yankees history, added team histories for the Brooklyn Dodgers and the New York Giants. Chicago sports editor and journalist Warren Brown, once dubbed the Mencken of the sports page, wrote both the Chicago Cubs and the White Sox team histories. Legendary Fred Lieb, who, at the time of his death in 1980 at the age of ninety-two, held the lowest numbered membership card in the Baseball Writers Association, contributed six team histories to the Putnam series. He also wrote the Connie Mack biography for Putnam.

For our reprints of the Putnam series, we add a foreword for each team history by one of today's most renowned baseball writers. The bibliography committee of the Society for American Baseball Research has also provided an index for each team history. Other than these additions and a few minor alterations, we have preserved the original state of the books, including any possible historical inaccuracies.

The Putnam team histories have been described as the "Cadillacs" of the team history genre. With their colorful prose and their delightful narratives of baseball history as the game moved into its postwar golden age, the Putnam books have also become among the most prized collectibles for baseball historians.

Richard Peterson

The
Baltimore Orioles

*The History of a Colorful Team
in Baltimore and St. Louis*

Frederick G. Lieb

With a New Foreword by Bob Broeg on the St. Louis Browns

SOUTHERN ILLINOIS UNIVERSITY PRESS
Carbondale

First published 1955 by G. P. Putnam's Sons. Copyright © 1955 Frederick G. Lieb

Writing Baseball series edition published 2005 by Southern Illinois University Press

Series editor's note copyright © 2001 and foreword copyright © 2005 by the Board of Trustees, Southern Illinois University
Printed in the United States of America

08 07 06 05   4 3 2 1

Library of Congress Cataloging-in-Publication Data

Lieb, Frederick George, 1888–
The Baltimore Orioles : the history of a colorful team in Baltimore and
St. Louis / Frederick G. Lieb ; with a new foreword by Bob Broeg on the
St. Louis Browns.
    p. cm. — (Writing baseball)
Includes index.
1. Baltimore Orioles (Baseball team) I. Title. II. Series.
GV875.B2L5 2005
796.357'64'097526—dc22   2004024302
ISBN 0-8093-2619-1 (pbk. : alk. paper)

Reprinted from the original 1955 edition published by G. P. Putnam's Sons.

The paper used in this publication meets the minimum requirements of American National Standard for Information Sciences—Permanence of Paper for Printed Library Materials, ANSI Z39.48-1992. ♾

Writing Baseball Series Editor: Richard Peterson

Contents

Illustrations

Foreword

ONCE upon a time when sportswriters rhymed *spoon* with *moon*, poets in the press box also used meter to joke about clubs or teams: for instance, "Washington first in war, first in peace, and last in the American League." But when the St. Louis Browns finished far behind, noting the city's fine economy, they used both meter and rhyme: "First in booze, first in shoes, and last in the American League" (and by many a metric mile).

The poor old Brownies lost so many games that their losses prevailed 1,049 more times than did their victories. Fact is, they had the lousiest record in the major leagues, finishing last in their division for ten of their fifty-three seasons. Yet the Browns had charm, if not beauty, and left behind treasured moments. There were triumphs under Chris Von Der Ahe, but by the time his ball club fell from its lofty perch in 1886–88, good old Chris mounted a chute-to-chute amusement park ride in a distant outfield to add interest. It was forever thus; in its fifty-three American League seasons, the Brownies boasted a one-armed outfielder, a hired hypnotist, the mighty midget, and even the best ballplayer in the land, George Sisler. Sisler's record 257 base hits in 1920 extended into the new century, still comfortably intact despite his having played only 154 games a season.

And, above all, the Browns displayed the one and only Babe Ruth. Otherwise the Bambino would have come to town only to face the Cards in the 1926 and 1928 World Series, when he destroyed their dollhouse Sportsman's Park. The Babe hit three home runs in each series, one so far that they said it hit the center field north side of the YMCA across Grand Boulevard but actually on a couple bounces rather than on a fly.

Why Babe and me? Because I first saw him in 1928 when I was ten years old. My father, dear Pop, who had been a lightweight boxer even though by heavyweight standards, told my mother a story he shouldn't have told near a rabbit-eared little boy. Briefly, in the wee hours of the morning, as pop walked to work as a bread salesman for the Baby-label (later Wonder Bread) bakery on Vandeventer, he heard a booming voice coming from down the street. It was the Babe being carried to a cab by a couple of cuddling cuties from May Traynor's brothel, which served hot drinks, hot girls, and cold beer. When Pop arrived at home later that afternoon, the Babe had already hit two home runs with a classic hangover.

That did it. Pop had to take me to see my first American League game. I never forgot the sight of the Babe with a slight tummy and small, yellow outfield glove, and I never forgot what he did that day. Man and boy, I've seen probably more than six thousand ball games, but I never saw a play in which the defensive left fielder was the first ballplayer to leave the field. With the score tied in the fifteenth inning, the Browns' winning run was scored on a short-looping fly ball to left field. Even though playing shallow, the Babe charged, reached down, and felt nothing. He let the ball die of exhaustion on the grass in short left field, which he played in St. Louis, and he realized that the third base runner dancing toward home plate would score easily. So as the Brownies celebrated a seldom-achieved victory over the Yankees, the Babe kept on running, stepped on third base and pivoted, and was out of sight into the third base home dugout.

I covered the National League and the man whom the Cardinals stole from the Browns and who turned around the history of the two ball clubs, Branch Rickey. When Mr. Rickey encouraged Cardinals owner Sam Breadon to invest in the grow-your-own ball club, I was only two years old. From the time I was eight until I was twenty-eight, meaning when I first saw the Redbirds and first covered them for the *St. Louis Post-Dispatch* in the 1946 world championship, I saw nine pennants and six world championships in twenty-one seasons. The Browns? Aw, shucks. They won only one pennant despite colorful George "Rube" Waddell, whom Pop admired as a boy early in the last century and with whom he had too many beers at a St. Louis neighborhood bar at Chippewa and California Avenues.

Thanks to American League founder Ban Johnson, St. Louis had no American League plans, but he moved the Milwaukee franchise to the rival sudsville in 1902. On a tip from a fellow Cincinnatian, Robert Lee Hedges, Johnson used the penurious National League individual salary limit of only twenty-four hundred dollars to lure several key National Leaguers to briefly bolster the ball club. Later, he and Hedges acted together to acquire several players, including box office wonder Waddell.

In a rousing four-club finish, sadly finishing at fourth place, the Brownies drew 618,947, a whopping total for that date, 1908. Hedges, a showman who invented ladies' day, rewarded feminine fans with free passes to the first concrete and steel stadium west of the Mississippi. His improved Sportsman's Park seated eighteen thousand. The Browns' good fortunes, however, left a brown taste in the mouth until Phil Ball, a sports-minded, curmudgeonly coal company magnate, bought the club. He was finally rewarded for having the St. Louis Terriers Federal League club from 1914 to 1915. Meanwhile Hedges had lured a once sore-armed Brownie catcher away from his law practice, the famous and fabulous "B.R.," or Branch Rickey, who brought the best and most controversial player ever to grace the Brownie uniform, George Sisler.

The "Sizzler" was poetry in motion—a graceful pitcher, a superb fielding first baseman, a great base stealer, and a masterful hitter. Rickey had paid his own way through law school by coaching Michigan's ball club and was enamored of his greatest player, George Sisler. Sisler called him "Coach" before leveling it off to "Mr. Rickey." Fact is, even dear Jane never addressed hubby Branch anywhere in public except by "Mr. Rickey."

Thanks again to Rickey—that is, Mr. Rickey—the Brownies prevailed in a bitter fight with Pittsburgh of the National League over contract rights to Sisler. When Pittsburgh owner Barney Dreyfuss was overruled by an archaic three-man commission, he was extremely bitter and refused to talk to the National League representative, Augie Herrmann, the Cincinnati owner who ruled against him. This disaffection, plus other developments, led to Judge Landis becoming the baseball czar in 1920.

In 1922 Ball inherited new Sportsman's Park and drew a rousing 712,918. The Browns finished only one game behind the Yankees in 1922. A second-game loss to Babe Ruth and company in a pivotal three-game series lived on bitterly in the minds of many Brownie fans. After Sisler hit .407 in 1920 and .422 two years later, that season of the desperate near miss, Ball, Sisler, and the Brownie fans developed hard luck when eye trouble barred the first baseman in 1923. Yet Ball was optimistic enough to extend into the 1926 season a remarkable face-lift of Sportsman's Park from eighteen thousand to thirty-four thousand seats. Oddly enough, Ball by that time couldn't stand Rickey as player-manager or business manager, giving him short shrift in all personal contacts, yet he was contrary enough to prevent B.R. from trying to leave.

When Helene Hathaway Robison Britton sold the Cardinals she had inherited from her late uncle and father in 1916, lawyer James C. Jones prevailed on St. Louisans to muster up enough bucks to keep the Redbirds in town. Seven St. Louis sports editors recommended hiring Rickey, and B.R. prevailed in a court of law.

Three years later, in one of Ball's weak moments, Breadon, a converted New York area bank clerk, rising automobile dealership owner, and newly elected president of the Cardinals, sweet-talked Ball into letting him use newly expanded Sportsman's Park. The Cards immediately benefited from the extra seating. In their first pennant season, 1926, a young kid named Bob Broeg profited from the Rickey-approved Knot Hole Gang, by which kids from ten to sixteen were admitted free on weekdays. The combination of a winning National League ball club coupled with free attendance for kids many days and for ladies some days was the most diabolical double-play combination since Tinker to Evers to Chance.

Poor old sportsman Phil Ball had shot himself in the foot, but he was still a sportsman. One midweek day when empty green seats in a steady light rain yawned at Ball, the Brownies were to play the BoSox. Willis Johnson, a former newspaperman and Ball's traveling secretary, was aware that a rainout and an early-season Sunday makeup doubleheader with the rich "Gold" Sox would be a natural.

"But there's nobody here, boss," said Johnson.

"I'm here," said Ball, softly.

Only 283 other fans showed up that day, and the traveling secretary of the Red Sox, Phil York, moaned, "Cripes, we couldn't get a box of baseballs out of that." That was when major league baseballs cost $1.50.

Unfortunately, like many other club owners, the boss stuck his nose into the action too often. As a result, by 1925 Ball's entire outfield was playing for the surprising, pennant-winning Washington Senators—Leon "Goose" Goslin, Fred Schulte, and Henry "Heinie" Manush.

By the way, the Browns overall were an effective team on the attack from the time of George Stone, the batting champion of 1906, but the Browns had few A-1 pitchers, like the long-gone Rube Waddell and the four-time twenty-game winner Urban Shocker of the roaring twenties. As a result, in June of 1929, owner Ball dictated that a screen be erected from the right field foul line 310 feet to a point 354 feet in right center. The screen extended the height of the concrete barrier from a dozen to about thirty-two feet. As a result, Cardinal players also suffered offensively.

Years later, at a Hall of Fame ceremony, I recalled to Heinie Manush that he had hit the right field screen three times that day in June of 1929, denying him three home runs. He sneered and put me in my smart-aleck place, saying, "You don't think they would have pitched me the same way [inside rather than outside] if that screen hadn't been up?" Come to think of it, the left-handed-hitting Manush was pitched away often rather than inside.

When Ball died in 1933, his estate was stuck with the club and Sportsman's Park and was left in the hands of a trustee who wanted a way out. It wasn't until 1936 that Rickey, for whom Ball had no affection, persuaded the Browns to allow Bill DeWitt, Rickey's longtime assistant, and Don Barnes, a small-loan operator, to purchase the Browns and Sportsman's Park for $325,000.

En route, the Brownies used up a supply of good old ex-Redbird heroes such as Rogers Hornsby, Jim Bottomley, and Gabby Street as managers. Hornsby's team drew an astonishingly low eighty-one thousand for seventy-seven home games in 1935, finishing in seventh place. Yet the slugging Rajah left his American League calling card when he pinch-hit in midseason of 1933. His first time up in the American League—and I saw this—he came up as a pinch hitter, facing the great Yankees who chortled sarcastically, "This is the great *National* League hitter Mr. Hornsby." Raj then hit Lefty Gomez's first pitch onto the right center field roof for a game-winning home run. As he trundled toward home plate and the Yankees took a shortcut to the third base dugout, he snapped, "Yes, you buzzards, that was the great *National* League hitter, Mr. Hornsby."

In 1939, by the time Fred Haney managed the Browns into the eighth-place coal hole with 43 wins and 111 losses and only 109,000 suffering souls bearing witness, DeWitt had a bright idea that manifested itself two years later in a Chicago winter meeting at which he proposed expansion to the West Coast by train. Trouble was, that meeting date was December 8, 1941.

From that potential surrender of his hometown, St. Louis, DeWitt produced the Browns' finest hour. In 1942 he pushed them up to the first division since 1929 and then followed it with a capable coup despite the taking of established players from his club and many teams by the war. He had castoffs and cutthroats, overage players and 4Fs. It was quite a picture of rags to pennant riches.

Maybe it was foreordained from spring training in 1944 when the Brownies gathered at Cape Girardeau, Missouri, to help with a fund-raising pancake supper. Manager Luke Sewell was courtly as usual, and coaches Zack Taylor and Freddie "Boot" Hofmann were a peach of a pair, especially Old Bootnose.

When the natives were fed, with Hofmann entertaining one

and all, Sewell and Taylor urged Old Bootnose to entertain the ladies while they went to the kitchen to prepare stacks of flapjacks just for him—lavish butter, paper doily, heavy syrup, followed by more flapjacks, paper doilies, butter, and heavy syrup. In awe, after consuming the stacks of pancakes including the doilies, the Bootnose crowed, "These are the best pancakes I ever had."

The downtrodden Browns began their season with an American League record of nine consecutive victories, a margin by which they prevailed all season. Then with four dramatic dates left, the Brownies faced the champion New York Yankees, who were just two games behind and tied with Detroit. Incredibly, the Browns won four in a row over Joe McCarthy's shell of a contender.

By the time the Browns beat the memory of Babe Ruth three straight and were tied with Detroit in the final day, Pandora's box opened and so did the Brownies' box office. They drew for the Sunday crowd showdown an overflow 34,625 and turned away twenty thousand. When a flip of the coin would have assigned the Tigers a one-game playoff, the climax proved dramatically unnecessary. An hour beforehand, Detroit had been upset by Washington's Emil "Dutch" Leonard, four to one.

More interesting, Dutch was offered by phone in his hotel room an incentive to throw the game. He recommended what Rogers Hornsby said to Sam Breadon, ruining his managerial stay with the Redbirds with what my former mentor, J. Roy Stockton, delicately phrased "an utterly impossible disposition to the game."

So the Dutchman came through, and all that the Brownies had to do for their one and only pennant was to win. Discouragingly, Sig "Jack" Jackucki gave up two early runs. Happily, excused briefly from war duty, stubby little Detroit outfielder Chet Laabs did the impossible and Vernon "Junior" Stephens did the expected. They hit three home runs in a five-to-two victory. Laabs, who hit two homers with men on base, had previously distinguished himself in 1938 by striking out five times for the Tigers against Cleveland's Bob Feller, who pitched a record eighteen-strikeout game.

Dancing in the green after the one and only all–St. Louis World Series in 1944, the Browns outdrew the Cardinals 508,644 to

461,968. In the two-team Sportsman's Park with an underpaid and overworked ground crew, the series could have been embarrassing for the three-time National League champions, but it was barely and fairly won by the Cards four games to two. Actually if Sylvester "Blix" Donnelly hadn't made a remarkable extra-inning play fielding a bunt, the Browns might have gone up by three, after winning the first two games.

Now that all was well financially with the Browns, Barnes sold out to associate Dick Muckerman after a third-place finish in 1946. They had six hundred thousand dollars in the bank, but it lasted only as long as postwar inflation. The Browns finished eighth the next year under Herold "Muddy" Ruel and drew only 320,474.

The Browns were financially embarrassed again, but an adroit general manager, the senior DeWitt brother, Bill, kept the franchise alive and Muckerman out of bankruptcy by selling their outstanding players—pitchers Jack Kramer, Jack Sanford, Ellis Kinder, Sam Zoldak, and shortstop Stephens. While DeWitt saved Muckerman's investment, he completely lost a chance at improvement, because you just can't play Joe Cash at second base.

The Brownies tried to make every day like New Year's Eve. Charley DeWitt even tried to help by suggesting and obtaining a one-armed outfielder and a so-called helpful hypnotist. The one-armed outfielder, Peter "Wyshner" Gray of Nanticoke, Pennsylvania, was an independent soul, heavy on the independence, and a physical marvel. Left-handed, he naturally wore the glove only on his left hand and, with fingertip catches, he'd throw the ball in the air, throw away his glove, and magically catch the ball again to make the throw. At bat, the lean and strong-armed poor Pete was the victim of the high fast ball when high strikes were called. In postwar baseball, he batted only .218 in seventy-seven games. Charley DeWitt tried to persuade him to accept a reported twenty-five thousand dollars to inspire rehabbed servicemen, but he declined, retreating to his favorite bar stool at home in Nanticoke. Only years later did he lend his name to a successful TV movie.

As for the hypnotist, I traveled a lot with the Browns that 1950 spring in Hollywood, Florida, and was delighted with the gimmick and the get-up-and-go of the portly Dr. David Tracey. Dr. Tracey was full of beans and beer but charming, and when he bragged he had put Coach Hofmann under hypnosis, fellow coach Zack Taylor scoffed, "Hell, I can do that with a couple of beers." The good doctor was released shortly after the 1950 season.

Within two years the brothers DeWitt, Bill as general manager and Charley as traveling secretary, sold out to flamboyant Bill Veeck, who had produced baseball's first $2 million gate (actually $2.6 million) with Cleveland in 1948. Veeck was between jobs because he could amuse some and annoy many, including the powers-that-be. A self-styled bleacher bum, Veeck wore no man's collar, not even his own. He was the game's greatest iconoclast, a turncoat to other club owners even though he wore no coat on the coldest days. He was indeed the Barnum of baseball and deserves to be remembered for many things. But, indubitably, he will be remembered best for the day he played a midget.

Within several months of taking over ownership of the Browns, Veeck was shot down for assuming he could coax, cajole, or annoy little Fred Saigh out of town. Saigh, with Bob Hannegan along for the ride, had acquired the Cardinals from Sam Breadon at the end of the 1947 season.

Veeck was convinced that if Milwaukee would build a big-league ballpark, the major leagues would come: that is, probably the Cardinals and, if not them, then the Browns. So Veeck's conniving heart missed a beat when Saigh, in tax trouble, sold the Cardinals to Anheuser-Busch in 1953, assuring St. Louis a better ball club. I think Bill gave up when Gussie Busch kept him on a dog trot with his artificial leg—he'd lost it in the marines—while Busch inspected Veeck's Sportsman's Park. The Big Eagle growled, "I'd just as soon see *my* ball club play in Forest Park" (rather than run down Sportsman's Park).

Soon Veeck tried to move into Milwaukee, a half century since the Brewers went to St. Louis to become the Browns, but the Boston Braves franchise owner, Lou Perini, had other designs, with prior rights to minor league territory. His 1948 National League pennant winners had dropped to seventh place and 270,000 in attendance by 1952. When Veeck then tried to move to Baltimore, the Browns became lame ducks and attendance spiraled downward to a "who cares" 297,238 in 1953. Veeck's effort to move to Baltimore, where the Browns would eventually have an orange-covered great success, was thwarted because many stuffed American League shirts, notably the Yankees, refused to let him move. By the time the Browns traded uniforms with Baltimore in 1954, Veeck was out.

Over the years, Veeck loved doing the unexpected. He had the unique notion that everybody should enjoy a ball game, win or lose. Oh, now and then Veeck would announce a giveaway of an orchid to each woman who attended, but he preferred surprises, like a ballpark lottery for a spanking new automobile. Or he would have a crate of cackling chickens delivered to a "lucky" fan or have a hundred-pound cake of ice deposited at a customer's seat on a hot night. If he was going to provide a can of fruit or vegetables to all, he would have the wrappers removed. If you loved peaches, you might end up with a can of peas.

But back to the day Veeck played a midget. The occasion was the St. Louis fiftieth-anniversary celebration of the American League. Veeck caught up with me after the Sunday paper had gone to press. He wondered what I thought. I was indignant. I wouldn't spoil it, but I was glad he told me. At my suggestion, *Post-Dispatch* photographer Jack January knelt down on what would be the first-base batting circle. As a result, he got one of the most precious pictures in sports history. By the way, photographers, along with players' scattered gloves, were allowed on the field until 1954, and this was 1951. Veeck, by game time, had told only the necessary few about his pièce de résistance. The Cecil B. DeMille of the diamond had gone up to the rooftop of the grandstand to direct the between-game show, with one admonition. Earlier, he had seen the little guy swinging a toy bat and he said, "If you so much as swing at a pitch I'll shoot you—and I was an expert rifleman in the marines." From the rooftop, Veeck waved on an eight-piece roving band dressed in uniforms of the naughty nineties. Aerial bombs exploded, casting miniature flags onto the field. A hand balancer performed at first base, trampoline artists tumbled at second, and a juggler juggled at third. A four-piece band of Brownie players walked onto the middle of the field—Satchel Paige on the drums, Al Widmar with a bull fiddle, Ed Redys with an accordion, and Johnny Berardino maneuvering the maracas.

Suddenly a giant papier-mâché cake was wheeled onto the field. The band played "Happy Birthday," and up and out through the top layer popped a little guy with a fractional number on his back. Quickly he ran off into the home team's third-base dugout. The crowd laughed happily.

After the Browns lost the first game as usual, manager Zack Taylor visited little Eddie Gaedel, the midget holed up in the empty Cardinals clubhouse. He was wearing a miniature Browns uniform usually worn by the former owner's son, Billy DeWitt, then age six and now the president of the St. Louis Cardinals. Gaedel's confidence was wavering. It shook further when Taylor tied Gaedel's miniature baseball shoes and said, with a touch of truth as well as humor, "I think you'll be all right, kid. I don't think they'll throw *at* you."

The nervous little guy jumped to his feet, ready to grab his fashionable duds and head back to Chicago, but looming in the doorway was the Browns' traveling secretary.

"Listen, kid, if you don't do what you've been told and when, I'll pinch your head," said Bill Durney, feigning anger, "and you heard Bill Veeck. He'll be on the rooftop with a high-powered rifle."

After Detroit failed to score in the first inning, field announcer Bernie Ebert droned, "For the Browns, number ⅛, Eddie Gaedel, batting for Frank Saucier.

I held my breath. The crowd gasped as the cute little man came out, vigorously swinging miniature bats. Would Ed Hurley, the hot-tempered Boston Irishman umpiring behind the plate, spoil the show?

Arms folded firmly across his chest, staring straight ahead, Hurley merely wiggled the fingers of his right hand toward the third-base dugout: Taylor, get your butt out here to home plate. And out came Taylor, tugging characteristically at his knee-length baseball bloomers with one hand and waving a telegraph approval contract in the other. Glancing at the contract, Hurley didn't flinch. He shrugged, motioned Gaedel to the plate, and beckoned to the pitcher, Bob Cain, age twenty-six, the same age as the midget.

Catcher Bob Swift went out to Cain. The left-hander wondered whether he could throw the ball underhanded—as in softball? No, the catcher told him, Hurley wouldn't permit that. Maybe, Swift suggested, he could go back and lie down behind the plate? No, if this time the pitcher threw cold water, the umpire really would get into a huff. Swift nodded and retreated behind the plate.

Small became smaller as the midget crouched. Cain could not get the ball low enough, lobbing it, and Gaedel dutifully did not swing. At ball four, Eddie triumphantly threw aside his bat and dashed to first base. Quickly, Jim Delsing, who would replace Saucier in right field and is still identified as "the man who ran for the midget," came out to replace Gaedel. Little Eddie, relieved to be alive, grandly patted Delsing on the fanny and disappeared into the dugout.

I wondered aloud to the Browns PR chief, Robert O. Fishel, later assistant president of the American League, how long Gaedel would remain in the park? Minutes later, Fishel introduced us, and I picked up the little man and sat him on the press-box tabletop. His attire is still fresh in my mind's eye. He wore light tan slacks, a yellow sport shirt, neatly draped by a chocolate sport coat.

He swung his feet merrily from the tabletop and said excitedly, "I feel like Babe Ruth."

"You know, Eddie, you little S.O.B., you're now what I always wanted to be."

"What's that?" he asked me.

"An ex–big leaguer."

The significance of the day sank in. Gaedel straightened, puffed out his chest with obvious pride, and smiled as he leaped from the counter and stalked off with a cheery good-bye.

Three nights later in Cincinnati, little Eddie Gaedel was arrested for abusing a cop. Ten years later the little man with a big-league thirst was beaten up outside a bar. He crawled to the home he shared with his mother, climbed the stairs, and died in bed. The Cook County coroner's jury ruled a heart attack, not homicide. When the littlest man was buried, only one baseball man appeared. He was Bob Cain, who coincidentally was traded the following spring to the Browns, for whom he pitched a record double one-hitter victory over Cleveland's Bob Feller.

Years later I wondered why Cain made the effort to travel to the funeral from Cleveland, where he made a living as a goodwill ambassador for Kraft Foods. Cain smiled, "I guess I'm a religious sort, but mainly I believe the Gaedel story is probably the best story I tell."

Mine, too!

Bob Broeg

Preface

IT has been fifty-nine years since the Baltimore Orioles last won a major league championship, yet there is no more fabulous name in baseball than the Orioles. Ever since the author was a small lad, he has heard older boys and young men speak of the past glories of the old Orioles. They were swashbuckling knights of the baseball trails—men who could run, hit, field, and, primarily, think. For, there never was a ball club, in the nineteenth or twentieth century, that was sharper witted than Ned Hanlon's fabulous Orioles, National League champions of 1894-95-96 and runner-up to Boston in 1897-98.

It was the author's good fortune to know many of the famous old Orioles—John McGraw, Wilbert Robinson, Joe Kelley, Kid Gleason, Willie Keeler, Sadie McMahon, Roger Bresnahan, and Joe McGinnity. The author's experience as a baseball writer overlapped most of John McGraw's memorable career as Giant manager. McGraw never tired of boasting about the old Orioles. Frequently, in the course of a bridge game in his Pullman compartment, as the Giant entourage was being whisked over the farmlands of Indiana and Illinois, something would remind him of the old Orioles, and the other members of the foursome were in for another vivid story of the prowess of this great team. Though John McGraw won ten pennants in New York, the Orioles of the nineties always remained the team closest to his heart. He managed the Giants, but he was the vital factor—the spark plug—of the old Orioles.

In autumn evenings at the old big league hunting lodge at Dover Hall, Georgia, Wilbert Robinson, our affectionate Uncle Robbie, tired after a day on the deer trails and mellowed by the concoctions of southeastern Georgia, also would entertain by the hour as he related tales of the Orioles and how he had matched wits with such catchers as Connie Mack, King Kelly, and Doc Bushong, and base runners Billy Hamilton, John Ward, Topsy Hartsel, and Jimmy Sheckard.

The author also had the good fortune to start his New York baseball writing career under James R. "Jim" Price, a native Baltimorean and early Baltimore baseball writer. *New York Press* sports editor Price never tired of reminiscing about his favorite team. On long winter nights, after the first edition had been put to bed, Jim would sit on my desk, give a graphic illustration of how Willie Keeler stuck his bare hand and arm through the barbed wire fence in Washington to make a circus catch. He would tell of how the 135-pound Irish terrier, McGraw, frightened, intimidated, and dominated men twice his size; of how McGraw, Jennings, and Keeler rehearsed their plays at Baltimore's old Union Park at 8 A.M.; of the good nature of Wilbert Robinson; of the keen wit and aggressiveness of Hugh Jennings and Joe Kelley; and the one-punch fights won by Kid Gleason.

Yet, Baltimore's baseball history was by no means confined to the glorious National League Orioles; there was the early major American Association team, with Baltimore's beloved Frank Foreman and Matt Kilroy, the 505 strike-out pitcher; the dramatic but ill-fated Baltimore Americans of 1901 and 1902. And there was Jack Dunn's ever-interesting International League Orioles, the team of Babe Ruth, Ernie Shore, Fritzie Maisel, Lefty Grove, Jack Bentley, George Earnshaw, Max Bishop, Joe Boley, Alphonse Thomas, and Johnny Ogden, that set a record for organized baseball by snagging seven straight pennants from 1919 to 1926. Dunn's Orioles had many of the characteristics of the old National League champions, and it shouldn't take too long before the old Oriole spirit takes possession of the present American League team.

The author valued the friendship of Jack Dunn. He shared in his confidence when Dunn berated Judge Landis and others who sought to put back the draft on his crack International League team. As a young New York baseball writer, he scored Baltimore Fritzie Maisel's 74 stolen bases with the 1914 Yankees; he was on terms of intimacy with Babe Ruth from the time this Baltimore waif came to New York in 1920 until Babe's untimely death in 1948. In 1931, the author made a baseball mission to Japan with the old Oriole, Lefty Grove, the year of Bob's 31-4 record with the Athletics, and learned that after one cracked Lefty's protective armor of suspicion and gruffness, he found a warm, friendly, fun-loving character.

Baltimore's baseball history goes back to the pre-Civil War period, and Hall of Famer William "Candy" Cummings, alleged inventor of the curve ball, played for the Lord Baltimores of the National Association as early as 1873. Despite the fact that Baltimore was without big league ball for half a century, no city has a better Hall of Fame representation than the Maryland metropolis with ten men enshrined at Cooperstown, New York: Will Cummings, John McGraw, Wilbert Robinson, Willie Keeler, Hugh Jennings, Dan Brouthers, Roger Bresnahan, Joe McGinnity, Babe Ruth, and Robert Grove. And somehow the committee on old-timers seems to have overlooked two great Baltimore old-timers—Ned Hanlon, manager of the fabulous Orioles, and Joe Kelley, the team's slashing left fielder. Ned and Joe surely belong.

It has been fun to write about Baltimore, and the city's great players and great teams. And, though the writer was born in Philadelphia and spent most of his adult life as a New York baseball writer, he does not feel presumptuous in writing the Baltimore baseball story. He has known, and in a fashion understood, Baltimore for many years. As a kid in his teens, he used to go on annual camping trips to Betterton, Maryland, on upper Chesapeake Bay. Each year a group of us would make regular pilgrimages to Baltimore; several camping associates married Baltimore sweethearts, and we got to know the town almost as well as our native Philadelphia. The rows of Baltimore houses were so like those of Philadelphia that we always felt at home.

Yet, there always seemed to be something missing in the Baltimore picture. The city wasn't in the big leagues, and seemingly in size, affluence, and commercial importance, it belonged there, just as do New York, Chicago, Philadelphia, Boston, Detroit, and the others. An avid fan since he was "knee-high to a grasshopper," the author knew Baltimore had been in the early National and American Leagues. He knew the old stories that the city supposedly hadn't supported its early teams, but somehow the author never felt convinced. He looked upon earlier attempts to bring big league ball back to Baltimore with friendly interest, and when the Orioles finally were re-admitted to the American League in 1953, it looked like the restoration of something that always should have been.

Baltimore's enthusiastic welcome for the modern American League Orioles and the city's warm support for its 1954 team, which bobbed in and out of seventh and eighth places for most of the season, gives some indication of what the city may do if it ever gets a real contender. But it isn't in the Oriole tradition for a team wearing the bird insignia to remain down for long.

In writing this book the author wishes to thank many for their generous assistance: Paul Menton, C. M. "Abe" Gibbs, and J. Murray Wieman of the *Baltimore Sun;* Rodger Pippin and Hugh Trader of the *Baltimore News-Post;* Hugh Bradley of the *New York Journal-American,* a *Baltimore News* staff writer during the years of Jack Dunn's greatest teams; George Weiss, vice-president of the Yankees and general manager of the Orioles after Dunn's demise; Ernest J. Lanigan, historian of the Cooperstown Hall of Fame and Baseball Museum; Lowell Reidenbaugh of the *Sporting News;* Dick Armstrong and Jack Dunn III of the Oriole organization; Earl Hilligan, publicity director of the American League; and John H. Lancaster of Baltimore. For the St. Louis Brown part of the narrative, I am indebted to the friendly help of Sid Keener, director of the Baseball Hall of Fame and former sports editor of the *St. Louis Star-Times.*

In addition the author consulted such books as *My Thirty Years in Baseball* by John McGraw, published in 1923; *Touching Second,* by John Evers and Hugh Fullerton; *The Real McGraw,* by Mrs. John J. McGraw and Arthur Mann; *America's National Game,* by Albert G. Spalding; *Balldom* by George Moreland; and the files of Taylor Spink's *Sporting News,* the national baseball weekly.

FREDERICK G. LIEB

The Baltimore Orioles

CHAPTER I

Baltimore—An Early Baseball Convert

BALTIMORE, great Chesapeake port of Maryland, always was a sporting town. Since the early 1800's, the city was partial to beautiful women, fast horses, games of chance, and appetizing foods. But catering to a man's palate did not stop at the city's fine hotels and night spots. Whoever concocted a more savory dish than the devilled crabs sold by Negro pushcart venders on Baltimore's streets a half-century ago?

A town with such sporting inclinations was bound to be an early pushover for the American game of baseball. As in New York, Philadelphia, and Boston, the game flourished in Baltimore in the pre-Civil War period and was played by the Monument City's "better young gentlemen." For one thing, the workers along the docks, in the warehouses, and even in the counting houses, toiled such long hours that there was little opportunity for them to participate in afternoon play.

The young gentlemen, playing baseball in long, well-laundered trousers and often wearing little round straw hats, took tallyhos to their places of sport in what were then the northern and western suburbs, territory which has long since been included in the very heart of present-day Baltimore. Crass white workers of the oyster beds looked at the gentlemen ball players with more or less tolerant amusement, and termed the uniformed, well-groomed young fops "pretty boys." "Don't get

3

your pretty suits dirty," they would call out as a tallyho-load of singing young ball players went whisking by.

As for the Negro dockhands, draymen, and other manual workers, they looked up at the happy athletes as though they were Arabian Nights princes from another world. Little did they suspect that less than a century later, some of their own boys—the Jackie Robinsons, Larry Dobys, Roy Campanellas, and Minnie Minosos—would rub shoulders with white boys in this game of baseball and win recognition as top-rank performers.

Early Baltimore baseball folk showed a preference for what was then called the "New England Game," an outgrowth of Town Ball, liking it better than the "New York Game." In the New England version of baseball, it was possible to retire the runner by hitting him with a thrown ball. How the rough-and-ready Orioles who came later would have reveled in such a practice! However, by the 1850's, Baltimore, along with most baseball-minded cities, adopted the New York Game, which used the rules of the great baseball pioneer, Alexander Cartwright, whereby the batsman and other base runners were retired by throwing to the base ahead of the runner.

Baltimore figured in the first Southern trip made by a Northern team, the famed Excelsiors of Brooklyn, in the summer of 1860. An earlier Excelsior trip through up-state New York had been so successful that the Brooklyn baseball knights next decided to go South, and scheduled a series of games in Maryland, Delaware, and southeastern Pennsylvania. The first game of this expedition was scheduled for Baltimore on July 22, 1860, and an opposition team was selected carefully from the best players then in Baltimore. The slogan of the team was "We must make a good showing for Baltimore against the Excelsiors."

The featured Excelsior player was the Brooklyn pitcher, James P. Creighton, unquestionably the ace pitcher of his day. Creighton already had mastered a wrinkle of a curve, and legends had him unhittable. The Baltimore All-Stars, among

4

them Arthur Pue Gorman, later United States Senator from Maryland, had their expected difficulty in hitting Creighton, but no one felt disappointed or let down when the crack Brooklyn team won by a score of 51 to 6. "Getting six runs off Creighton was quite a feat; we were far from being disgraced," said Gorman. The visit of the Excelsiors was topped by a big banquet at Guy's Hotel, where everyone feasted on oysters, crab meat, Maryland duck, roast beef, and other viands, only to be washed down by the choicest wines from the Guy's Hotel cellar.

"I see in this visit of the Excelsiors a precedent for further visits of New York and Brooklyn teams to Baltimore, and perhaps in the foreseeable future, our teams, too, will travel to New York, Philadelphia, and other great cities," said Gorman at the dinner. Already the future Senator was quite an orator. Gorman really was being farsighted, but little did he suspect that within a quarter of a century, paid teams from New York, Philadelphia, Pittsburgh, even from far-away St. Louis, would make regular calls on the Chesapeake metropolis.

The gunfire at Fort Sumter, which started the American Civil War, did not slow down baseball in the Eastern seaboard cities. In the great fratricidal struggle, Maryland, the old Free State—all of it below the Mason and Dixon line—was a state of divided loyalties. The same was true of Baltimore, Maryland's metropolis and No. 1 seaport, but war prosperity was bound to follow in the wake of war. Beginning with Ellsworth's New York Zouaves, who had some difficulty getting through the city, a great stream of Union soldiers passed through Baltimore on their way to Washington and the Virginia battlefields. Millions of dollars' worth of war supplies was deposited on the city's docks. War plants, supplying the needs of the enlarged Army, Navy, and the bureaucrats of expanded Washington, sprang up all over town. The result was a war boom, and lots of loose money.

In fact, there was so much ready cash around Baltimore in 1863 that the Chesapeake city vied with Philadelphia for

5

the services of the first professional ball player, Alfred J. Reach, star player of the Brooklyn Eckfords. Al Reach, an English-born former cricketter, was the Babe Ruth of his day, baseball's greatest batsman of the 1860's. The tragic death of Jimmy Creighton in 1862 left Reach the young game's outstanding star. It may seem incongruous that in 1863, the summer of Gettysburg, two cities as near the famous battle-field as Baltimore and Philadelphia should enter into spirited bidding for the services of a hard-hitting second baseman. Arthur Gorman made two trips to New York and Brooklyn in his efforts to snag Reach for Baltimore. His rival was Col. Fitzgerald, owner of the Philadelphia *Item,* who was acting for the early Philadelphia Athletics.

Reach was a silversmith and jeweler, employed in New York when he wasn't playing ball. At one point, Gorman thought he landed the prize; he had topped Fitzgerald's best offer, only to lose Reach to the Philadelphia Athletics because of a matter of geography.

"I like your offer, Mr. Gorman; you have been most liberal," said Reach. "But, if I accept Col. Fitzgerald's offer, I can continue to live with my family in Brooklyn. After games, I will have time to catch the evening train for New York, and on days when no game is scheduled, I can continue at my business in New York."

Thus Al Reach played war prosperity both ways—through baseball and jewelry—and Baltimore missed engaging the first all-out professional.

Shortly after the war, in 1866, Baltimore became the capital of organized baseball—as it then existed. Arthur Pue Gorman, Maryland's early enthusiast, was elected president of the National Association of Base Ball Players. This honor was bestowed upon him at the tenth annual convention of the Association; 237 clubs were represented, 20 of them from Maryland.

In 1867, Gorman found himself faced with what promised to be the game's first scandal. As president of the National

Association, he accompanied the crack team from neighboring Washington, the Nationals, on the first Western trip made by an Eastern club. In fact, Baltimorean Gorman gave the expedition his personal aid and encouragement.

The Nationals were made up largely of government clerks, but they had as their star, captain-shortstop George Wright, one of the game's early immortals. After the Nationals scored 532 runs in six lopsided victories, an average of nearly 90 runs a game, they were rudely stopped in Chicago by a 17-year-old pitcher, Al Spalding, toiling for the Forest City club of Rockford, Illinois. In a stunning upset, Forest City defeated the Nationals, 29 to 23. The ugly head of betting already had raised its head in baseball, and nasty rumors circulated around Chicago that the Nationals had held back in order to influence betting on the next day's game, when the Washington team was to play the Chicago Excelsiors, a supposedly stronger team than Rockford. The *Chicago Tribune* printed the rumors, even going so far as to say, "The Nationals threw the game to Rockford for betting purposes." The *Tribune* hadn't realized what a pitcher Rockford had in Al Spalding.

Arthur Gorman's eyes blazed with anger, as he and Col. Frank Jones, president of the Nationals, invaded the editorial sanctum of the *Tribune,* demanding an apology and retraction. "That was a terrible thing to write about our fine young men," stormed Gorman. "Even their jobs in Washington are in jeopardy." Arthur Pue got some kind of an apology, and the Washingtons then defeated the Excelsiors, 49 to 4.

In 1869, when the Cincinnati Reds, the first all-salaried club, was sweeping the country without a defeat, they played a game in Baltimore against the Marylands, July 24, 1869, on grounds situated on Madison Avenue. This was supposed to be quite a contest, as the Marylands proudly termed themselves "Champions of the South." Even though the Marylands lost, 47 to 7, everyone was happy, and the Cincinnati visit was one of the high spots in early Baltimore baseball. Players on the

Marylands that day were Hooper, Cook, Whitington, Mingher, Lennon, Wilson, Goldsmith, Kearl, and Armstrong.

Baltimore was not a charter member of the first professional league, the National Association of Professional Base Ball Players, when it took the field in 1871, but the Chesapeake city entered a team, the Lord Baltimores, in the Association's second season. The Lord Baltimores did all right, too, winding up third with 35 victories, 19 defeats, and a percentage of .648. They were topped only by the Red Stockings of Boston and the Athletics of Philadelphia. As was the custom in that day, the Lord Baltimores also played many exhibition games.

Albert Henderson was the manager, and he assembled quite a ball club, headed by Robert T. "Bobby" Mathews, a Baltimore product, who had a great season, winning 26 games and losing 16. When not busy on the mound, Bobby filled in at third base and in the outfield. Though one of Baltimore's most famous home-grown ball players, he remained with the Lord Baltimores only one season, moving on to the Mutuals of New York in 1873. He won 42 games for the latter club in 1874, and pitched big league ball until 1887, when he wound up with the Philadelphia Athletics.

First baseman Everett and center fielder George Hall came to that first Baltimore major league club from the Washington Olympics. Second baseman Lip Pike, left fielder Tom York, and catcher-infielder Bill Craver, were acquisitions from the Troy, New York, club. Pike was an early slugger, and York later played for many years in the National League. Tom, a Brooklynite, was custodian of the New York press box as late as the middle 1920's.

William Charles "Cherokee" Fisher, who came from Rockford, Illinois, was the right fielder when not helping Mathews with the pitching or playing second and third base. Shortstop John Radcliffe moved to Baltimore from the Philadelphia Athletics and third baseman Dick Higham transferred from the New York Mutuals. George Hall and Bill Craver were destined to leave the game in disgrace six years later, when in

1877 they were members of the infamous Louisville National League quartet that was drummed out of baseball for throwing games.

The 1873 record of the Lord Baltimores was almost a duplicate of the year before. They again finished third behind Boston and Philadelphia. This time they won 34 games and lost 22 for a .607 percentage. It was to be Baltimore's last first-division team in many a year. A new pitching acquisition was Baltimore's first Hall of Fame player, William Arthur "Candy" Cummings, credited by baseball historians as being the inventor of the curve ball. At least, that's the legend on his plaque at Cooperstown. "Candy" came from the Mutuals of New York, and did most of Baltimore's 1873 pitching, winning 31 of the team's 34 league victories and losing 14. Cummings also took an occasional whirl at third base. When "Candy" wasn't on the mound, Manager Henderson employed Asa Brainard, a part-time outfielder, as his pitcher. Asa had moved over from the Washington Olympics. Brainard was one of the game's outstanding post-Civil War pitchers and early eligible for a House of David nine. Asa, fully bearded, was the Cincinnati hurler in 1869 when the unbeaten Red Stockings swamped the Marylands.

The following season, 1874, was a dark one for Baltimore baseball. Cummings moved on to the Philadelphia Athletics, and the once unbeaten Brainard had a sad record of 5 victories and 23 defeats. He also played second base and the outfield. Henderson had made a number of changes in his line-ups of the first two years, and there is no doubt that his players let him down. After the club won nine straight games, it began to lose game after game, some under most unsavory conditions. It was pretty well established that some players actually threw games, and the proud Lord Baltimores dropped to the cellar as the city's first tail-ender. The fans facetiously referred to them as the Mosquitoes, when not calling them worse names. Fights and brawls at the grounds were frequent, as fans fought with players, gamblers, and among themselves.

9

It was the unhappiest period of professional baseball's splendid history. Gone were the days of the 1850's, when scions of Baltimore's best families went to ball games in their tallyhos, and celebrated with feasts and oratory on the eves of games. Arthur Gorman retained his interest in Baltimore baseball, but most of the nicer people had been crowded out. It had become a game for rowdies, roughnecks, and tin horn gamblers. Conditions were equally bad in all National Association cities. Writing of this period in his *America's National Game*, Albert G. Spalding, one of the game's great pioneers and the young chap who stopped the Washington Nationals in 1867, said: "The occasional throwing of games was practiced by some, and no punishment meted out to the offenders. . . . Liquor selling, either on the grounds or in close proximity thereto, was so general as to make scenes of drunkenness and riot of every day occurrence, not only among the spectators, but now and then in the ranks of the players themselves. Many games had fist fights, and almost every team had its lushers."

Writing of this same National Association period, Henry "Father" Chadwick, the game's first historian, wrote that the outcome of the games depended to a large degree on the pool-selling, with pools as high as $20,000 for a game. Wrote Henry: "Hence the temptation to fraudulent arrangements for losing matches for betting purposes became so great as to be almost unresistable."

The 1874 tailender, and conditions which prevailed to make the Lord Baltimores the butt of the league, left an ugly taste in the mouths of Baltimore fans. They had no further stomach for National Association ball. The Lord Baltimores resigned from the Association, and though Baltimore fielded strong independent professional teams, the Monument City was without big league representation for the next eight years.

10

CHAPTER II

Orioles Join Beer
and Whiskey League

THE NATIONAL ASSOCIATION, under the leadership of William A. Hulbert and Al Spalding, had a complete reorganization in 1876, and emerged as the present National League. It went all the way from sin to virtue, barred liquor selling, clamped down on the early crooks, and put a stipulation in its constitution that any club playing a Sunday game automatically would forfeit its franchise.

Using iron discipline, the National League threw the Philadelphia Athletics and New York Mutuals out of the league in its first season, for failure to make their last Western trips. Louisville, another charter city, became fallow territory after the 1877 scandals, in which four players, including the former Lord Baltimore men, Craver and Hall, were expelled. Another charter city, St. Louis, called it quits after two seasons, while Cincinnati was kicked out after the 1880 season when the club insisted on selling beer and leasing out its park for Sunday amusements.

It left a lot of idle territory, which was capable of supporting less Puritanic big league ball. In 1881, some of the Eastern clubs, the Athletics of Philadelphia, the Metropolitans of New York, and the Quicksteps of Brooklyn, had a loose league known as the Eastern Championship Association. These clubs played numerous extra games with the clubs in Baltimore, Pittsburgh, Louisville, and Cincinnati.

Owners of these powerful independent teams then con-

11

ceived the idea of a second major league, the American Association, which was to operate as a rival to the National League, by then in its sixth season. Some credit O. P. Caylor, a cantankerous Cincinnati sports writer with a caustic pen, with conceiving the idea of the new league. Pittsburgh says the league was built around a conversation between H. D. "Denny" McKnight, president of the Pittsburgh Alleghenies, and Justus Thorner, president of Cincinnati's rebellious National League club of 1880.

"Why don't we have a league of our own?" McKnight asked of Thorner. "We have the population, the baseball crowds and the interest. Why, we draw better at our independent games than does the National League for its league contests."

Out of this conversation came organization meetings in Cincinnati and Philadelphia in the off-season of 1881-82, when the American Association was formed with Eastern clubs of Baltimore, Philadelphia, and Pittsburgh and Western clubs of Cincinnati, Louisville, and St. Louis. The Metropolitans of New York and Columbus, Ohio, were added after the 1882 season to increase the loop to the customary eight clubs. The bewhiskered Pittsburgher, Denny McKnight, was elected league president even though he continued to head the club in Allegheny.

The league was as different from the white ribbon National League as day is from night. In fact, it is doubtful if the former Colorado Senator, Edwin Johnson, would have approved Denny McKnight's club owners. In 1953, Senator Johnson tried to push Senate action to divorce Gussie Busch, president of the Anheuser Busch breweries, from the St. Louis Cardinals.

In Baltimore, the new baseball sponsor was Harry Von Der Horst who, in connection with his brother, Herman, owned the Von Der Horst Brewing Company of Baltimore. In St. Louis, Al Spink, who launched *Sporting News* in 1886 and uncle of Taylor Spink, the present publisher, enlisted a second Von Der to the Association's line-up of club owners, the fabulous Chris Von Der Ahe. Chris owned a popular St. Louis saloon and grocery store. In Louisville, the Bernheim distilleries, with which the late Barney Dreyfuss got his start in baseball, backed the Louisville Eclipses, and there was a smell of malt and hard liquor through the other clubs of the circuit.

The new American Association was situated in cities with substantial German population; it featured Sunday ball and beer. In the bailiwicks of the two Von Ders, Horst and Ahe, the ball parks actually were glorified beer gardens. And both of these colorful Germans would have been the last to deny that they entered baseball for no other reason than to push their beer sales.

In reply to a question of how business was, Harry Von Der Horst replied, "Vell, ve don't vin many baseball games, but ve sell lots of beer."

The new league also announced its appeal to the average fan; it stressed 25 cent ball, in contrast to the National League's alleged "aristocratic 50 cent ball." "Put baseball within the reach of everyone" was one of the Association's slogans.

Is it any wonder that the National League, in derision and with some feeling of superiority, referred to the new circuit as the "Beer and Whiskey League"? It fought the Association for a year, but eventually the two leagues entered an agreement and for nearly a decade the white ribbon National and the Beer and Whiskey League operated peacefully and their champions met in seven World Series.

In Baltimore, Harry Von Der Horst leased a large lot at Huntingdon Avenue, now 25th Street, near Greenmount Avenue. There Harry built Union Park, a rather good-sized ballyard for that era. He had a double-decked grandstand, with small bleachers and ample space for picnic tables and stabling horses. He could seat around 6,000. You came out to Union Park in your own carriage or used the old Greenmount horse car line. While Union Park was built for baseball, it was

13

essentially an amusement park. One could take along the entire family; grown-ups paid two bits, kids were free. After the ball game, you could dine, dance, and listen to the band concert. Harry got his returns largely from his restaurant and the big thirsts of his beer-drinking customers.

A chap with a face full of whiskers, Von Der Horst was a gemütlich but smart beer merchant. He was a much more intelligent man than the egocentric St. Louis exhibitionist, Von Der Ahe. Later, as baseball developed, Von Der Horst was to go into baseball more seriously. Oddly enough, in their Association years, Von Der Ahe felt sorry for Von Der Horst, saying, "Harry runs a ball team like a dumkopf. He iss a dumkopf! He should run a ball club more like me." Yet, later, when both were in the National League, Chris, worn out by excesses and dissipation, was the dumkopf, and Harry Von Der Horst was the smartie.

Henry C. Myers, a Philadelphian, was Von Der Horst's first manager; Henry came from the Providence National League club and helped out at shortstop and in pitching. Myers' team never got off the ground; it didn't win a game until June and finished a poor last with 19 victories against 54 defeats for a lowly .260. Even so, that was better than manager Myers' .223 batting average, compiled in 69 games. Baltimore used 22 players in 1882, including Tom Evers, uncle of the Chicago Cub Hall of Fame immortal, Johnny Evers.

The following winter Von der Horst sold a minority interest in the Baltimore club to William S. Barnie, a New Yorker, and for the next eight years Barnie was to be Mr. Baltimore Baseball. Billy, a bill-poster when not otherwise busy in baseball, took over the management and in 1883 helped out behind the bat. Barnie had lots of experience in early baseball; he had caught in the old National Association for Hartford, the Westerns of Keokuk, and the Mutuals of New York. Billy then became interested in the Brooklyn Atlantics, and in 1882 he had sought the Eastern franchise

14

for Brooklyn which subsequently was awarded to Baltimore. He brought some of his former Atlantic players with him and while the club again ran last, it managed to win 28 games while losing 68. And, more important to Harry Von Der Horst, the 1883 club showed a profit of $30,000. After all, it wasn't imperative for Harry's trade to look at the ball game. One always could talk politics over one's beer stein, or dance to the dreamy strains of the Vienna Waltz.

Yet the 1883 season was more historic than Harry Von Der Horst's $30,000 profit. It was the year the Baltimore club first became known as the Orioles, a name which was to be one of the historic team nicknames in baseball. Who first named them the Orioles is not known, though some credit bill-poster Barnie with thinking it up. Ornithologists long before had termed the beautiful black and yellow, and black and orange Chesapeake bird, the Baltimore oriole (*Icterus galbula*) as different from the Old World oriole species. And, with the exception of one year, 1900, there have been baseball Baltimore Orioles ever since, whether they were in the American Association, National League, American League, Eastern League, International League, and again in 1954 in the American.

In 1884, Baltimore had two clubs claiming major league status for the only time in its history. A third major league, the Union Association, took the field. It had an Abe Lincoln platform; it intended to free baseball players from their slavery by doing away with the reserve rule. Despite its high ideals, and its theory that any player could sell his services to the highest bidder, the Union Association blew up after one unhappy season. The Baltimore Unions had a satisfactory season in the club standing, finishing third under the leadership of Charles Levis and Bill Henderson.

The Unions didn't take the play away from Union Park, where Von Der Horst and Barnie had their most successful season up to that time. The American Association had expanded to twelve clubs, in which the Orioles' vastly improved percentage of .594 got them no better than sixth. But, it was a near-perfect race; the Orioles had a pennant chance up to September, eventually finishing 12 games out of first and five out of second. A race as close as that today would make a mint of money for American or National League clubs fortunate enough to wind up in such a blanket finish. The first six clubs came over the finish line as follows: Metropolitans (New York) 75-21, .701; Columbus, 69-39, .639; Eclipse (Louisville) 68-40, .630; St. Louis, 67-40, .626; Cincinnati, 68-41, .624; Baltimore, 63-43, .594.

The Orioles again made a tidy profit, and Von Der Horst was well pleased. "Mr. Barnie, maybe ve should have finished higher, but all in all I think you did very vell," he told his manager. "Von of these days I hope you finish ahead of that rude St. Louis Dutchman, Von Der Ahe. I've got a lot of confidence in you, and I'm sure before long ve'll vin the pennant."

Von Der Horst wasn't so pleased in 1885 and 1886, when the Orioles flopped back to the cellar, while Chris Von Der Ahe's Browns soared to the top, to win the first two of their string of four successive pennants. But Barnie introduced a pitcher in 1885 who made Baltimore fans forget all about their tailender. The pitcher was Matthew Aloysius "Matches" Kilroy, a left-hander from Philadelphia, who struck out the imposing total of 505 enemy batsmen that season. The pitching distance then still was 50 feet, but Matt's 505 remains the major league record today. It is a record more endurable than Babe Ruth's 60 home runs a season; it is doubtful if it ever will be bettered, as Bobbie Feller, with 348 strikeouts in 1946, has the best seasonal record for this century.

Coming from the Augusta, Georgia, Southern League club, where Kilroy enjoyed a sensational season, Matt won 29 games and lost 34 for Barnie's 1885 tailender. Baseball historian Ernie Lanigan of the Cooperstown Hall of Fame also reports "Kilroy was the greatest pitcher of all times for picking runners off first base." That amused Baltimore fans, but they shouted with glee when Matt rocked backed and then shot over third strikes on such famed American Association batsmen as Dave Orr, Tip O'Neill, Arlie Latham, and Charley Comiskey.

"Make 'em like it, Matt; make 'em like it!" "One, two, three, and yu'r out," yelled the pleased crowds in the Union Park stands. The batters never got to like it, but Matt liked his role as Strike Out King, and so did his Baltimore loyal legion of well-wishers.

Matt Kilroy later had a saloon in Philadelphia near the old Athletic field, Columbia Park. He wore a big black moustache, and used to tend bar himself. When the author was a kid, he and some of his friends would push in the swinging doors of Kilroy's saloon to get a peep at the man who had struck out 505 batsmen one season. We knew Rube Waddell, then the Athletic southpaw star, had struck out over 300. So we looked at Kilroy, who had beaten Rube's best mark by nearly 200, as a sort of superman.

Matches Kilroy really made his presence felt in 1887, when he won 46 games and lost 20. That's the most victories turned in by a left-handed pitcher in one season in the annals of big league baseball. Matt couldn't match his 505 strike-outs of the year before, but his superb pitching had all of Baltimore talking.

The Orioles climbed from the cellar to a respectable third with 77 victories, 58 defeats and a percentage of .570. That was well behind the .704 of Von Der Ahe's pennant-winning Browns, but Von Der Horst again was pleased; Billy Barnie was pleased, and the Baltimore fans were pleased. This unquestionably was the best ball club Baltimore had had up to that time, and one again heard talk of pennants in Von Der Horst's baseball beer garden. Barnie had spent a busy winter, and came up with some fine replacements, the most important being outfielder Mike Griffin from Utica, N. Y., and first baseman Tom Tucker and pitcher John "Phenomenal" Smith from the Newark club. Tucker, who later became a crack

National League first baseman in Boston, hit .315, while Phenomenal Smith was quite a left-handed side-kick for Matt Kilroy. His 1887 record was 29 victories and as many defeats. It meant that Matt and Phenomenal John won 75 of the club's 77 victories. The pair worked 135 games, 73 for Matches and 62 for Phenomenal. The other two Baltimore victories were credited to Louie Shreve.

Billy Greenwood, a new second baseman Barnie brought along from Philadelphia, also helped. It was the year they scored bases on balls as hits and Oyster Tom Burns, who played shortstop and third base, hit a mighty .401. He first had come to the Orioles as a pitcher and extra infielder in 1885. Griffin, the Utica acquisition, hit .386, in the year of the inflated batting averages. The other outfielders were Joe Sommer, .355, and Blondy Bill Purcell, .305; Purcell had come from the Boston Nationals the year before. Jumbo Jim Davis, a New Yorker, who shifted between shortstop and third with Oyster Tom Burns, hit .345. If you didn't hit .300 that year, you were a nobody.

However, whenever Baltimore had a team which seemingly was going somewhere, some one always was pulling the rug from under it. In 1888, Kilroy was neither as hot as Matches nor Matchless, and John Smith was anything but Phenomenal. Matt won 16 games and lost 21, and Smith won 15 and lost 20. From working in 135 games in 1887, the two lefties appeared in only 78 the following summer. Late in the season, Barnie sold old Phenomenal to the Philadelphia Athletics. Smith never did much of note after that until 1900, when, as manager of the Norfolk club, he taught Christy Mathewson, a young fast-throwing collegian, all the pitching tricks he knew and helped develop Matty for the big league market.

With bases on balls again merely exempting a batsman from a time at bat, Oriole averages tumbled sharply in 1888. Oyster Bill Burns came down from .401 to .308 and Mike Griffin tumbled from .368 to .261. Bill Purcell was released to the Athletics, Bill Burns to Brooklyn, and other players were fined and suspended for drinking and general hell-raising. The Oriole fans, disappointed with the fadeout back into the second division, began to belabor the players much in the way the earlier National Association rooters pilloried the Lord Baltimores in their tailend year of 1874. With the help of some hastily recruited semi-pro pitchers, Barnie managed to finish fifth with a 57-80, .416 showing.

Kilroy snapped back in 1889, not to what he was in 1886 and 1887, but he participated in 65 games, winning 28 and losing 25. In his outstanding four-year Oriole sojourn—three with second division clubs—he won 119 games and lost an even 100.

Rendering first-rate assistance to Kilroy in 1889 was Baltimore's most beloved baseball figure, Francis Isaiah Foreman. Because of his antics on the field and the way he could screw up his face, he was known as "Monkey" Foreman. Foreman is one of the Monument City's most famous baseball names. He was born in Baltimore during the crucial days of the Civil War, May 1, 1863. The oldest of the old Orioles, he was within a fortnight of his ninety-first birthday when the new Orioles celebrated their official return to the majors on April 15, 1954. Foreman served briefly with the Birds as a pitcher-outfielder in 1885; in 1889, Monkey, who boasted he never had a sore arm, won 25 games and lost 21.

With Lefty Matches Kilroy and Monkey Foreman doing almost all of Barnie's pitching, Billie's 1889 club finished 103 points higher than the 1888 club, but it again added up to fifth place in an eight-club league. The Orioles wound up on the right side of the .500 mark—70 victories, 65 defeats, .519 percentage—but they still trailed Brooklyn, the St. Louis Browns, the Athletics, and the Cincinnati Reds.

The season of 1890 was the toughest that big league ball had to face up to during that time. Seventy-five percent of the National League's top players and a good part of the American Association's better talent jumped to a new league, the Players

19

League, supported by an early player union, the Baseball Brotherhood. Ball players were to be cut in on the profits. It was a wild, unsettled time in baseball. Matt Kilroy jumped to the Brotherhood team in Boston; first baseman Tom Tucker also bobbed up in the Hub, but landed with the Boston Nationals. Foreman also jumped, but eventually bounced up with Cincinnati. At the same time Von Der Horst was in a rebellious mood against his fellow American Association club owners, claiming that Baltimore constantly was being pushed around by Western owners, particularly Chris Von Der Ahe of St. Louis and Denny McKnight and his Allegheny associates before Pittsburgh shifted to the National League.

Unwilling to pay the big salaries of the Brotherhood War and irked by Von Der Ahe's dictatorial tactics, Von Der Horst resigned from the American Association and placed the Orioles in a weaker all-Eastern league, the Atlantic Association. "They'll come out to Union Park to drink beer, dance and have their picnics just the same," said Harry. The Orioles found the pickings rather easy in this new company and had a record of 77 victories and 24 defeats, when on August 27, Von Der Horst suddenly reversed himself and climbed back on the American Association band wagon. He took over the vacated franchise of the last-place Brooklyns. Brooklyn started that season with clubs in three major leagues, the National, Players, and American Association. As the N. L. Dodgers won their first pennant, and John Ward's Players League Brooklyns ran second, there were only crumbs for the Brooklyn A. A. team. But there already were portents that the Brotherhood-sponsored league would blow up after the 1890 season.

In what was left of the 1890 American Association season, the Orioles won 15 games and lost 19. That 1890 Brotherhood year would have little significance for present-day Baltimore fans, but for the players brought to the Monument City in that late season shift. Left fielder George Van Haltern jumped from the Brooklyn Players League club, and to strengthen the Orioles the Athletics passed along catcher Wilbert Robinson, pitcher "Sadie" McMahon, and outfielder Curt Welch. George "Rip" Van Haltern, a handsome St. Louisan with a big black cavalryman's moustache, was one of the most picturesque figures then in baseball. A big strong chap, he played big league ball for 17 years. Originally a pitcher with Cap Anson's Chicago White Stockings, he was converted into an outfielder because of his hitting. Rip was a dominant man on a ball club, and Von Der Horst immediately named big George his team captain.

Curt Welch had won fame as the fast-running center fielder and lead-off man for Von Der Ahe's and Comiskey's St. Louis Browns champions and in the 1886 Browns-Chicago World Series, his name had become a household word as the result of Curt stealing home for the winning run under the nose of the immortal King Kelly, Chicago's great catcher, in the tenth inning of the crucial sixth game. As it was a winners-take-all World Series, the play became known nationally as "Curt Welch's $15,000 slide."

However, the athlete who was to win the heart of Baltimore was big, gruff, genial and kindly Wilbert Robinson, heavyweight catcher. Though he later was to become captain and a star member of baseball's rowdiest club, Robinson was one of the game's most lovable characters until his untimely death in 1934 in an Atlanta hotel bathtub, while serving as president of the Atlanta Crackers.

The old chestnut, "Nobody loves a fat man," certainly never applied to Wilbert Robinson. In a period of feuds, animosities, and general bitterness in baseball, Robbie had no enemies. People not only loved him, but he scattered good will and affection wherever he went. Years later, at a spring training party at Venice, Florida, Uncle Robbie, then manager of the Brooklyn Dodgers, already was seated when Connie Mack, manager of the Athletics, entered the banquet room. Throwing both arms around Mack's neck, Robbie kissed him affectionately on both cheeks, saying, "You lovable old son-of-a-sea

21

cook." Probably no other man in baseball, certainly no other ex-fighting Oriole, would have kissed another baseball man in public, but it was Robbie's inherent affection and good nature bubbling forth.

Robbie was no saint; he loved good living and in his later years he was a good two-fisted drinker. Some of his crudities and quaint expressions still are repeated today; many are Robinsonian gems. During the tough days in the South Pacific in World War II, the author recalls a correspondent writing of the language of the men in the jungle foxholes, "profanity that was not profane; vulgarity that was not vulgar." If it had been written about Wilbert Robinson, no one could have expressed it better.

He became one of baseball's best catchers, was an able general behind the plate, and an always dangerous batsman. In Robinson's Philadelphia and early Baltimore days, his nicknames were Billy and Yank, the latter a name that never particularly appealed to him. He came from Hudson, Mass., and an earlier infielder on the Browns had been nicknamed "Yank" Robinson. "Hell, why should they call me after that guy?" protested Robbie. "Yank Robinson once made six errors in one game."

Real intimates used to call him "Billy Fish," and it always got a rise out of him. As a youngster in Hudson, he worked for a butcher and fish dealer. One phase of his job was to hawk his boss's fish about town. One day an irate housewife called after him, "Come back here, Billy Fish, and take away your fish. They smell!" The Orioles got hold of that bit of gossip, and never let Robbie live it down.

Though Robbie already was quite portly when he came to Baltimore in 1890, in his first year with the Athletics as a catcher-outfielder in 1887, he was surprisingly fast and stole 42 bases in 87 games. During his sojourn with the Athletics, he married an Irish girl who was on a visit to a girl friend in Philadelphia. The colleen never returned to Ireland; she

22

married the good-natured, fun-loving, moustachioed Athletic catcher, later settled with Robbie in Baltimore, gave him four fine children, and during Robinson's later years as Brooklyn manager she became the beloved "Ma" Robinson and "Aunt Mary" of the Dodgers to millions of fans.

Baltimore had a reasonably strong club in 1891, the last season of the Beer and Whiskey circuit. The Orioles finished fourth, winning 71 games and losing 64. Yet, Von Der Horst didn't think Barnie had gotten enough out of such players as Van Haltern, Welch, Robinson, Perry Werden, Pete Gilbert, Pitcher "Egyptian" Healy, and others, and late in the season he fired his bill-poster, and turned the club over to the left fielder-captain, George Van Haltern. Billie subsequently caught on with the Washington and Louisville National League clubs. With the latter team, he was to do the Orioles a singularly good turn a few years later.

The 1891 season was one of strife and ill will between the National League and the rival American Association. After the Players League blew up after one season, contract and reserve jumpers were ordered returned to the National or American Association clubs to which they belonged before the Brotherhood War. However, through some oversight, the Philadelphia Athletics neglected to place the names of two of their returned jumpers, second baseman Louie Bierbauer and Harry Stovey, one of the game's greatest base-runners, on their 1891 reserve list. The Pittsburgh Pirates signed Bierbauer and the Boston Nationals engaged Stovey. The American Association termed this action piratical, giving the Pirates their present nickname. A neutral board of arbitration awarded the disputed players to Pittsburgh and Boston, respectively, but the American Association took the decision in poor grace, and the two leagues engaged in a cold war all season.

The outcome of this latest friction was a merger between the two leagues, whereby Harry Von Der Horst was awarded the Baltimore franchise in a new rather top-heavy, twelve-club

23

league, termed "The National League and American Association of Baseball Clubs." In the merger, the National League also took in the former A. A. clubs in St. Louis, Washington, and Louisville. In this way, such famous names as Chris Von Der Ahe and Barney Dreyfuss came into the National League with Von Der Horst.

CHAPTER III

Truculent John McGraw
Comes to the Chesapeake

LATE IN THE 1891 American Association season, before Barnie severed his nine-year term with the Orioles, he introduced to Baltimore fans a bundle of dynamite hidden in a pint-sized 5-foot 6-inch, 121-pound body. The dynamite was an eighteen-year-old boy with snapping black eyes from Truxton, New York, named John Joseph McGraw, who was to leave a deep impress first on Baltimore baseball, and then on National League baseball in New York.

McGraw was destined to become one of Baltimore's most controversial sports figures, first as an outstanding Oriole player and later as manager of the Orioles in both the National and early American Leagues. He left Baltimore in midseason of 1902, under circumstances that still are debatable among baseball fans, to develop into the super-manager of the New York Giants. Many regard him as the No. 1 manager of all time. In his 29 complete seasons in charge of the Giants, from 1903 to 1931, he won ten pennants, was the runner-up ten times, and finished out of the first division only twice. Only in recent years have the Giants regained some of the prestige and popularity that they enjoyed in the heyday of McGraw.

From the time he cut his eye-teeth John McGraw was cocky, sharp spoken, and a kid with a splendid idea of himself and his ability. No one but a McGraw would have had the temerity to try for a big league job against the toughies of the 1890's when he was no bigger than a grasshopper.

25

A candy butcher on New York trains in his early youth, John McGraw began his professional ball career in 1890 with the Oleon, New York, club when he was only seventeen. He started out as a pitcher, and always felt he was a specialist on pitching. However, early managers moved the eager boy to the infield. Before the brash kid was eighteen, he enlisted with a baseball expedition, Al Lawson's Stars, to Cuba and Key West. John was the tiniest of the Stars. Later he played winter ball in Gainesville, Florida, and helped that club gain the Florida winter title. When baseball earnings dried up, he supported himself selling men's clothes in Gainesville's ready-made clothing store. By 1892, he played for Cedar Rapids in the Illinois-Iowa League, sassed Cap Anson, the famous Chicago manager, in an exhibition game, produced a batting average of .275 in 85 games and stole 21 bases.

While McGraw was playing for Cedar Rapids, the first Bill Gleason, a former shortstop on the Browns, told John that he had been writing about him to Bill Barnie of the Baltimore Orioles. Of course, John perked up his ears and his dark eyes glistened. After more correspondence, Barnie wrote Gleason to have McGraw report to him, and sent along John's railroad tickets. McGraw jumped at the opportunity. He didn't have to get his release, as the Illinois-Iowa League was in dire financial straits and the young New York Stater was considering join-ing a California team when the good news came to report to Baltimore.

In his book, *My Thirty Years in Baseball,* McGraw reports how Bill Barnie had the surprise of his life when the frail-looking kid showed up in the Union Park clubhouse, saying, "I'm John McGraw."

"Good God, you don't mean to tell me you're the player I've been corresponding with Bill Gleason about," stammered Barnie, not trying to hide his chagrin and disappointment. "Why, you're nothing but a boy. Can you play ball?"

"Sure, I can play ball," snapped McGraw. "That's why

26

I'm here. Come out and see me and watch my smoke. I'm bigger and stronger than I look."

"Well, you talk big," commented Barnie.

They didn't have many spare uniforms in a clubhouse in those days. Barnie had just released a 6-foot, 190-pound infielder, George Wise, to Washington. His Oriole uniform was the only one available. "Get into this," said Barnie, and added with a laugh, "Don't get lost in it."

No one ever laughed at John McGraw after he became an established player and manager, but when he made his first Oriole appearance against Columbus, August 26, 1891, he looked like something out of a comic strip. Wise's big uniform fitted him like a Mother Hubbard wrapper. Perhaps the roomy uniform made even this cocky kid self-conscious. Barnie injected him into the Oriole line-up at shortstop, and McGraw booted his first chance and struck out in his first time at bat against Phil Knell, Columbus's best pitcher with a 27-26 record in the 1891 season.

"I'm still looking for the smoke," taunted Barnie.

McGraw merely gritted his teeth. He got one single off Knell and fielded faultlessly the rest of the way. Barnie, and then Van Haltern, kept McGraw at shortstop for the balance of the season, and the 18-year-old hit .245 for 31 games.

With the merger of the National League and American Association into a twelve-club National League in 1892, the players from four discarded clubs were on the open market. It meant tougher competition for all positions and McGraw hung on in Baltimore as a part-time second baseman and utility player. It wasn't until 1893, when he was 20, that he became a full-time Oriole regular.

From the start McGraw was truculent and combative. He was small, but that never kept him out of a fight. He took his share of lickings, but that never deterred him. He was like an Irish terrier, ever ready to snap at umpires or players who outweighed him from 50 to 75 pounds. He also had an Irish temper, and when he erupted his language was blistering and vituperative.

During his stay in Baltimore and early in his New York career, his nickname was Muggsy. It was used by rival players, sometimes by the Orioles, and frequently by the sports writers in the nation's press. There was a small time Baltimore politician named Muggsy McGraw about that time, and somehow talk got around Union Park that young Muggsy was the elder Muggsy McGraw's son. There also was a crude, illiterate character in the comic strips called Muggsy. McGraw detested the name, much as the late umpire, Bill Klem, detested "Catfish," and in John's later years, Muggsy was a fighting word.

In 1919, years after he left the Orioles, McGraw celebrated his April 7 birthday with a training trip party in Baltimore. A naive motion picture actor, John Sainpolis, extolling McGraw, made frequent references to him as Muggsy. "Now, I don't know why John should object to the word, Mugg-sy," Sainpolis orated. "To me, the nickname Muggsy always was a term of endearment."

Frank Graham, Sam Crane, Jimmy Sinnott, the author, and other New York writers were at the party. We could see McGraw's face get redder and redder, as the veins stood out on his neck. At any moment, we expected to see him break out and commit mayhem on Sainpolis. Another of the New York writers was Harry Schumacher, of the old New York *Globe,* a big fellow but with a little giggly laugh. Every time Sainpolis uttered the detested word, "Mugg-sy," giving it the actor's full flourish, Schumacher giggled. McGraw paid no further attention to Sainpolis but turned on Schumacher and gave Harry a tongue-lashing with the full McGravian flavor.

McGraw's language was salty, especially when he got into a quarrel or argument. But he was proud of his diction and ability to speak correct English. While he had had little more than a grade-school education before leaving Truxton for his first baseball job, later, during his career as an Oriole player, he and Hugh Jennings, a team mate, spent four off-seasons at

Allegany College, now St. Bonaventure's College, at Allegany, New York. McGraw and Jennings helped pay for their education by coaching the baseball squad before reporting for spring training with the Orioles. It was at St. Bonaventure's that McGraw brushed up on the King's English, and he hotly resented any implication that he talked like a Muggsy McGraw.

Weed Dickinson, baseball writer on the *New York Morning Telegraph*, once began his story of a Giant defeat with an opening line: "Z'in da dirt! Z'in da dirt!"

The quote supposedly was from a fuming McGraw. In a ninth-inning Giant rally, the tying run was thrown out at the plate. While the players and fans were leaving the field, McGraw stood at the plate raging at the umpire. He claimed the opposing catcher had failed to hold the ball, and that it was in the dirt when the umpire called the last man out.

The next day McGraw called Weed Dickinson to the railing in front of the old field press box at the Polo Grounds. In his hand he waved a clipping of the *Telegraph's* baseball story.

"Dickinson," he said with strong feeling. "I don't talk that way, and don't ever quote me talking that way again."

McGraw was smart, even brilliant. In the days of his greatest renown, many persons in and out of the New York press box considered him the biggest man in baseball. He had a hair-trigger mind, and was contemptuous of others whose mental apparatus did not function as quickly as his. He was without doubt a genius in baseball—when it came to judging young players, in team strategy, and in picking the weak spots of his opponents. He was an absolute tyrant and dictator on his ball club. He managed every moment, even called practically every pitched ball in many of his pennant-winning campaigns. Once a player started to say, "I think. . ." McGraw quickly interrupted him, saying: "You play your position; I get paid for doing the thinking around here."

He was intensely proud of his career as a Baltimore player, as a batsman, base-runner, and third baseman. Without a

29

moment's thought, he could give his batting average and stolen base total for any season in which he played. Once in correcting the flaws of a young infielder in spring training, McGraw started his remarks, "Now, when I played ball, I did it this way."

"Oh, did you play ball, Mr. McGraw?" asked the poor rookie.

McGraw stormed all over the place, and burned the kid to a crisp. The author played bridge with McGraw the night after the incident, and John couldn't get this piece of unintended sacrilegiousness out of his mind. Several times during the evening, he said with his salty irony: "Did I ever play ball, Mr. McGraw? That stupid so-and-so!" Needless to say, that rookie never got to New York.

McGraw was a man of many facets. Most of the time he was good company and a pleasant host; he liked to give parties. The baseball writers attached to the Giants usually were invited to these sessions. But when McGraw was crossed or angered, he could be a Tartar.

He was generous to a fault, and was a soft touch for any broke or rundown ex-manager or ball player. He had feuded and exchanged barbed compliments with most of them, but in their time of need, he stood by. With the exception of a few isolated cases, he was intensely loyal to his own men, yet he knew no sentiment in conducting his managerial job. He traded away players that he liked, Art Fletcher, Larry Doyle, Arthur Nehf, and took on others he disliked if he felt it helped his ball team. He heartily disliked the Baltimore-born player, Charley "Buck" Herzog, but twice after the Giants had traded Buck away, McGraw regained his services in subsequent transactions.

While there are a few references to Jack McGraw and Johnny McGraw in accounts of his early playing days, such terms of intimacy and affection had disappeared long before he left Baltimore. One just couldn't think of that sizzling firebrand as Johnny McGraw. He knew thousands of persons,

30

but had few intimates, other than fellow ex-Orioles—Hughie
Jennings and Wilbert Robinson (he broke with Robbie in
1913)—Christy Mathewson, and a few cronies from the New
York Lambs' Club. Few ever called him by his Christian name
of John; Jennings, Matty, and such veteran reporters as Boze
Bulger, Sid Mercer, Damon Runyon, and Sam Crane addressed him as "Mac." Though Frankie Graham, his biog-
rapher, traveled with the Giants for many years, he never
addressed the Giant leader as anything but "Mr. McGraw."
Eddie Brannick, Giant secretary for nearly four decades, still
would consider it sacrilege to speak of his old boss other than
as "Mr. McGraw," and outside of Mathewson the writer never
heard any of his ball players address him otherwise. Out of
his hearing, such untrammeled spirits as Frank Frisch, Bill
Terry, and Freddy Lindstrom spoke of him as "the old man"
or "the little round man," and after Earl Smith left the Giants
he used to call him Muggsy, and McGraw hated him as he
did no other athlete who had played for him.

In his later years, McGraw said and wrote, "It is foolish,
and a waste of time, to fight umpires," but he was an umpire
fighter most of his life, as a Baltimore player and manager,
and in his greater role as manager of the Giants.

He feuded with such National League club owners as
Barney Dreyfuss, Charley Ebbets, Charley Murphy, and William Baker, and found it difficult to accept discipline from
his league presidents. As manager and a substantial stockholder of the early Baltimore American League Orioles, he
constantly was in Ban Johnson's doghouse for baiting the
young executive's umpires. But it was much the same when
John transferred back to the National League. He was fined
$150 and suspended fifteen days for a tongue-lashing he gave
former National League president Harry Pulliam over the
phone. He tangled with John K. Tener, the former Pennsylvania Governor, and when Tener told the league it had to
choose between him and McGraw, the latter repudiated an interview with Sid Mercer, the well-known New York baseball

writer. That cost him another $1,000. In his later years, he seared the sensitive soul of John A. Heydler, Tener's successor, by barbed diatribes in the Cincinnati and St. Louis ball parks.

But McGraw was a graduate of a hard baseball school. He knew only one way to play baseball: hard—and to win. With him a ball game was more than just a contest between two rival teams; it was miniature war in which he gave no quarter, and expected none. From the day the little Irish terrier from Truxton first introduced himself to Bill Barnie in Baltimore in 1891, John McGraw was a fighter and a battler.

CHAPTER IV

Orioles Land Managerial Genius

BALTIMORE'S shift from the American Association to the National League in 1892 was not an immediate success. At first, Baltimore fans got a big kick out of the transfer. It meant they would see such National League headliners as Cap Anson, Ed Delehanty, Cy Young, Sam Thompson, Kid Nichols, and Bobbie Lowe. And despite the National League's shortcomings, Baltimore fans knew the old loop had more class than the now defunct Beer and Whiskey circuit. But when the Orioles quickly sank to the bottom of the new twelve-club league, and trailed dismally at the finish, the bang was pretty well gone. The Birds won a scant 46 games, and suffered 101 defeats for a poor percentage of .313. Von Der Ahe of the new National League Browns finished eleventh, but his .373 percentage still was 60 points higher than that of Von Der Horst. "What's the good of being in the National League if everybody kicks hell out of us?" was the complaint of many loyal Oriole fans.

Yet, despite the lowly finish of the 1892 Birds, something happened that season which before too long was to lift the Orioles out of the depths to the very pinnacle of baseball. Van Haltern was dumped early as manager, and while Von Der Horst was shopping around for a successor, he put the club in charge of Jack Waltz, his head beer salesman.

The man Von Der Horst was negotiating with during Waltz's temporary occupancy of the driver's seat was the former Pittsburgh pilot, Edward Hugh "Ned" Hanlon, who was destined to become one of the game's real managerial wizards and for years thereafter remained a top figure in Baltimore baseball.

There was no particular elation in Baltimore when Hanlon took the Oriole reins in late May. "What's he done as a manager?" asked the fans. Hanlon managed Pittsburgh to a fifth place finish in 1889. One of the top rebels of the Baseball Brotherhood, he managed the Pittsburgh Players League team in 1890, and wound up sixth. Back with the Pittsburgh Pirates as playing manager in 1891, he was fired after his club finished a dead last. Not too much to recommend him as a managerial genius, yet Hanlon was that in the making. Soon he was to startle baseball with his inside ball and diamond tricks never thought up heretofore.

A shrewd Irisher from Montville, Conn., Ned proved the David Harum of all baseball traders. The custom of earlier Connecticut traders in disposing of wooden nutmegs to guileless victims was nothing to some of the trades Hanlon worked off on unsuspecting National League club owners and managers.

Hanlon, of course, had established quite a reputation as a National League player before coming to Baltimore. The author has heard old-timers rave about his outfielding. His old sports editor, Jim Price, used to speak of Hanlon as "a Tris Speaker without a glove." Price used to say, "In some respects, Hanlon was better than Speaker, because he played during the greater part of his career without a glove. How he could snatch long drives out of the air with his bare hands was uncanny."

Hanlon was a player of the same stripe as Jim Piersall, prize outfielder of the 1954 Boston Red Sox. Ned was only a fair hitter, but a fielding fool. After playing one season in Cleveland, Hanlon was with Detroit in the full eight years in which that city had representation in the National League, from 1881 to 1888. Ned was the captain-center fielder of

34

the Detroit World's Champions of 1887 under Manager Watty Watkins. In those days a captain had much more authority than he has today, and Ned directed these early Detroits on the field.

Hanlon batted over .300 only once—in 1887, the year of the trick batting averages. He played 115 games with the 1891 Pirates, but suffered a leg injury, and Baltimore fans saw little of his rare outfielding skill. He played only eight games for the 1892 Orioles, hit .233, and then put his uniform aside. From then on, he managed in mufti.

One of Hanlon's first smart deals was to get rid of George "Rip" Van Haltern, his managerial predecessor. Rip of the big moustache was traded to Pittsburgh for a 20-year old outfielder, Joseph James Kelley. Like Ned, Joe was a New Englander, coming from Cambridge, Mass., and like Hanlon, he was to settle in Baltimore and make it his home for the remainder of his life. Detecting young Joe's great inherent talent was another proof of Hanlon's Irish second sight. In 1891, young Kelley had played only 14 National League games, 12 with his home-town Boston team and 2 with Pittsburgh. Joe had hit .245 in 56 games for the 1892 Pirates before the trade that brought him to the Orioles. He looked like just a promising kid and many Baltimore fans thought their new manager was crazy for giving up an experienced regular, Van Haltern, for a green youth. But under Hanlon's tuition, Kelley soon developed into a slashing clean-up hitter, and beginning with 1893 he hit over .300 for twelve consecutive seasons with a high of .391 in 1894. Joe was fast, batted third, hit for many extra bases, and was well up in the stolen-base department. He also was a splendid rangy outfielder, covering acres of ground. With some of McGraw's truculence, Kelley was a fighter at the drop of the hat and one of the really great Orioles.

Early in the 1892 season, Van Haltern had benched young scrappy John McGraw, but when Hanlon took over he put the little Truxton gamecock at second base. But apparently

Ned didn't think the kid was ready for regular duty, as he obtained "Cub" Stricker from the St. Louis Browns to play the midway bag. Hanlon then almost broke McGraw's young heart, when he suggested, "John, I think I'll send you to Mobile for a little experience. You can play there every day. It'll be good for you."

"Good nothing!" yelled back McGraw. "I know all about Mobile, and how it gets 130 in the sun on their diamond in July and August. It's a hell hole, that's what it is. I'm trying to put on a little weight, and I'd just melt away down there. I'd quit playing ball before I would go to Mobile. Besides, what's the matter with the way I've been playing around here?" Young Mac argued so loudly and intensely that Hanlon said, "All right, I won't send you there. We can always use you as a utility player."

It was about this time that Hanlon turned down an offered trade which was as smart as some of the great deals he made. Cap Anson, the Chicago manager, who had liked McGraw ever since the obstreperous kid sassed him in a Cedar Rapids exhibition game, approached Hanlon and said, "I notice you're not playing that fighting young rooster, McGraw, regularly. I think I could use him every day. I might let you have Jim Ryan for him, if you want to talk turkey."

That must have been a tempting offer for Hanlon. Though Jim Ryan was a playful fellow who liked his grog, he was an established .300-hitting outfield regular. But, Hanlon must have recognized McGraw's potentialities, as he replied, "Thanks, Cap, but I think I'll keep my little fighting rooster."

One of the things about McGraw's play that caught Hanlon's eye was the brash New Yorker's ability to hit to all fields. McGraw was a left-handed hitter, but he was quite adept in stepping into a pitch and punching the ball into left field. Most of Hanlon's orthodox left-handed hitters pulled 19 out of 20 balls to right field.

"Who taught you to hit to left field?" Hanlon asked, with more or less admiration.

"Taught myself—in my first season with Oleon," said McGraw. "Nobody is a real hitter, unless he can hit to all fields."

Hanlon was impressed. "You've got something there, young fellow," he said. "Always remember it." McGraw always did; to the end of his baseball days, he always insisted no man was a real hitter unless he could master the faculty of hitting to all fields and upsetting any strategic deployment which the defensive side attempted to use against him.

Even on that 1892 Baltimore tailender, the Orioles were an exciting lot, and Wilbert Robinson, the hefty catcher, wrote a record into the book which has held up to the present day. In the first game of a double-header with Von Der Ahe's Browns on June 10, 1892, Robbie got seven hits in as many times at bat, the only player ever to get "7 for 7" in a nine-inning game. Wilbert rapped out three singles, punched out a double, and then finished with three more singles.

Though St. Louis eventually beat out the Birds for eleventh place, on the day of this double-header the Orioles looked like the greatest team in the world. A 6-6 darkness tie the preceding day had brought about the bargain bill. Baltimore won the first game, 25 to 4, and the second, 9 to 3, smacking out 44 hits in the two games. Robbie tapered down to one hit in the second game.

Most of the Orioles then wore moustaches. Even little 19-year-old John McGraw had a few thin black hairs on his upper lip. But Robbie had a soup-strainer that was his pride and joy. It was a luxuriant affair and before Wilbert left his home for the ball game, "Ma" Robinson would put wax on it and carefully curl the ends. In a game with Philadelphia, Robinson threw down to "Cub" Stricker at second base and apparently had Ed Delahanty trapped off base. But, Tim Hurst, the single umpire working behind the plate, yelled, "Safe!"

Wilbert Robinson sputtered. "Safe, my eye!" he fumed. "What's wrong with you, Tim? Have you suddenly lost your eyesight? It never was too good, anyway. Gosh almighty, I had Delahanty frozen off second base."

Hurst playfully twisted the ends of Robbie's big moustache. "Now, let's not be angry, Wilbert," he said. "We'll just say that one man was frozen on that play. Now, if it's all right with you, we'll proceed with the ball game."

Robbie continued to sputter. It was bad enough to have Hurst call the play wrong on him, but the colorful Tim twisting the ends of his moustache was worse than an indignity; it was lese majesty. To make matters worse for Wilbert, fellow Orioles kidded him about the indignity throughout the remainder of the game. By the end of the ninth inning, the usually good-natured Robinson was ready to crown Hurst with a bat, and other players had to pull him away from the umpire.

There was substantial improvement in the Orioles in 1893. They won 14 more games and lost 31 less than the 1892 tailender, winding up eighth with 60 victories and 70 defeats. This year the once famous Chicago White Stockings, the St. Louis Browns, Louisville, and Washington finished below Baltimore. Von Der Horst finally got ahead of Von Der Ahe, and now it was Chris who was the dumkopf. Yet, it irked Hanlon that his improved team could win only two of twelve games from the Boston champions. "We'll never be any good until we can knock off some of those top teams," he confided to Jack Waltz.

Hanlon again made one of his smart deals, but at the time the trade was made, it looked strictly routine. He made this swap with Bill Barnie, the old Oriole chieftain, now trying his luck with Louisville. The Colonels had a weak-hitting shortstop, Hugh Ambrose Jennings, hailing from Pittston, Pa., in the Pennsylvania hard coal country. Like McGraw, Jennings broke into the bigtime in the last year of the American Association—with the 1891 Louisville Sluggers. With the new Louisville National League club, Hughie was anything

38

but a slugger. Playing a full 152-game season in 1892, he hit a fair .232. But by the spring of 1893, he couldn't beg, borrow, or steal a hit. After 23 games, he was hitting an anemic .148. Who would want a .148 hitter? No one, but the canny Hanlon, who again had looked into his crystal ball with highly satisfactory results.

Hanlon arranged to have a few beers with Barnie after the game. Making conversation, Ned said: "That noisy freckle face you have playing shortstop isn't hitting a lick, is he?"

Barnie agreed heartily. "He couldn't hit a barn with a paddle," he griped.

"Maybe I could teach him something about hitting," continued Ned. "Want to fix up some kind of a deal."

Barnie, little suspecting that he was to play the role of a kindly Santa Claus, was all ears. "I'm listening, Ned," he said. "What've you got to offer?"

"I might let you have Tim O'Rourke and Bill Brown if you'd let us have Jennings and that pitcher, Harry Taylor."

Barnie grabbed Hanlon's hand before Ned had a chance to change his mind. "It's deal," he said happily. O'Rourke, known as Voiceless Tim, was Baltimore's regular shortstop and hitting .379 when the trade was made. Brown was a first baseman. Taylor, the Louisville pitcher wanted by Hanlon, was a part-time player who played baseball between law courses. He didn't stay long in baseball and wound up a Justice of the New York Supreme Court in Buffalo.

Baltimore writers and fans questioned the wisdom of the deal. It looked absolutely asinine trading a .379-hitting shortstop for a .148 batsman, but Hanlon gradually was getting rid of his booze-fighters and had just picked up another Hall of Fame immortal. Jennings rode the Oriole bench the rest of the season, getting into only 15 Baltimore games, but he did pull his batting average up to .192 and showed some of the speed which enabled him to steal as high as 72 bases a season.

Hugh Jennings was a sandy-red-haired, freckle-faced, chattering baseball enthusiast, who loved baseball as much as did

39

McGraw, Kelley, and Robinson. In the hot Louisville and Baltimore sun, his genial Irish face was broiled to a deep red. Though not as tough as McGraw, he was a hard-playing, aggressive, hustling, thinking ball player. He talked constantly on the ball field. Once Cap Anson, himself quite a talker, yelled at Jennings, "For God's sake, Hughie, don't you ever close that trap?" "Why should he close it, you big garrulous baboon?" interjected the fiery McGraw.

As McGraw had started as a pitcher, so Jennings began on the other end of the battery—as a catcher. In a game in the anthracite country, Hughie almost killed a batsman while trying to throw out a runner at second. The catcher then stood ten feet behind the plate, and Hughie's throw hit the batter on the base of the skull, knocking him out cold. Jennings then had trouble with his throwing arm. He used to put clay around it, and baked it in a brickyard kiln. The treatment apparently worked, as Hughie gave up catching and became a hard-throwing shortstop.

Hughie and McGraw clicked immediately, and were to remain pals up to the time of Jennings' untimely death of tuberculosis in 1928. Perhaps the closeness of their birthdays built a sort of astrological bond between them. Hughie, four years older than Mac, was born on April 6, 1869, bringing his birthday one day ahead of McGraw's. For years they celebrated a joint birthday party. Soon after Jennings joined the Orioles, the pair roomed together and became inseparable. They attended St. Bonaventure's together. Jennings later went in for still higher education, was graduated from the Cornell law school, admitted to the bar in Pennsylvania, and for a time Hughie practiced law in Scranton between baseball seasons.

Teams then had no scouting systems, but depended on friendly tips for promising players. Former teammates of Hanlon residing on the West Coast tipped him off on a quartet of players then playing independent ball in California; catcher Bill Clarke, infielder Heinie Reitz, outfielder

George Treadway, and pitcher Edgar McNabb. Hanlon signed the quartet to Oriole contracts. Boilermaker Clarke, a native New Yorker, was to serve as second-string catcher to Robbie for six seasons, and hustling Reitz, a Chicagoan, quickly nailed down the second base job.

With the trading of Tim O'Rourke to Louisville, McGraw, rather than Jennings, went to shortstop. Mac came fast that season. The young infielder whom Hanlon wanted to farm out the year before played in 127 games, hit .328, and stole 40 bases. John was right when he said he was doing all right in Baltimore. By this time he had grown to his full 5 feet, 7 inches, and weighed 145 pounds.

In the pitching department, John J. "Sadie" McMahon did a superb job. McMahon, who came from Wilmington, Delaware, was the work horse of the staff. He had come from the Athletics with Robbie late in the 1890 season, and in Baltimore's last A. A. season, 1891, Sadie was pretty much the entire pitching staff, winning 35 games and losing 24. He wasn't so good with the National League tailender of 1892, winning 19 and losing 25, but bounced back on the winning side in 1893, registering 24 wins against 16 setbacks. Sadie later became a scout for McGraw on the Giants.

An interesting Oriole character of the 1892-93 period was left-handed pitcher, Fred "Crazy" Schmidt. McGraw, an inveterate storyteller, used to love to tell stories about Crazy. "Schmidt kept a notebook, in which he put down what he thought were the weaknesses of opposing batsmen," McGraw would relate. "One day, when we were playing Chicago, Cap Anson came to the plate. Schmidt pulled out his notebook to see what he should pitch to the great 'Anse.' I moved in from my position, looked over his shoulder, and asked, 'What does it say?' 'It says here I should give Anson a base on balls; that's his weakness,' replied Crazy." When it suited McGraw's mood, he sometimes made Hans Wagner the famous hitter, but Honus did not come into the league until 1897. The Anson version is the correct one.

41

In the meantime, the status of Hanlon had changed from that of merely manager to president-manager. During the 1893 season, Von Der Horst sold a big block of his Oriole stock to the enterprising Hanlon. It was announced that Ned had acquired a majority interest, but most Baltimoreans doubted it. They believed the brewer still held control, but passed responsibilities over to Hanlon. "I'm tired of the players coming to me with their complaints," said Von Der Horst. "Let them take their beefs to the new boss, Hanlon. Anyway he knows more about baseball, and I know more about beer." Under the new setup he was treasurer, and Jack Waltz, the beer salesman, vice-president.

Hanlon, one of the smartest players of his day, had amassed quite a sum of money for an athlete of that period. As captain-center fielder of the old Detroits, he was one of the highest-salaried players on the club. He made a good salary when he went to Pittsburgh as manager in 1899, and while many players lost their shirts in the Brotherhood War, Hanlon, who had been awarded the Pittsburgh Players League franchise, got out of this venture with a tidy profit. Hanlon also had an early knack of putting his money into profitable investments. No wonder people already were calling him "Foxy Ned."

CHAPTER V

Foxy Ned's Miracle

Two EVENTS of early 1894 were to have an amazing effect on the Baltimore team's fortune. They were to change the status of the Orioles from that of a National League doormat to kings of the sport. The first took place in the National League's winter trading marts; the second in the batting cage of St. Bonaventure College.

Hanlon, the super-trader, pulled the greatest deal of his fabulous career with Brooklyn in January. He gave up his regular third baseman Billy Shindle and outfielder George Treadway to the Dodgers in exchange for Dennis "Big Dan" Brouthers, 35-year old clouting first baseman, and a young squirt, Willie Keeler, who had played in only 42 National League games. The young man's full name was William H. Keeler; he was 5 feet, 4½ inches tall, and in his prime his weight never got any higher than 140 pounds. Though a left-handed thrower and batsman with the Giants and Brooklyn, he had appeared for these clubs in the odd role of a third baseman.

Did Hanlon make this deal primarily to get the slugging Brouthers, with a long list of imposing batting averages, and was Willie Keeler thrown in to sweeten the deal? Or, did Foxy Ned again have some kind of a sixth sense that made him realize the amazing possibilities of little Keeler. Wee Willie, as he was affectionately known, was a product of the Brooklyn sand lots and son of a Brooklyn trolley switchman. He was such a mite that he looked more like an errand boy or junior clerk than a big league ball player. Yet, he developed

43

into baseball's most scientific hitter, a batsman capable of hitting an incredible .432—second highest in the majors—and a player who did his full part in making the Orioles a national byword.

What did Ned have to go on when he made this spectacular deal? Keeler was picked off the Brooklyn sand lots by the Giants in 1892 when Willie was twenty. They farmed the kid to Binghamton, where he hit .374. In 13 games with the Giants that year, he hit an acceptable .306. Even so, no one yet had any thought of Keeler as a full-time big league performer. He was sent out again to Binghamton in 1893, where he hit .294. Recalled by the Giants, Willie was held lightly by manager John Montgomery Ward, one of the outstanding managers of the early nineties. Ward traded Keeler in mid-season to his native Brooklyn for a nonentity. Between New York and Brooklyn, Keeler played in 29 National League 1893 games and hit whenever they let him play. He rapped out 30 hits, including two homers, for an average of .333 and stole seven bases. And he impressed Ned Hanlon, even though Ward of the Giants and the Brooklyn high command, Charles Byrne, Charley Ebbets and Manager Dave Foutz, saw Keeler only as an underweight runt, who never could stand the rigors of a full National League season, and no doubt a boy batting far over his head.

The acquisition of Keeler was important to Baltimore success, but the miracle change of Hugh Jennings from a sucker hitter to one of the top batsmen of the National League was equally important. We have told how McGraw and Jennings coached the St. Bonaventure baseball team in exchange for their tuition.

"There's no reason for you being such a sucker hitter," McGraw told Jennings. "You can't stay in the big league hitting .192. Let's see whether we can't do something about it."

In the college batting cage, Mac showed Hughie how he was pulling away from curve balls and inside pitches. Jennings had a bad case of what ball players call "the foot in the water

44

bucket." Some players such as Al Simmons, former American League batting champion, could hit that way; Jennings couldn't.

McGraw put the home plate so close to the wire netting of the cage that Hughie couldn't step back. If he did he scraped his elbows. McGraw also changed Jennings's batting style, turned him around, and taught him how to step into a pitch. McGraw, who later pitched batting practice for the Giants until he was past 50, then pitched to Hughie by the hour. As Jennings would connect solidly, John would express his pleasure, exclaiming, "Now, you're doing it. When I hear that kind of a crack, I know you're really putting the wood to the ball."

When Jennings reported to Hanlon's Macon, Ga., training camp, Ned beheld a changed Hugh Jennings. The freckle-faced redhead soon was plastering balls all over the field in a manner which dazzled Hanlon. "That's how I like to see you hit," beamed Ned. Shindle, his regular third baseman, had gone to Brooklyn in the Keeler swap, and he told McGraw, "From now on, you'll play third base, and Jennings will take over at shortstop."

The Macon camp was one of the most interesting training camps ever held in baseball. History was made there. Keeler, by this time twenty-two, holding his bat with his hands well apart, sprayed hits to all corners of the field. McGraw never looked better. Walter "Steve" Brodie, an outfielder acquired from the St. Louis Browns for $1,000 late in the 1893 season, got into the act, along with big Brouthers, Kelley, Reitz, Clarke, and Wilbert Robinson.

Hanlon told Keeler earlier, "Forget that you ever played the infield. On my team, you're an outfielder. You'll play right field, unless you show me you can't play it."

Baseball managers still were playing the old army game. Stolen bases were frequent; there was some sacrificing but the usual strategy was to hit straight away. In Hanlon's early exhibition games, he had McGraw lead off and Keeler batting second. Both could stand at the plate indefinitely, fouling off balls until they walked or got a good ball to hit. Both were good bunters, and could hit to any field.

By the hour, they practiced the hit-and-run play, whereby after McGraw reached first base, Keeler would punch the ball through the hole, advancing Mac to third. McGraw would go down as on an attempted steal; if the shortstop covered second base, Willie jabbed the ball into left field. If the second baseman covered, Keeler pulled the ball and prodded it to right. If it was a bad ball, Willie merely fouled it off. It was a play which soon would have the league dizzy.

Everybody on the club, including the pitchers, had to be an expert bunter. The pitching distance had been changed in 1893 from 50 feet to the present 60 feet, 6 inches, and the Orioles were the first team to take full advantage of the new conditions. They introduced what still is known as the "Baltimore chop." It was a play executed by a fast runner and usually required a fast, sun-baked diamond. The batter chopped the ball so hard into the turf that it took a high bound, sufficiently high for the batter to reach base. Keeler, McGraw, Jennings, and Kelley soon became adept at executing the play. The Orioles made it tough for any wretch who missed a sign, or failed to bunt when that play was on top. Hanlon didn't have to punish the culprit; the entire bench jumped down his neck.

Not only did the Birds introduce new unheard of offensive tactics, but they introduced new styles of defensive play. The Orioles didn't invent everything; there were smart ball players before them, but they shook the complacency of nineteenth century baseball, and were the forerunners of the game of today. On the attempted double steal, they first introduced the cut-off play. With runners on third and first, when the runner on first lit out for second, either shortstop Jennings or second baseman Reitz came well into the diamond to be in position to take catcher Robinson's throw. In the meantime, the other covered second base. If the runner on third made no attempt

46

to steal home, the throw went through to second base. However, if this runner tried to score, either the pitcher or the infielder who had crossed in front of second base cut in on the throw and snapped the ball back to Robbie at the plate. In a similar situation, Wilbert also had what the Orioles termed "the old sucker throw." He made a full motion as if to throw to second, but the ball never left his hand. Instead, he rifled the ball to McGraw at third base, and often trapped the runner off that bag.

We speak of such plays today as "inside baseball." In the nineties, they referred to them as "Baltimore baseball" and "Oriole baseball." In fact, John Montgomery Ward of the Giants insisted it wasn't even baseball, and tried unsuccessfully to have the league enact legislation against some of Hanlon's plays. And Ward, an attorney, was supposedly a clever man. Ward, Hanlon, and John K. Tener were the Brotherhood high command during the Players League war, but Ned apparently never let in John Montgomery on any of his secret weapons.

Were these plays thought up by Hanlon, or were they the brain children of such clever players as McGraw, Jennings, Keeler, Kelley, McMahon, and Robinson? Perhaps, a combination of both. It is significant that in his book, *Thirty Years in Baseball,* McGraw remarked of Hanlon: "Ned had a wonderful faculty of organization. He was hailed as the developer of inside baseball, which was right, but I always have thought that he was a greater organizer and team builder than a field general."

The inference must be that McGraw gave Hanlon full credit for gathering this remarkable caste together, but that his nimble-witted hands, particularly the astute McGraw, deserve large assists in the All-Time Baltimore box score for thinking up the plays which made the old Orioles immortal.

Anyway, when the 1894 National League race got under way, no one outside of Baltimore gave the Orioles a tumble. Rival managers and old line baseball writers regarded them as the same club which had finished twelfth in 1892 and eighth in 1893. With what they termed "experiments" and "untried youngsters," they weren't sure they'd be as good as in 1893. The Boston Beaneaters had won three straight pennants, and Connie Mack's Pittsburgh Pirates, 1893 runner-up, were considered a hot candidate to dethrone the men from Boston. John Ward's Giants, strengthened by winter deals, and Harry Wright's Philadelphia sluggers also were regarded highly.

The schedule brought the Giants to Baltimore for the opening series. There had been good reports of the hustling young Orioles from Macon and an overflow crowd of 15,000 filled Von Der Horst's Union Park to the rafters and spilled all over the outfield and the picnic grove. The crowd was in for a highly pleasant afternoon, and the Giants for a shocking surprise. The Orioles began running in the first inning, putting the famous Giant fast-ball pitcher Amos Rusie, and his complacent catcher, Duke Farrell, in a state of utter confusion as they repeatedly put on the hit and run. Sadie McMahon had no difficulty in beating Rusie, 8 to 3.

Hanlon's line-up that day was John McGraw, third base; Willie Keeler, right field; Joe Kelley, left field; Dan Brouthers, first base; Hugh Jennings, shortstop; Steve Brodie, center field; Heinie Reitz, second base; Wilbert Robinson, catcher; McMahon, pitcher.

McGraw and Keeler still were standing the Giants on their ears in the second game; Jennings had their mouths open by the manner in which he was stepping into all pitches; all the Orioles still were running, and the Birds ran off with this one, 12 to 6. They eventually swept the four-game series with New York, and sent Ward on his way muttering and cursing. "That's trick stuff by a lot of kids," he insisted. "Maybe they are better trained than we are, but we'll show them up in our next series. They'll blow up long before the season is over. Besides, I'm not sure what they're doing is legal. As soon

48

as we get to Washington, I'll ask Nick Young, the League president, about it."

Shortly afterwards, the Boston champions, and their crack pitcher, Kid Nichols, also got a sample of the trick stuff of Hanlon's kids. Nichols, seemingly in his best form, had the Orioles throttled for eight innings, and Boston led, 3 to 1. Then, the Birds suddenly erupted for 14 runs in the ninth inning to win by 15 to 3. The home team then usually chose to bat first. And, McGraw and Keller pulled their new hit and run thirteen consecutive times before they were stopped.

To make life still more joyful—and profitable—for Hanlon, Von Der Horst, and Waltz, the Baltimore street transportation system chose this very auspicious spring to introduce its new electric cars and soon express trolleys ran to Union Park in place of the old Greenmount Avenue horse cars.

Despite Baltimore's newly found run-making ability, it soon became evident that Hanlon had only one dependable pitcher, John McMahon. Sadie was winning regularly, but the club would have collapsed, as Ward had predicted, if Hanlon and Von Der Horst hadn't bolstered their weak pitching staff. The need for more pitching was emphasized early when the Beaneaters celebrated Bunker Hill Day by shelling Tony Mullane for a 16-run inning. Tony faced 22 batsmen in that frame, and stone-hearted Hanlon didn't relieve Mullane, a handsome dude from Cork, Ireland, until the seventh inning. Mullane, a former 36-game winner, had been one of the game's early pitching stars, but by 1894 had reached the twilight of a great career. The Orioles lost the morning Bunker Hill game in Boston, 24-7, but evened things by taking the afternoon affair.

In midseason forays on second division clubs in need of money, Hanlon purchased Bill "Kid" Gleason from the St. Louis Browns; Charles "Duke" Esper from Washington; and late in the season, George Hemming from Louisville. These pitchers were like a transfusion of fresh red blood, both to the Orioles and themselves. Gleason had won two out of ten games for the 1894 Browns before coming to Baltimore; with

49

the Birds he won fifteen and lost six. Esper's record with Washington was six won and nine lost; with Baltimore it was nine won and two lost. Hemming had won four and lost fourteen for Louisville; with the Orioles he won each of his five games.

Kid Gleason was the most distinguished, and colorful, of these midseason pitching acquisitions. As his name also was Bill, he often is mistaken for the earlier Bill Gleason, former St. Louis shortstop, who in 1891 recommended McGraw to Bill Barnie. The later Bill Gleason was a product of the Camden, N. J., waterfront, and as tough as nails. He fitted perfectly into the rough and rowdy Oriole picture. He was only a little taller than McGraw, but at that time more robust and could lick men fifty pounds heavier. Furthermore, the Kid never ducked a fight, and usually emerged the victor. While his fifteen 1894 victories were a tremendous lift to Hanlon and his Birds, Gleason, who always could hit, eventually went to second base for the Orioles. He is best remembered as the manager of the 1919 Chicago White Sox, generally dubbed the Black Sox, the team that threw the World Series that year and broke Kid Gleason's heart.

Baltimore went baseball crazy as the club held up week after week, and appreciative loyal crowds jammed the double-decked stands at Union Park as the Orioles successfully repelled the drives of the Giants, the defending champion Beaneaters, and the slugging Phillies. However, it wasn't until the Fourth of July that other National League clubs actually admitted that the Orioles had a real pennant chance. Along with John Ward, they had kidded themselves along with the theory that Hanlon's kids would blow. But Hanlon's kids declined to blow. In fact, as the season moved along they thought up new tricks and wiles to dumbfound, irk, and pester their enemies. This was a ball club that talked, ate, drank, and slept baseball.

After McGraw and Jennings had talked baseball all night, they thought nothing of reporting at the ball park at 8 o'clock in the morning and trying out newly thought up plays with Keeler, Kelley, and Robinson. It frequently has been told how Ty Cobb, great batsman and base runner of the Detroit Tigers, used to sharpen his spikes on the bench to intimidate rival infielders and catchers. The Orioles beat Ty Cobb to that practice by over a decade. They filed their spikes to razor edge fineness, and if anyone got into the way, it was just too bad. The new Orioles ran, ran, and ran.

They weren't too ethical in their attempts to win and stay in first place, nor in how they ran. In the days of the single umpire, John McGraw would run from first base to third, by way of the pitcher's box, if he could get away with it. If the umpire's back was turned, and his attention was directed to a play at the plate, he couldn't call a play he hadn't seen.

One day when McGraw pulled this piece of larceny in a game with Washington, with Honest John Kelly the umpire, Gus Schmelz, the Senator manager, stormed at Kelly, "Well, how in the hell do you think Muggsy got over to third base? You know he didn't have time to go around by second base. Do you think he flew there?"

"I don't know whether he flew there or not, but I didn't see it," said Honest John. "But he's there now, and nothing I can do about it." To retain his reputation for honesty, Kelly could not call out McGraw for something he didn't see.

McGraw had other plays which enraged rivals. He always stood on the inside corner of his bag as a runner attempted to score from second base. That forced the runner to run around McGraw to tag the third base bag on his journey to the plate. The delay often proved fatal. Another McGraw play they talk about to this day was his efforts to hold back runners trying to score on outfield flys. And, we mean "hold back" literally. The single umpire couldn't watch the outfielder and McGraw at the same time, so John would hook his fingers into the base runner's belt and hold him for several moments after the catch. Once Pete Browning of Louisville unbuckled his belt and struggled loose. John was left holding the belt, while

Browning ran down the third base line and scored the run while holding up his pants.

The Orioles enlisted the services of their congenial groundkeeper, Tom Murphy, in some other snide tricks. As the Orioles were developing into a team of expert bunters, the ground around third base was built up hill so bunts would remain in fair ground. Murphy also would mix finely chipped soap into the soil around the pitcher's box. This would bother opposing pitchers, as their hands would get slippery as they pitched the ball. Oriole pitchers knew the exact area where there was good clean sandy loam.

Murphy also had been instructed by Hanlon, captain Robinson, McGraw, and lesser lights to let the grass grow high in the outfield. Extra balls then were planted in this high grass, and when an enemy batsman hit into the tall grass, it frequently was to the advantage of the Orioles to dig up and field one of the planted balls. Steve Brodie's experience with the tall grass and a planted ball is one of the oldest legends in baseball. There are different versions, but the following was told to me by Jim Price, the Baltimore sports writer of the nineties, who claimed he was at Union Park when the amusing incident occurred.

"The St. Louis Browns were playing at Baltimore, and with Joe Quinn on first, Tommy Dowd hit a sharp drive to left center," reminisced Price. "Kelley cut across the path of the ball, apparently scooped it up, and threw to McGraw to catch Quinn at third base. Just as the single umpire was about to call Quinn out, Brodie, who had been chasing the real ball to the fence, threw it in from deep center, and gave away another of Baltimore's famous inside plays. After an argument, the umpire forfeited the game to St. Louis."

Brodie was another character McGraw, Robbie, and Jennings could tell stories about by the hour. "Mac" listed Brodie as one of baseball's six most picturesque characters, the others being Rube Waddell, Bugs Raymond, Ossee Schreckengost,

Larry McLean, and Babe Ruth. He made the listing before Dizzy Dean won his big league spurs.

"But Brodie was unconsciously funny," McGraw used to say. "He didn't mean to be funny, and actually took baseball quite seriously. It was his efforts to be serious and to take everything in its full literal sense that made him so amusing to the rest of us on the ball club."

Hanlon had been bawling out a group of players for not waiting out pitchers, and for hitting at bad balls. "That goes especially for you, Steve," he said. "You've been hitting at balls over your head. There's no harm in having a strike called on you once in a while. Now, if you don't take a strike now and then, and wait out the pitcher I'll fine you."

Brodie went to the plate with this idea firmly implanted in his mind. He took strike one, strike two, strike three.

Returning to the bench, he threw his bat down and remarked to Hanlon with unfeigned disgust. "Now, don't tell me I can't take 'em," he bellowed. "And, what's more, I could a knocked any of them fat pitches out of the park."

As the 1894 race went into its latter stage, Baltimore's leading rival was the New York Giants. The New Yorkers still were trying to overcome the effects of those four straight April defeats at Union Park. John Montgomery Ward had a strong club, and in Amos Rusie and Jouett Meekim he had two of the best pitchers in the league. This pair was good for 72 of the Giants' 88 victories. The Orioles started their final Western trip leading New York by only a half game. But, on this trip the Orioles showed their real greatness by winning 24 games out of 25, nailing down Baltimore's first pennant in Cleveland. They enjoyed one winning streak of eighteen straight. They had won thirteen in a row at home, and picked up five more on the road before they were stopped. McGraw used to like to tell how the Orioles might have won the entire 25 games. "We lost one game in Pittsburgh, when Robbie, the big fat lummox, couldn't get his feet out of the sticky mud in a wet game in Pittsburgh and missed an easy foul fly," he said. The tough season again had McGraw down to 123 pounds, including a big black moustache he had succeeded in raising.

In their first pennant-winning season, the Orioles won 89 games and lost 39 for a percentage of .695. Ward's second-place Giants had 88 victories and 44 defeats while the third-place Beaneaters won 83 and lost 49. The Baltimores had a club batting average of around .340, but they were under the all-time record batting average of .343 made by the fourth place Philadelphia Phillies in the same year. The Orioles also stole upward of 300 bases.

As mentioned earlier, 1894 was the first year of the new 60-foot, 6-inch pitching distance, and batting averages were higher than any year since then. Every regular on Hanlon's team batted better than .300. Joe Kelley led with a majestic .391; in one double-header, September 3, Joe clicked off nine hits, eight singles, and a two-bagger, in as many times at bat. The other Oriole regulars fared as follows: Brodie, .369; Keeler, .365; Robinson, .348; Brouthers, .344; McGraw, .340; Jennings, .332 (a gain of .140 points over 1893); Reitz, .306. Hanlon used as many as ten pitchers that season, though some remained briefly. Sadie McMahon was the big winner, with 26 victories and 8 defeats. Alas, it was his last big season! Of the pitchers who started the season only one other, Bill Hawke, with a 14-10 record, won more than six games. It showed the importance of the investments in Gleason, Esper, and Hemming.

Baltimore, with its string of second division teams behind it, almost blew its top over its new National League champions. The Chesapeake city celebrated with the wildest expression of pure unalloyed joy any pennant had brought to a municipality up to that time. Half the town was congregated at the railroad station to welcome the club home from its pennant-clinching western trip. Hundreds of Baltimore's finest had to save the Orioles from their proud but hysterical admirers. Even so a

54

number of the players were mauled by friendly fans who wanted to pat the heroes on the back.

Mayor Latrobe thanked each player personally for what he had done for the greater glory of Baltimore, the National Guard was called out in honor of the Orioles, and the city celebrated with the biggest baseball parade held in Baltimore prior to the great celebration of April 15, 1954, when the modern American League Orioles were welcomed back to Baltimore. All of this was climaxed with a big feast at the Hotel Rennert, where the Orioles, in full dress—including Steve Brodie—were wined, dined, and eulogized by city, state, and national officials.

Unfortunately, the wining and dining of the Orioles didn't stop with the city's big banquet. Every one wanted to buy the heroes a drink, and some of the heroes were accepting all invitations. Even the town's sporting girls, not to be outdone by the city's swells, partied the Oriole ball tossers, treating them to their best viands, wines, and other diversions. In fact, the Birds were wined and diverted to such a degree that they were easy picking for the New York Giants in the Temple Cup Series which followed the close of the regular season.

The Temple Cup Series was something like the present Shaughnessy play-offs in the International League, a four-out-of-seven series between the first and second clubs in the twelve-club National League. The Series was the brain-child of Col. William C. Temple, a Pittsburgh sportsman, and was intended to be a substitute for the earlier World Series between the champions of the National League and American Association. He offered a beautiful cup which was to be fought for at the end of each league season. For a while the Temple Cup was exhibited at the Baseball Museum in Cooperstown, N. Y.; it is now in the possession of the donor's son-in-law in Orlando, Fla.

Temple's rules provided for a players' pool, as in the modern World Series, with the winners taking 60 percent of the spoils and the losers 40 percent. However, individual Oriole and

Giant players, playing it most conservatively, entered into private agreements to pool a winner's and loser's share and split the difference.

With the exception of McGraw, who didn't drink until his playing days were over, and a few others, the Orioles still were groggy and bleary-eyed from days and nights of continuous entertainment when the first Temple Cup Series started in Baltimore, October 2. Von Der Horst and Hanlon doubled their normal scale of admission prices; Baltimore fans paid the hiked tariff but they saw a poor show. Sadie McMahon, Hanlon's best pitcher, was out of condition and didn't start a game. Duke Esper took on the bullet-firing Amos Rusie in the first game, and went down, 4 to 1. The fans saw a lot of hitting and base-running the next day, but the Orioles again finished on the wrong end, 9 to 6, as Meekim triumphed over Kid Gleason.

When the Series moved to New York for games on October 6 and 8, the teams followed the same pattern as in Baltimore. The third game was an exact replica of the first, with Amos Rusie winning a second 4 to 1 decision. This time Hanlon's defeated pitcher was George Hemming. An off day, October 7, didn't sober up the Birds, as Meekim annihilated Bill Hawke in the fourth and final tussle, 16 to 3.

Thus the Orioles, who started their season with four straight over New York, wound up by losing four straight to the haughty New Yorkers. Ward was contemptuous of the Birds when it was over. "I said all along that we had the better team," he insisted. "Baltimore owes its flag to its early start, and the team's rowdy tactics, intimidating and bull-dozing all umpires. But I am glad we showed them up before the fans of the nation." All of which made bad reading in Baltimore, and took some of the joy out of the championship.

The Series left many unpleasant repercussions. A winner's share was $768 and a loser's $360. That meant that a pooled winning and losing share was $1128, and players entering the private agreements each should have drawn $564. But most of the Giants welched and refused to abide by their side agreements. It started a feud that lasted as long as the Orioles remained a power in National League baseball. Whenever they caught up with the Giants, or players who had been on Ward's 1894 club, they greeted them with cries of "You dirty welchers! Filthy cheaters! You'd sell out your own mothers!"

However, McGraw and the few Baltimore players who had remained in condition felt the club had let them down and hadn't acted like real Orioles. Years later McGraw discussed the loss of this first Temple Cup Series in four straight games. "I was pretty sore at the time, but maybe the years have tempered my views," he said. "For most of the fellows, the race was over when we clinched the pennant in Cleveland. We had accomplished what we had set out to do—win the flag. And once the boys broke training, it wasn't easy to get back. Besides most of them looked at the Temple Cup Series as a series of glorified exhibitions. We'd won the pennant; that's all that counted. And, the side agreements the Orioles entered into with individual Giants killed any financial incentive to win. Not knowing that most of Ward's players would welch, they thought they'd get the same, win or lose. That, of course, was bad."

CHAPTER VI

Orioles Repeat
in 1895 and 1896

BECAUSE OF THE Giants' four straight victories in the 1894 Temple Cup Series, John Montgomery Ward insisted he had the best club in the country, despite Baltimore's unexpected pennant triumph. Many of the nation's fans felt the same way about it. But, when the Orioles repeated in 1895, and made it three straight in 1896, the entire country was willing to doff its hat to one of the great teams of baseball history. In fact, Foxy Ned's team made such a deep impress on the game that six decades have been unable to erase it. Not only in Baltimore, but wherever baseball is played, we still hear of the strategy and tactics of the old Orioles, the guts and fortitude of the old Orioles, and their never-say-die spirit.

Yet, Hanlon had no easy task in making it three straight. While the main cogs of the team were Keeler, Kelley, McGraw, Robinson, and Jennings, exigencies required numerous changes in the remainder of the caste. Oriole pitching never came up to the general caliber of the team, and the corps with which Ned finished the 1896 season had few carryovers from the staff assembled at Baltimore's 1894 Macon training camp. Kelley, Brodie, and Keeler remained the regular outfield trio on all three championship teams; Robbie and Bill Clarke made up the catching staff, but there were numerous changes in the infield, especially at first and second bases. And, at third, McGraw was incapacitated for most of the 1896 season.

Only the once light-hitting Jennings played through all three pennant-winning campaigns.

Hanlon's most important newcomer in 1895 was pitcher William Hoffer from Buffalo. They called him Willie, Bill, and Chick. He hailed from Cedar Rapids, where as a boy in his teens he had played on the same team with McGraw. Willie was in his early twenties; he had a good fast ball, great courage, and was a horse for work. Without Hoffer's superb pitching, the 1895 flag would not have been possible. He became the bellwether of the staff, winning 31 games and losing 7. He took up the slack when Sadie McMahon, bothered with arm trouble, slumped from 26-8 in 1894 to 10-4 in 1895. After the 1894 Temple Cup fiasco, pitchers Tony Mullane, Albert Inks, and Bill Hawke were dropped, the latter because of a serious illness.

George Hemming, the 1894 Washington acquisition, did well in 1895, winning twenty games and losing ten. Von Der Ahe of St. Louis still needed money, so Hanlon slipped him cash and Bill Kissinger for Art Clarkson. Clarkson, who had won only one game and lost seven for the 1895 Browns, won eleven and lost only three with the flashy Orioles behind him. Late in the 1895 season, Hanlon engaged Dr. Erasmus Arlington "Arlie" Pond, of Rutland, Vermont, who was to enjoy several successful pitching seasons with the Orioles before going to the Philippines as an Army doctor and surgeon during the Spanish-American War. Dr. Arlie remained in Manila as a practicing physician up to the time of his death in 1930.

Kid Gleason's arm was acting up, and when Heinie Reitz sprained an ankle, Hanlon assigned the Kid to second base, a position he was to play for the remainder of his long major league career. Gleason's presence in the regular line-up did not slow up the team's punch, as the aggressive Camden boy hit a lusty .323. However, the following winter, the busy trader, Hanlon, swapped the Jersey Kid to the Giants for first baseman Jack Doyle. Jack had the not entirely undeserved nickname of "Dirty" Doyle. He was one of the three managers Andy Freedman employed to help him run his 1895 Giants. An octogenarian, Jack Doyle still was listed as an active Cub scout in 1954.

Hanlon also developed first-base difficulties. Dennis Brouthers, in his seventeenth big league season, slowed down perceptibly, and after playing only five 1895 Oriole games Big Dan was shipped to Louisville. George Carey, a Western Leaguer, then played first base for the 1895 champions, but hit only .271, too light for a first baseman of that period, and in 1896 he was succeeded by Dirty Jack Doyle.

John McGraw also missed many games in these last two championship years. He played only 93 games in 1895, missing some thirty games at the close of the season because of malaria and loss of weight. It was to his credit that in the games he did play, he batted .374 and stole 69 bases. Reitz then filled in at third base. In 1896, McGraw's career was threatened by typhoid, which kept him out of Hanlon's line-up until August 25. He took part in only 19 late season games as Jim Donnelly, a hasty pick-up, filled in for him in 103 contests. Donnelly had played for the Washington National League club and with the Browns and Columbus of the old American Association. To fill other infield gaps the same season, Hanlon signed Billy Keister, a local Baltimore boy, Joe Quinn, formerly of the Browns, and John Irwin. Frank Bowerman, a big raw-boned kid from Michigan, who was to do a lot of catching for McGraw in New York, caught a few late-season Oriole games in 1895 and 1896.

The Giants, Baltimore's stubborn foe of 1894, stumbled into the second division in 1895, and the Orioles' leading rivals for the first half of the new season were the Pittsburgh Pirates led by Connie Mack. At the age of 33, the tall New Englander, serving his team as manager-catcher, was making a bold bid for his first pennant. During the months of April, May, and June, the Orioles and Pirates bobbed in and out of first place. "They're a good team," Hanlon advised his players, "and don't take them lightly. In Frank Killen, they've got the best left-handed pitcher since Matt Kilroy."

Then, on June 11, that very pitcher, Frank Killen, was severely spiked while covering the home plate at Union Park. We have told of the way the Orioles defiantly filed their spikes to frighten opponents. They also had a saying, "Git out of our way, if you don't want to git hurt." Another version was, "if you don't want to git killed." But, there is no reason to believe that the spiking was other than accidental. When a wild throw got away from Mack, Killen covered the plate, and the Oriole slider cut open the pitcher's right leg from thigh to ankle. Killen was confined to a Baltimore hospital for 49 days. The year before Killen had won 35 games, the most for any National League southpaw in one season. Out of action with his spike wounds for most of 1895, Killen won only seven games.

Even so, the Pirates managed to hang on until early August with Mack alternating his other two first-string pitchers, Pink Hawley and Bill Hart, every other day. Feeling between the clubs ran high.

"If ya hadn't almost killed Killen, we'd now be ten games in front," barked Jake Beckley, the Pittsburgh first baseman.

"Talking about killing, what's Mack doing to Pink Hawley? He's killing him, using him the way he does," chirped McGraw.

Mack interposed, "Hawley'll hold up, unless one of you Orioles cut him down like you did to Frank Killen."

"How you staying up there, you long-legged galoot—using black magic?" asked Hughie Jennings.

"Can't you control your drunks, Connie?" offered Joe Kelley. "They tell me they are running away with your club."

The Pittsburgh pitching staff eventually collapsed from overwork, as the Orioles had prophesied, and on August 10 the Orioles shoved the Pirates out of first place, this time for good. The Pirates died a lingering death, slipping from first to seventh in the last month and a half of the season.

With Pittsburgh disposed of, the Orioles' toughest rival

was Pat Tebeau's Cleveland Spiders, as tough and fighting a ball club as the Orioles. Tebeau managed the club from first base, and was as bellicose a character as ever played big league ball. Tebeau's pitching staff was headed by the great Cy Young (35-10) and George Cuppy (25-15), while Jesse Burkett, slashing crabby outfielder, led the league in 1895 with a spectacular .423. They called Jesse "the Crab." Other outstanding Spiders were catcher John Joseph "Rowdy" O'Connor and center fielder Jim "Loafer" McAleer. Jim was a center fielder much like Ned Hanlon, a great fly-hawk but only mediocre with the bat.

Sparks flashed whenever the Orioles and Spiders clashed, and it wasn't until Baltimore's last series of the season that the Birds finally shook off the persistent pursuers from Ohio. It made all of the Orioles feel good when they clinched their 1895 flag at New York's Polo Grounds, where they had fared so poorly against the Giants in the Temple Cup Series just a year before. Baltimore took its second pennant with 87 victories, 43 defeats and percentage of .669, three games ahead of Cleveland with 84-46, .646. The Phillies were a good third; and far down the list, in ninth place, were the Giants.

Baltimore fans got no more fun out of the 1895 Temple Cup Series than out of the 1894 rout. Again the Orioles were trounced soundly by the second-place club. This year the Orioles took the games more seriously than in the preceding fall, but there again was a tendency to break training and let down, after the pennant was clinched in New York. However, they again were up against determined opposition. Where the 1894 Birds knocked their heads out against the fast-ball pitching of Rusie and Meekim, in their second Temple Cup venture, they were the victims of one of the greatest pitchers of them all, the venerable Cy Young, winner of 511 big league victories. The Ohio farmer then was 28, and in his very prime. The Orioles got one game out of five from the Spiders, but three times they were blown over by the formidable Young.

62

This year the Series started in Cleveland, and the Birds were two down before they reached Union Park. As in 1894, the Series opened October 2, and the first game proved the best, the closest, and most exciting of the Series. Sadie McMahon, who had closed the season strongly, was selected by Hanlon to face Young, and the Wilmingtonian gave a good account of himself before losing in the ninth, 5 to 4. With the game all tied up, Chief Zimmer, the Cleveland catcher, singled home Pat Tebeau with the winning run. A crowd of 9,000, considered splendid for that period, attended the game and helped liven things with a vegetable shower against the detested Orioles.

Willie Hoffer, the young 35-game winner, failed in the second game, losing to George "Nig" Cuppy, 7 to 2. Cuppy's real name was George Maceo Koppe, and the Orioles tried to make something out of it. Their bench bench jockeys demanded to know, "Where did you get that Cuppy, Kopps?" But Cuppy, Koppe, or Kopps refused to let their verbal barbs get under his skin.

By the time the Series shifted to Baltimore after a lapse of a day, the oyster town's citizenry had become rather bored with the Temple Cup and the string of Oriole defeats. Only a mediocre crowd marched through Von Der Horst's turnstiles. Encouraged by McMahon's strong effort against Young in the first game, Hanlon gave Sadie a chance to even things up with Cy before the home folk. But, it was another boring exhibition for Baltimore, as Young triumphed easily in this one, 7 to 1. That made seven straight Temple Cup reverses for the Birds. There was a short respite for Baltimore when Duke Esper won a 5-0 shutout in the fourth game, but Young applied the clamps in the fifth and closing contest, when he downed Hoffer, 5 to 2. That made the two-year Temple Cup showing of the fabulous Orioles one victory and eight defeats for a dismal .111.

The Orioles heard plenty about it in 1896, when in Cleveland, New York, and other hostile towns, they were greeted with taunts of "Fake Champions!" "Quitters!" and "Can't take it when the chips are down."

Such diatribes served to stir up the Orioles to their highest endeavors, and in 1896 they won their easiest pennant. The second-place club again was Tebeau's pugnacious Spiders, but this year there was quite a bit of daylight between the three-time champions and the Cleveland runner-up, a matter of nine and a half games. The Orioles reached their highest peak that season, .698, with 90 victories and 39 defeats. With the spark-plug, McGraw, idle most of the year, this really was a surpass-ing achievement. Cleveland followed with 80 victories, 48 defeats and .625. In Baltimore's three pennant-winning years, Von Der Ahe saw his Browns finish ninth in 1894 and eleventh in both 1895 and 1896. Now surely Chris was the dumkopf, and Von Der Horst the real smartie.

Willie Hoffer again was the pitching leader of the 1896 champions, winning 26 games and losing 7. McMahon did more work than in 1895, winning 12 and losing 8. Charlie Esper won 14 and lost 5, while George Hemming and the new man, Dr. Arlie Pond, had almost identical records, 15-7 and 15-8, respectively. Joe Corbett, brother of Gentleman Jim Corbett, the heavyweight champ, closed the season in a blaze of smoke, winning three out of four games. The club again stole over 300 bases, hit over .300, and guess who was high man on the roost? None other than the old banjo hitter, Hughie Jennings, who hit an imposing .397.

This year the Orioles were determined to wipe out the stigma of their earlier Temple Cup defeats. The taunts and insults of the season had a chastening effect. Hanlon, Jennings, McGraw, and Robinson impressed on their fellow players that if they lost again they really would be the laughing stock of baseball, and would deserve the hated term of "Fake Champions." This autumn there was no breaking of training after the pennant was clinched. All players were honor bound to put off all partying and heavy drinking until the Temple Cup Series was over. They kept as keyed up as are present-day major league champions on the eve of a World Series. McGraw further encouraged the club by announcing he would play the entire Series.

The result was a smashing victory for the Orioles in which they reversed the order of 1895, rolling the sputtering, protesting Spiders in the dust four straight. That October the brilliant Young had no terror for the Birds, as they even reversed the one-side scores of the preceding fall. In the opener, Willie Hoffer easily downed Young, 7 to 1. Though a 29-game National League winner, Cy wasn't in good condition for the Series and did not pitch after this game. Impressed by Joe Corbett's late-season form, Hanlon sent him against Bobbie Wallace in the second game. The Orioles lit into young Bobbie for four runs in the first inning and Corbett breezed home an easy 7 to 2 winner. Wallace, the defeated pitcher, later turned to infielding and became a Hall of Fame shortstop.

After these one-sided victories, the Orioles were sure they had their aggressive rivals on the run. They yipped, chortled, gnashed their teeth, and told the Spiders they always had been a bunch of bums. Hoffer came back to win the third game from Cuppy, 6-2, and when the Series was resumed in Cleveland three days later, Joe Corbett wound it up with a 5-0 shutout as Cuppy again was the defeated Spider pitcher.

Even if the Orioles got a big moral uplift from winning their first Temple Cup Series, it was a poor Series financially. Though the Temple Cup Series was planned as a four-out-of-seven affair—as is the present World Series—clubs were winning and losing so quickly that it never could build up any suspense or dramatic interest. After the second game in Baltimore, Von Der Horst and Hanlon slashed their prices for the third game, and with the Spiders behind, three games to nothing, when the Series shifted to Cleveland, only a Corporal's guard was on hand for the fourth game.

Winners of three straight pennants, and now finally Temple Cup winners, the fame of the Orioles spread all over the country. The sports writers were hailing them as the greatest team baseball had produced to that day, greater than Anson's old Chicago White Stockings and Frank Selee's Boston champions of 1891-92-93. The nation especially took little Willie Keeler, the club's brilliant right fielder, to its heart, as Wee Willie displaced such earlier favorites as Cap Anson, "Old Hoss" Radbourne, King Kelly, and Hughie Duffy in the country's affections. Willie was such a mite; he made his hits through use of his wits, rather than brawn. His explanation for his sturdy hitting, "I hit 'em where they ain't," fascinated both the cultured and uncultured. It was a perfect recipe for successful hitting. For Willie truly was a magician with a bat. He could bunt, line the ball through holes in the infield, or dump little flys over the heads of the infielders. If the outfielders played him too close, he had enough power to drive the ball over their heads.

Like all the other Orioles, Keeler dearly loved to play baseball. One day, when he was in his cups, he burst out laughing. When fellow players questioned him about his hilarity, he replied, "I'm laughing about those suckers, the club owners, paying me for playing ball. Why, I would pay my way into their parks, if that was the only way I had of getting into a ball game."

Willie always was a bachelor. In some ways, he was like a little boy who never grew up. He always felt the Fourth of July should be fittingly celebrated. When it was customary to play morning and afternoon games on this holiday, Willie would go out to his position, with a revolver, loaded with blanks, in his rear pocket. At regular intervals during the game, Willie would empty his revolver into the sky.

So much has been written of Keeler's hitting that one gets the impression that his talent was only in that direction. But he could run bases with McGraw and Jennings. He stole 73 bases for the 1896 champions, and his fielding was on a par with his hitting and base-running.

Jim Price told me of a catch he once saw Keeler make in a holiday game in Washington. There was a rusty barbed wire fence outside of right field. A Washington player hit a ball which was dropping on the other side of the barbed wire, when Willie leaped, thrust his left arm through the barbed wire and caught the ball bare-handed. Keeler's arm was badly scratched from the barbed wire, but another Oriole had got his man. "It was the greatest catch I ever saw in my long career as a baseball writer and sports editor," Price told me.

Steve Brodie had so much respect for Keeler's fielding ability that he felt Willie could play both Steve's center field patch and his own right field. A fan sitting in the center field bleachers had been riding Brodie unmercifully, and after some difficulty Steve located the abusive rooter. Bringing a ladder from the clubhouse, he said to Keeler, "Do you mind covering center field as well as right field in this inning. I got that guy spotted, and I'm going up there to give him a going over."

Overhearing the conversation other players protested, "But, you can't do that, Steve. Having only eight players on the field is illegal. They might forfeit the game against us."

"What's illegal about it?" Brodie blurted. "Willie can play both fields. He plays 'em better than I do."

Of course, the Orioles were fighters and umpire baiters, about the worst in baseball. During the author's career as a New York baseball writer, he knew former National League presidents Tom Lynch and John Heydler quite intimately. Both had been National League umpires in the nineties— during the period of Oriole greatness—and in reminiscent moods they have told of some of their troubles with the old Orioles. Lynch especially had trouble with the Birds. Though Tom was the most honest of men, the Orioles constantly accused him of being biased against them and of being pro-Boston, because he was a New Englander coming from New Britain, Conn. "Unquestionably, the Orioles and the Cleveland Spiders were the worst two teams I ever umpired against," said Tom. "When I umpired Baltimore games, I thought the Orioles were the worst, but when I worked in Cleveland, I wasn't sure. Maybe, they were even tougher and meaner than the Orioles. As for individual players who were toughest on umpires, I'd say it was a tie between McGraw and Pat Tebeau."

Once, while discussing the difficult periods of the past, the usually mild-mannered John Heydler really pitched into the Orioles. "We hear a lot of the glories of the old Orioles," he said. "Yes, they were a great team: they could run, hit, steal bases, and introduced a lot of fine plays into baseball. But there is another side of the picture which seldom is told today. The Orioles were mean, vicious, ready at any time to maim a rival player or an umpire, if it helped their cause. The things they would say to an umpire were unbelievably vile, and they broke the spirits of some fine men. I've seen umpires bathe their feet by the hour after McGraw and others spiked them through their shoes. The worst of it was that they got away with much of their browbeating and hooliganism. Seeing them unpunished for flagrant misconduct on the field, other clubs patterned after them, and I feel the lot of the umpire never was worse than in the years that the Orioles were flying high."

However, even this umpire-baiting had its amusing phases. An aggregation of Joe Kelley hero worshippers presented the hard-hitting Cambridge Irishman with a watch before a game in Union Park. Kelley thanked his well-wishers and handed the watch to a clubhouse attendant to keep until after the game. The clubhouse man had to go out on an errand and he asked Umpire George Burnham, "Would you mind taking care of Joe Kelley's watch until I get back." Burnham stuck the watch in his pocket as he walked out to start the game.

Burnham later called Kelley out on a close play at second. It resulted in quite a rhubarb, with Kelley boiling over and giving Burnham the full Oriole treatment.

"Now, for saying that, you're out of the game," snapped Burnham.

Kelley beefed some more. "For that, I ought to bash your ugly face in," he roared.

68

Burnham reached into his pocket for a watch, and said, "Now, I'm giving you just one minute to get off the field."

Kelley slapped the watch out of his hand, and kicked it around the field.

"Now, that will cost you $25, and the watch will cost you $100," said Burnham.

"What'd you mean that watch will cost me $100?" shot back Kelley. "You're crazy if you think that $3.00 Waterbury of yours is worth anything like that."

"It's not my watch; it's yours," said Burnham. From then on Burnham's nickname was "Watch" Burnham.

Because of Washington's numerous government workers, who were the capital city's best fans, games in the District of Columbia did not start until 4.30 P.M. The contests usually were finished in twilight, and there were constant arguments about calling games. As Washington usually was behind, the Senators wanted to continue playing; the visiting club wanted the game called.

The Orioles had a good lead on Washington in the seventh inning, and it was so dark that it was difficult to follow the ball. With two out, and the count two strikes on the batsman, Robinson did not throw the ball back to McMahon. Sadie went through the motion of delivering the ball, and a few moments later Robbie smacked his glove and produced the ball, which never had left his hand.

"Three strikes; you're out," called Umpire Gaffney.

The enraged Washington batsman jumped in front of Gaffney and raged, "How do you get that way, you blind bat? That ball was two feet outside."

On another occasion in Washington, Captain Robinson was trying to have Umpire Jack Kerns call the game because of darkness, but Kerns was adamant and said, "It's light enough for one more inning." Robbie then had pitcher Art Clarkson pitch him a lemon, and Kerns ruled it a strike. The rotund catcher showed the lemon to Kerns, saying, "We left the ball on the bench." Kerns dryly admitted, "Well, I guess that will be enough! Game called on account of darkness!"

On a team of fire eaters and wildcats, Captain Robinson was the jollier and peacemaker. If McGraw, Jennings, or Kelley got an umpire or player badly riled, Robbie would rub salve in the man's wounds and say, "Now don't mind what McGraw has called you. You know he goes off half-cocked, but he doesn't mean half that he says." It induced Arlie Latham, a fine colorful player who turned umpire in the nineties to quip: "Robbie and McGraw work both ends against the middle. Robbie sleeps in a salve factory, and McGraw eats gunpowder for breakfast and washes it down with blood."

Baltimore fans also got into the act. McGraw early learned the lesson of crowd psychology, and knew how to egg on the crowd against umpires and rivals. Oriole bleacher fans were among the first to bring small mirrors to the park as their baseball equipment. They never had any hesitancy in flashing the mirrors into a batsman's eyes, provided, of course, that the batter wasn't any Oriole.

For years we've heard the stories of the toughness of the Orioles in withstanding physical pain and playing despite injuries and illness. Even today when a player suffers a bruised finger or lesser leg injury, sports writers frequently call down from the press box, "Take it, like an old Oriole." It is true they stuck injured fingers into the ground, spit tobacco juice on spike wounds, and frequently played with fevers, broken fingers and maimed ankles. Yet, the numerous games missed by McGraw, and frequent substitutions in the Baltimore line-ups during the three championship years showed the Orioles were only human.

The Orioles were a clanish lot. With them it was "One for all, and all for one." Few teams ever had their club spirit, off the field as well as on the field. Players today wander off in groups of two and three, and all clubs have their lone wolves. On the Orioles, they did things together. If they went to the theatre, a legitimate drama or a burlesque house, the entire club went, sitting in one section. On off-days, they attended the races at Bowie or Pimlico. They bowled and played pool together; attended fights, got into fights, and always they talked baseball.

Long after the old Orioles were broken up, and players were scattered to the four winds, Oriole survivors held annual reunions, attended by Hanlon, McGraw, Robinson, Kelley, Keeler, Jennings, Gleason, Clarke, McMahon, and lesser Baltimore lights. And still they talked Oriole baseball.

CHAPTER VII

Beaneaters Check Brave Attempt for Four Straight

HAVING WON THREE successive flags, Ned Hanlon and his aggressive band of baseball warriors were keenly ambitious to make it four straight. Two of the early pioneering clubs of major league baseball had won four straight, the Boston Red Stockings of the National Association in 1872-73-74-75, and the St. Louis Browns of the American Association in 1885-86-87-88. But no club had done it in the National League. "That's no reason we can't do it," Hanlon told his players at the start of the 1897 season. "This still is a young club, right in its prime, and there is no reason why we shouldn't go on winning pennants for some time to come." To which Robbie, Jennings, McGraw, Keeler, and Kelley gave a vigorous "Amen."

In order to fortify the club for No. 4, Hanlon made another strengthening deal, giving up the colorful but not too smart Steve Brodie to Pittsburgh for Jake Stenzel. The Orioles tossed in $2,000 to sweeten the deal. It proved another of Ned's foxy moves. Stenzel, a Cincinnati German whose real name was Jacob Stelzle, was 30 but he had one more good year, and contributed a .351 batting average and a flock of stolen bases to the Oriole cause in 1897.

Stenzel was one of five Oriole regulars who hit better than .350 that season. Willie Keeler hit a phenomenal .432, second highest in major league baseball; Kelley followed with .389; Dirty Jack Doyle hit a lusty .356; and Hugh Jennings was right behind him with .353.

This was Wee Willie's finest hour, the season in which he

reached the baseball stratosphere and gave Baltimore its first batting championship. Keeler began a 44-game batting streak on the Orioles' opening day, April 22, and it lasted until June 18, nearly two months later. Game after game, the wee one bagged one, two, three, or four safe blows. Never was "hitting 'em where they ain't" so profitable, and so much fun. It was the longest batting streak in the majors until Joe DiMaggio, great player of the modern Yankees, hit in 56 successive games in 1941.

If Keeler was checked for a day, the little Brooklynite continued his assault on National League pitchers for the remainder of the season. He set a record for that period of 243 hits, while his 1897 record of 199 singles still stands today. Keeler played in only 128 games that year, contrasted with 154 games played by George Sisler of the Browns in 1920 when Gorgeous George hung up the present major league record of 257 hits. Frank O'Doul and Bill Terry, who jointly hold the National League mark with 254 hits, also both played through full 154 game seasons. How many hits Keeler could have made in 1897 had he had the advantage of an 154-game schedule can only be conjectured. However, as he averaged close to 1.9 hits a game, in 26 more contests he would have made 49 more hits, or a total of 292.

Hanlon also felt he had a strengthened pitching staff. Sadie McMahon, headliner of the 1894 champs and still of some service in 1895 and 1896, faded out completely. He appeared in only nine games, and did not fetch in a single victory. His defection was more than made up by the splendid progress of two youngsters of 1896, Joe Corbett and Jerry Nops. Corbett followed up his two 1896 Temple Cup victories with a superb 24-8 showing. It looked as though Joe would be as good a pitcher as his famous brother, Jim, was a fighter. Nops, a lefty who came from the Phillies late in 1896, turned in a 20-7 record. Willie Hoffer still was good enough to win 22 out of 32 decisions, while Doctor Arlie Pond won 18 and lost 9. A real formidable quartet for that day! A fifth pitcher, Morris

"Doc" Amole, who served in fill-in roles, won four and lost four.

As early as the spring months, the Orioles were satisfied they wouldn't have much to fear from their stubborn foe of 1895 and 1896, the Cleveland Spiders. Cy Young, who had averaged 32 victories for the five previous seasons, lacked his usual effectiveness, dropping to a 21-18 season, mediocre for Cy.

"Young isn't the pitcher he used to be, and without him winning his customary thirty to thirty-five games, the Spiders are just another ball club," fanned Robbie in the clubhouse. "I guess we can write them off."

"The Giants again look tough. Scrappy Bill Joyce has them hustling, and Rusie never was faster," offered Hugh Jennings. "They may be the team we have to beat."

"Aren't you fellows overlooking Boston?" asked Joe Kelley, the man from Cambridge. "They're better now than any time since they won the National League pennants in 1891, 1892, and 1893."

"You're right, Joe," said Hanlon, who had listened in on the discussion. "When the teams find their proper levels, Boston is the club we'll have to beat."

It just happened that the Orioles played a big, though involuntary, part in converting the Beaneaters from a good fighting club to a red hot penant threat that fought the Orioles every inch of the way. In an early series, the Orioles cleaned up the team from Boston three straight. In looking for the goat of these early reverses, Frank Selee, the Boston manager, decided it was the 33-year-old first baseman, Tom Tucker. He was the same Foghorn Tucker who had played for Baltimore before the Brotherhood War. A native of Holyoke, he had a strong following all over Massachusetts. But Selee decided Tom was showing his age; he first benched Tucker and later released him to Washington. And he moved Fred Tenney, Brown graduate, to first base. A left-hander, who had caught and played the outfield for Boston after graduating from

74

college, Tenney quickly blossomed into an all-time first-base great and became a member of that sterling Boston infield of Jimmy Collins, Herman Long, Bobbie Lowe, and Tenney.

During most of the season, it was a one-two race, with first the Orioles and then the Beaneaters in the front seat, and both clubs playing around .700 percent ball. Both Oriole players and Baltimore baseball writers accused Tom Lynch, who worked in many of their games, of favoritism toward Boston. It resulted in a bitter feud between the Birds and old Tom, which exploded into a terrific battle between Lynch and Jack Doyle at the Boston grounds. The two men swung hard and then rolled around the ground in fierce combat. Joe Corbett and Joe Kelley held Lynch, while others grabbed Doyle, but Lynch got it in his head that the two Joes had joined in the attack. He broke loose, and started swinging at the peacemakers. This gave some of the bleacherites an idea it was a Donnybrook, as they leaped over the bleacher rail to get into the melee. Others threw bottles at Baltimore players, but finally a platoon of Boston police, responding to a riot call, restored order. One of Lynch's eyes was closed by Doyle's punches, but Tom went on with the game, and umpired the remainder of the series with a beautiful shiner.

Eventually the clubs met in Baltimore in late September in the city's most memorable baseball series. The season had only a week to go, and Baltimore led by a single point, .707 to .706. A delegation of 125 Bostonians, the vanguard of what was to become Boston's famous Royal Rooters, accompanied their team to Baltimore and helped root the Beaneaters home, 6 to 4, in the first game. That enabled Boston to seesaw in front by a few points.

The Orioles regained their one point lead by winning the second game, 6 to 3, and then practically the entire season's play was put on the line in the third and concluding game. Unquestionably the cupidity of Von Der Horst and Hanlon was a big factor in the Orioles losing a burlesque by a score of 19 to 10. Von Der Horst agreed with such early baseball men as Von Der Ahe and Charley Ebbets in their contention, "Never let a dollar get away; you never know when you'll be needing it." The double-decked Union Park grandstand and bleachers seated approximately 9,500, but all Baltimore wanted to see this pennant-winning game and Von Der Horst was there to please. He sold so many tickets that the fans were massed behind the catcher, stood along the foul lines and stood so deep in the outfield that the outfielders played on the necks of the infielders.

The game quickly developed into a farce, as any kind of a pop fly was a ground-rule double. Of course, the crowded field worked the same handicap on both clubs, but Boston got the majority of these cheap hits. There was no chance to retrieve overthrows or poor pitches. They, too, were covered by ground rules. The Orioles had no room to spread for their inside tactics; if any balls had been hid in the high grass of the outfield they would have been trampled under the feet of the great overflow throng. Von Der Horst gave his paid attendance as 25,390, the best in Baltimore for many years and one of the big attendances of nineteenth century baseball. Even so, all present were not included in Von's official figures. Baltimore newspapers said another 2,000 got in by breaking down an outfield fence, while an additional 5,000 took in the game from adjacent housetops.

Hugh Fullerton, gifted Chicago baseball writer of the nineties and early decades of this century, tells of a catch Willie Keeler made in this final Baltimore-Boston series in his book, *Touching Second,* written in collaboration with John Evers. The catch took place in the second game, the one won by the Orioles. Right field, Willie's pasture, was rough and weedy, and back of it was a high fence used for advertising purposes. Inside the fence sloped at an angle of sixty-five degrees, though it was straight on the outside. With two runners on base, Chick Stahl, the crack Boston center fielder, hit a long fly to right, which looked like the winning clout for the Beaneaters. Fullerton reported that Keeler, running like a scared rabbit, mounted the fence, higher and higher, and with a final thrust caught the ball just as it was clearing the fence. Then, according to Hughie, the little outfielder's momentum was so great that he ran for another fifteen feet on top of the fence before falling some distance to the street below. The umpire ruled he had made a legal catch before tumbling out of the park.

Boston's 19-10 farcical victory in the third game enabled the Beaneaters to leave Baltimore a game to the good. Each club had one more series to play, and when it was over Boston had a record of 93 victories, 39 defeats, and a percentage of .705. Baltimore followed with 90 victories, 40 defeats, and a percentage of .693. In their battle to make it four straight, the Birds had been stopped by a mere twelve points. Since 1897 no major league club with a percentage of .693 ever has been defeated for a pennant. The highest second-place percentages since then were .680 by the 1909 Cubs and .675 by the 1942 Dodgers. Oddly enough, the .693 second-place Oriole percentage of 1897 was within a few points of the winning percentages of two of the previous pennant winners—.695 in 1894 and .698 in 1896. Only in 1895, when the club finished with .669, did it fall under this .690 to .700 average.

Injuries to iron men Orioles also were a big factor in the team's failure to make it four straight. The scrappy McGraw was back at his third base corner, but a bruised heel and other injuries limited his play to 105 games. Even so, he rallied sufficiently from his 1896 attack of typhoid to hit .326 and steal 42 bases. Jennings missed some 20 games because of spike wounds, and the club missed the steadying influence of Captain Wilbert Robinson behind the plate. Robbie suffered from a broken finger and leg injuries and took part in only 47 games. Bill Clarke, second-string catcher, caught 63 games, but when he hit only .274, Hanlon gave more work to Frank Bowerman, Michigan youngster, and Frank showed himself to be a real big leaguer, hitting .323 in 33 games.

After losing out to the Beaneaters by 12 points in the

77

National League race, the Orioles turned about and tore the Boston men to shreds in the 1897 Temple Cup Series. This post-season Series between the clubs which had just battled so furiously for the National League flag was definitely anticlimax. Except for a pretty good first game attendance in Boston, when the Beaneaters won by a score of 13 to 12, the crowds were poor. In Baltimore Von Der Horst had no occasion to put up his outfield ropes, as the Maryland fans still were exhausted from the late September series. Even though they were playing before empty benches, the Orioles rallied from their first game Temple Cup defeat to clean up the Beaneaters in the next four games, 13-11, 8-3, 12-11, and 9-3. It was a slam-bang Series, with extra-base hits a dime a dozen. In addition to winning the regularly scheduled Temple Cup Series, four games to one, the Orioles also defeated the Beaneaters in two exhibitions played outside of Boston, 11-10 in Springfield and 8-6 in Worcester. "What a crime we couldn't have won one of these when we needed a victory so badly in September," moaned the Birds.

So, the club which lost eight out of nine Temple Cup games in 1894 and 1895 wound up with eight out of nine victories in 1896 and 1897. Three times in the four Series, the second-place team was the victor. As a result of four one-sided Series, the three victories for the runner-up club, and the public's general apathy toward the games in 1896 and 1897, Col. Temple, with the consent of the National League, retired the cup after Baltimore had won temporary possession of it in 1896 and 1897.

Another interesting development in Baltimore baseball about this time was the opening of the Diamond Cafe by John McGraw and captain Wilbert Robinson. It was located at 519 North Howard Street, where the two popular Orioles leased three floors which were used for a dining room, a bar, bowling alleys, and pool and billiard rooms. It soon became a rendezvous for Baltimore's sporting blood—ball players, jockeys, horse trainers, fighters, runners. The Diamond Cafe today is

78

best remembered in sports history as the place where the game of duck pins was born.

Ned Hanlon made one more try for a fourth Baltimore pennant in 1898, the year of the Spanish-American War, but again had to be satisfied with second place. In many respects, this campaign was a repetition of 1897. Willie Keeler again was the National's batting champion, but with a reduced average of .379. And Willie's steals slumped from 62 to 26. The Orioles again provided the champion Beaneaters with their toughest competition, but they couldn't make it as close as they did the year before. In a new extended 150-game schedule, the Birds finished six games behind. Boston won 102 games and lost 47, while the Orioles won 96 and lost 53. The Birds led the third place Cincinnati Reds by five and a half games.

All baseball was hit hard by the Spanish-American War. The United States had not yet reached the status of a great world power. While Admiral Dewey made quick work of the Spanish fleet in Manila harbor early in the war, several other Spanish fleets were at large and there were frequent war scares in the Atlantic coast cities of Baltimore, New York, Philadelphia, Boston, and Charleston. With fans of former years massed in front of newspaper bulletin boards to read the latest war returns, the ball parks often were deserted. Despite a second-place club, business at Union Park was bad.

Before the war clouds broke, Hanlon was busy with his famous trades, and again put over some dandies. The best was a deal with Washington whereby he obtained first baseman Dennis "Dan" McGann, second baseman Gene DeMontreville and pitcher Doc Jim McJames from Washington for Jack Doyle and Heinie Reitz. Doyle went to Washington as manager, but soon got into a scrap and moved on to New York.

Dennis "Dan" McGann was a young first baseman, a hothead from Shelbyville, Kentucky, who was destined to go far in baseball. He played a bang-up first base for Hanlon that season and batted .298. Eugene Napoleon DeMontreville was a handsome, moustachioed French-Canadian from St. Paul, a dashing fellow who contributed a .325 batting average to the 1898 cause. Dr. McJames, who played baseball while working for his medical degree, was a polished South Carolinian. His pitching record zoomed like those of earlier Washington pitchers shifted to Baltimore; from 14-24 in 1897 to 27-14 in 1898.

It actually was little short of amazing how Hanlon could make over his pitching staff from one season to another and still run one-two. Of his "Big Four" of 1897—Hoffer, Corbett, Pond, and Nops—only the latter was of any service in 1898. Jerry, the left-hander, won nineteen games and lost ten. Hoffer's arm went bad, and after losing five games, Willie did some substitute outfield chores and then was released to Pittsburgh. Corbett did not report, and there were stories he was injured while serving as a sparring partner for his brother, Gentleman Jim. After Dr. Arlie Pond pitched only two games, winning one and losing one, he marched off to war, joining the Medical Corps.

Losing three pitchers such as Hoffer, Corbett, and Pond would have wrecked the average club, but Foxy Ned was ready for these new emergencies. He had a doctor already to fill Doc Pond's place in the previously mentioned Dr. McJames. Stepping into Willie Hoffer's former big pitching shoes was Jim Hughes, a brilliant 22-year-old youngster from Sacramento, who had a sensational freshman year, winning twenty-one games and losing eleven. Al Maul, a veteran who had been a star in Pittsburgh and Philadelphia, had been acquired from the Phillies late in the 1897 season; he won twenty and lost seven. A pretty good staff dug up in a jiffy!

After Stenzel's "one more good season," old Jake slumped to a .254 batting pace, and promptly was exiled to the St. Louis Browns, while good old Steve Brodie was regained in a deal with Pittsburgh for Frank Bowerman. And was Steve

80

happy to be back? "I feel like I been rescued from a grave-yard," was his greeting when he returned to the Orioles.

In addition to a second batting title for Keeler and the fine pitching of the youngsters, McJames and Hughes, other high spots of the 1898 second place finish were the continued strong hitting of Kelley and Jennings, and McGraw playing 141 games, the most he played in any season in his entire career. Johnny was pretty well over his health difficulties, batted .334 and oddly enough hit his 42 stolen bases of 1897 right on the nose

This was the last season all of the famous National League Orioles, most of them fighting Irishmen, were teamed together. But what careers they still had ahead of them! John McGraw, Hugh Jennings, Wilbert Robinson, Joe Kelley, Kid Gleason, and Frank Bowerman blossomed into big league managers. McGraw, after serving his managerial apprenticeship in Baltimore, directed the Giants for thirty years; Jennings handled the Detroit Tigers and the impetuous Ty Cobb through fourteen tempestuous seasons; while Robinson, by this time affectionately known as Uncle Robbie, led the so-called Brooklyn Daffiness Boys through twelve historic campaigns. Kelley directed National League clubs in both Cincinnati and Boston; Bowerman also managed the Braves; and Kid Gleason led the White Sox's greatest team. Sadie McMahon, Jack Doyle, and later Joe Kelley served long and meritorious careers as top-ranking scouts, while Bill Clarke was Princeton baseball coach for nearly four decades.

Between Hanlon and his famous alumni, McGraw, Jennings, Robinson and Gleason, they won 21 big league pennants. Yet, the bad luck in the early Baltimore Temple Cup Series clung to the old Orioles in later World Series competition. McGraw won only three out of nine Series; Jennings lost his three Series in Detroit; and Robbie dropped both the 1916 and 1920 Series in Brooklyn. Kid Gleason had a club good enough to win any World Series in Chicago in 1919, but traitors on his team sold him out for a mess of pottage.

CHAPTER VIII

Birds Victims of Syndicate Ball

SYNDICATE ball raised its ugly head in the National League in the nineties. Things then were permitted which never would pass the scrutiny of the well-run major leagues and the Commissioner's office today. As the result of financial difficulties of the Giants during the Brotherhood War, A. H. Soden, president of the Boston club, John T. Brush, Cincinnati Red president, and a brother of Al Spalding, Chicago owner, held substantial blocks of stock in the influential New York club. The Robinson brothers, who had made their money in Cleveland traction, owned both the Cleveland and St. Louis clubs. Because the Spiders, their better team, weren't drawing expected crowds in Cleveland, Frank Robinson shifted the Spiders to St. Louis, where they became the present-day Cardinals, and inflicted the leftovers of Chris Von Der Ahe's Browns on the defenseless fans of Cleveland.

It was at this time that the Baltimore Orioles and Brooklyn Dodgers got into the act, forming a two-team syndicate and pooling their players and other assets. Charles H. Byrne, early president and biggest stockholder of the Dodgers, died in 1898, and a former enterprising bookkeeper, Charles A. Ebbets, was elected president. Ferdinand Abell, a professional gambler, was Ebbets' associate. Von Der Horst and Hanlon purchased the old Byrne interest in the Brooklyn club, also stock owned by George Chauncey, former backer of the Brooklyn Brotherhood team who had been taken into the Brooklyn fold after the Players League collapsed. Ebbets and Abell, with the latter providing the money, then bought a substantial piece of the Orioles. After the stock purchases, Von Der Horst held controlling interest in both the Brooklyn and Baltimore clubs and each club had the same board of directors. Von Der Horst was satisfied to permit young Ebbets to remain president in Brooklyn, while Hanlon came out of the combine in a most anomalous role for a top-ranking baseball man. He was manager of the Brooklyn team, while still retaining the presidency of the Orioles.

Who was the author of this Brooklyn-Baltimore syndicate? Some think it was the brainchild of the imaginative young Brooklyn president, Ebbets, but more likely it originated with Hanlon and Von Der Horst, probably the shrewd Foxy Ned. Brooklyn, an independent city prior to 1898, had just been taken into Greater New York as one of the five boroughs. From visiting the city with the Orioles, Hanlon visualized the borough's future growth and its baseball possibilities. Also both Hanlon and Von Der Horst were disgruntled with the scant crowds that attended Union Park games in 1898 and with the continued rumors of shady business when the Orioles blew their chance for four straight in 1897.

Unquestionably the first objective of the move was to give Brooklyn, which had finished tenth in 1898, a championship as quickly as possible. Perhaps, using the same premise which actuated the Robinson brothers when they shifted Cy Young, Jesse Burkett, Pat Tebeau, Rhody Wallace, and other stars to St. Louis for the expected better draw, Hanlon and Von Der Horst assigned the Oriole greats, Willie Keeler, Joe Kelley, Hugh Jennings, and lesser lights, to Brooklyn. Oriole president Hanlon still wanted a presentable team in Baltimore, so long as it didn't interfere with Brooklyn manager Hanlon's plans for an early pennant winner.

The players of both clubs were pooled, with a stipulation that Ned Hanlon was to take no Oriole players after April 15. At first, it also was Hanlon's intention to take McGraw and Robinson to Brooklyn. Both objected, expressing their unwillingness to leave their profitable business, the Diamond

Cafe, and the upshot of the matter was that John McGraw, at that time only 26, was put in command of what remained of the Orioles. Hanlon had recognized the qualities of leadership in the young game cock, and even half-patronizingly told McGraw, "If you can bridle that Irish temper of yours, you could develop into a real manager."

When the players were drawn from the pool, Brooklyn had first choice, and Hanlon naturally gave himself the best of it. Not only did he take Keeler, the two-time batting champion, Kelley and Jennings, but also Dan McGann, the first base find of 1898, and three of Baltimore's first-line pitchers of 1898, Jim McJames, James Jay Hughes, and Al Maul, a trio who in the Spanish-American War years accounted for 68 of Baltimore's 96 victories. Ned, as baseball students know, worked another miracle in Brooklyn, winning the pennants of 1899 and 1900.

What did McGraw have left in Baltimore? Himself, Robbie, and pitchers Jerry Nops and Frank Kitson, the latter a promising pitching rookie of 1898. Also Steve Brodie, plucked back from the Pirates a year before, and Billy Keister, the second base-playing homebred, regained from Boston. From the tenth-place Dodgers of 1898 came catchers Jack Ryan and Alex Smith, first baseman "Candy" LaChance, outfielder Jimmy Sheckard, and pitchers Harry Howell and Jim McKenna.

These Brooklyn acquisitions were by no means nonentities. Jimmy Sheckard, then only a kid of twenty, was a fast-running Pennsylvania Dutchman from York County, who had joined Brooklyn late in 1897 after a sensational career with Brockton in the New England League. He later became the left fielder and crack lead-off man of the great championship Cubs of 1906-07-08-10. He held the National League's seasonal base-on-balls record until Eddie Stanky erased it from the book. LaChance, a French-Canadian from Waterbury, Conn., became first baseman for the early Red Sox, American League champions of 1903-04, while Harry Howell developed into one of the early pitching stars of the American League.

However, more important, McGraw acquired a sleeper in the discards and extra players Hanlon turned over to him from the pool. He was a sturdy young pitcher from Rock Island, Ill., Joseph Jerome McGinnity, drafted by Brooklyn from Peoria at the end of the 1898 season. Joe was the later-day famous "Iron Man" of the Giants champions of 1904-05. McGraw early recognized he had a jewel in the sturdy mid-westerner, and even kept the young pitcher under wraps. The Orioles trained in March, 1899, in Savannah, and Hanlon's Brooklyn Superbas conditioned in nearby Augusta. The two teams of the Von Der Horst-Hanlon-Ebbets-Abell axis naturally played a number of intrasyndicate exhibition games. McGraw ordered McGinnity to hold back his curve, Joe's best pitch, in all of these contests. He was so afraid Ned would grab McGinnity before the mid-April deadline, the closed season on Orioles.

From the start, McGraw took his managerial venture quite seriously. A man driven by an overpowering ambition, John realized it was his chance to show he could lead men and plan the strategy of a big league team. Immediately he became the boss and players accustomed to the former clubhouse intimacies were quickly called to order. Only Robbie could speak to the new manager as an equal.

"I know I'm still working for you, also that you will make every effort to win in Brooklyn," McGraw told Hanlon. "But, once our teams are on the field, I'll fight your club as hard as I'll fight any club in the league."

"That's right, John; that's the way I want it to be," echoed Hanlon.

McGraw, still playing a dashing third base, battled from the opening game, and soon Baltimore was surprised—and pleased—to learn it still had a fighting, aggressive hard-running and competent team. The Orioles lost early games as the result of outfield weaknesses, but the young manager put over deals whereby he acquired outfielder Ducky Holmes from St. Louis and Dave Fultz, another fly-chaser, from the Phillies. Both later became American League stars. Sheckard, Fultz, and Holmes quickly developed into a brilliant, fast-running outfield trio, and all were gazelles on the base paths. Fultz, a cultured Virginian and Brown graduate, was an odd figure on this cussing, umpire-baiting Oriole team. An earnest Y.M.C.A. man, Dave didn't swear, drink, smoke, or chew tobacco. But, he played the game to the hilt and won the respect of his rowdier teammates by his ability to hit and run. Fultz, a lawyer, later became president of the pre-World War I players' union, the Players' Fraternity.

During the previous winter, with the Baltimore-Brooklyn combine having an excess of players, Gene DeMontreville was sold to Chicago. Trying to strengthen his infield, McGraw, without consulting Hanlon, arranged for a deal with Chicago, trading his shortstop, George Magoon, for the return of DeMontreville. The deal irked Hanlon in Brooklyn; he didn't want the upstart, McGraw, to get his team too hot. Ned promptly arranged for a follow-up deal whereby he sent Hughie Jennings to Baltimore for DeMontreville and Jerry Nops, the last of the "Big Four of 1898." By this time Jennings had had a return of the sore arm that had plagued him in his early bush-league catching days. He no longer could make the long throw from shortstop and played only 63 games in 1899. McGraw hit the ceiling; there was a furious battle within the syndicate, with Ebbets, the young Brooklyn president, naturally backing up Hanlon.

"I thought I was doing you a favor, and that you would like to have your old buddy, Jennings, back with you in Baltimore," Hanlon told McGraw.

"Yes, you want to do me a favor," replied young McGraw in his best sarcasm. "You know Hughie can't throw across the room, let alone throw across the diamond. You want to ruin my ball club."

In the end, Von Der Horst sided with McGraw, and called

off the deal, though Jennings, with his sore arm, was permitted to finish the season under McGraw in Baltimore.

In the last two months of the season, McGraw really had his young team stepping, and the Orioles were playing the best ball in the league, the kind of baseball that had thrilled the nation's fans a few years before. They battled Hanlon's Brooklyns every time they met, and as late as middle September they had a pennant chance. Then McGraw's first wife became critically ill and died that month; during the young manager's absence the team lost its momentum and fell back, eventually finishing a good fourth with 84 victories, 58 defeats, and a percentage of .591. Only Hanlon's new Brooklyn Superbas, the former champion Beaneaters, and the Phillies finished ahead of McGraw, while eight clubs trailed in the wake of the Orioles.

Directing his own team inspired McGraw to the greatest batting year of his career. "Mac" hit .390 and stole 73 bases in a determined fight with Jimmy Sheckard for the league leadership. Jimmy stole 78, but to his dying day the Pennsylvania Dutchman insisted it was 79. In a late season game with Brooklyn, while the Sheckard-McGraw contest still was on, Jim lit out for second on a steal and thought he had it easy when Umpire Jack Hunt called him out. Sheckard flew into a terrific rage, and sprayed the umpire with tobacco juice. It was either intentional or simply the result of Jimmy's angry sputtering. The indignant Hunt ordered Jimmy out of the park, and when Sheckard refused to leave, he forfeited the game to Brooklyn.

If the 1899 Birds lost one game to Brooklyn by forfeit, they picked up a victory from the Giants the same way. In a game at New York's Polo Grounds, Andy Freedman, the pugnacious owner of the Giants, left his box to berate a former player, Ducky Holmes, and created such a rumpus on the field that Tom Lynch, the supposedly anti-Baltimore umpire, forfeited the game to the Orioles.

Next to McGraw the player most responsible for John's

fourth place finish with a team of remnants and rookies was the sleeper of the spring, Joe McGinnity. McGraw learned early that his midwestern curve-ball pitcher, with the rubber arm, was a real Iron Man. Joe started an impressive big league career by winning 27 games and losing 13. Young Frank Kitson was another horse for work, winning 20 and losing 16, while Handsome Harry Howell, Hanlon's contribution from Brooklyn, made himself useful with 14 wins and 7 defeats. Nops frequently was in McGraw's doghouse for failing to show up for games and for being guilty of transgressions against training rules, but the left-hander managed to win 16 games out of 28.

According to Mrs. McGraw's book, *The Real McGraw,* McGraw's fourth-place Orioles outdrew the new champion Dodgers at home, 123,416 to 122,575, and by 46,000 on the road; also that the 1899 Baltimore team showed a modest profit of $15,000. Nevertheless, a stunning blow was in store for the fans of Baltimore and the Free State of Maryland. They were to wake one morning and learn that they no longer had a ball team.

For some time, there had been a stubborn feud in the National League, centering around Andrew Freedman, the Giant owner. He insisted the loop was topheavy and out of balance, and led a crusade to "cut off the dead wood." The league still was suffering from the effects of the poor Spanish-American War year, and 1899 wasn't much better. Cleveland was woefully weak; the transplanted Browns were so bad that most of Cleveland's late home games were transferred to rival cities. Freedman, the hewer of dead wood, won his fight, as the league voted to streamline to eight clubs, lopping off Baltimore and Washington in the East and Cleveland and Louisville in the West. Freedman's particular feud was with neighboring Brooklyn, but he couldn't lop off Hanlon's new champion Superbas. It had to be Baltimore. So, after having continuous major league ball since entering the American Association as a charter member in 1882, proud Baltimore again found itself out of the big league picture. And it didn't like the role at all!

The National League spent a considerable sum of money in, streamlining itself. The withdrawal of Baltimore cost the league $30,000, and the club was permitted to retain its players and transfer its top stars to Brooklyn. Despite Cleveland's wretched 1899 showing, the Robinsons received $25,000, while the league also took over the Cleveland grounds, agreeing to pay an annual $5,000 rental for the next three years. Washington was paid $39,000, the agreement stipulating that the league would take title to any players not otherwise disposed of by March 9. Dreyfuss of Louisville seems to have fared the poorest, as Louisville was awarded only $10,000. But Barney took the $10,000, and with some other money that he succeeded in borrowing, he purchased a half interest in the Pittsburgh club. By combining the best players of the disbanded Louisville Colonels and the Pirates, he had the makings of the club that swept the National League for easy pennants in 1901-02-03.

Under the conditions of the retirement of the Baltimore franchise, Von Der Horst and Hanlon sent the better players of the 1899 Orioles to Brooklyn: McGraw, Robinson, McGinnity, Howell, Kitson, Nops, Keister, DeMontreville, and Sheckard. Hughie Jennings also went back to the Dodgers to experiment with a new position, first base.

McGraw and Robinson, still interested in their private Baltimore venture, both indicated early they had no wish to play under Hanlon in Brooklyn. Whereupon, Charley Ebbets, no doubt acting for Hanlon, advised McGraw, Robinson, and Billy Keister that they had been sold to the St. Louis Cardinals and to report to that club. According to news accounts of the time, Frank Robinson, Cardinal owner, paid $15,000 for the trio; it was not an inconsequential sum for the turn of the century.

Again there was no enthusiasm by McGraw and Robbie for their St. Louis transfer. They were determined holdouts

89

and at one time Ebbets threatened to ask the league to take disciplinary action if they did not report to St. Louis. Charley couldn't collect his $15,000 until they did.

Eventually on May 9, nearly a month after the start of the 1900 season, Frank Robinson induced McGraw, Robbie and Keister to come to St. Louis and talk terms. It was a gala occasion; Robinson met the players at the depot, paraded them around town, and threw a sumptuous meal at what then passed for a night club. Amid popping champagne bottles, the trio agreed to play the 1900 season in St. Louis. McGraw was to get $100 a game, far above the $2,400 National League salary limit then in force.

However, before signing, McGraw had a shock for Robinson who had eyed the young battler as his future team director. "Frank, I'll sign for only one season, and I'll give you the best while I am here," McGraw said. "But, I can't sign a contract with a reserve clause, and I must tell you I'll be with you for only this 1900 season."

"But, why Mac?" Robinson demanded. "You'll like it here; it's a great town; they'll like your style of play; they will be back of you just as they were in Baltimore. What's more I'm hopeful, you'll be manager some day."

"I'm sorry, Frank, but I can play with you only for one season."

He played that one season; his late start and injuries limited his play to 98 games, for which he drew roughly $9,500. He played on the same team with Cy Young, Nemesis of the 1895 Temple Cup Series, and Jesse Burkett; as a cardinal he hit .337 and stole 28 bases. And then he was off for another great adventure!

CHAPTER IX

Baltimore Finds Haven in New American League

WHEN John McGraw told Frank Robinson, president of the Cardinals, that he could not sign a 1900 contract with a reserve clause and would play in St. Louis only one season, he already had definite plans to return to Baltimore as a major league manager and part owner in 1901. Shortly after the National League cut down to eight clubs in the winter of 1900-1901, a group of baseball promoters started working on a plan to resurrect the old major American Association, which had been absorbed into the National League in 1892.

They were particularly interested in putting an American Association club back in Baltimore, and offered McGraw and Wilbert Robinson stock holdings in a new Oriole A. A. club. Both men definitely were interested, and McGraw agreed to manage such a team. Other franchises were awarded to Chicago, St. Louis, Detroit, Boston, Philadelphia, and Providence. Cap Anson was the proposed league's big card in Chicago, while such other well-known names as Tom McCarthy, Scrappy Bill Joyce, Patsy Donovan, and Billy Murray were included among the managerial prospects.

In the meantime, Byron Bancroft Johnson, youthful president of the young American League (it had been the Western League prior to 1900), started a series of moves to checkmate the proposed American Association, cross the Allegheny Mountains and blossom his own league into a full major. At first, Johnson hoped to do this in peaceful agreement with the National League, but when the National League showed an inclination to fight, and to encourage the American Association promoters, Ban fought the National League with all the ferocity and tenacity of his domineering nature. The bitterest of all baseball wars was in the making.

On October 14, 1900, Johnson held a historic meeting in Chicago, attended by Charles Comiskey, Connie Mack, Charles Sommers, and James Manning. It dissolved a five-year agreement entered into by the Western League clubs in 1895, voted to form a new league and to move clubs into Eastern territory. In his official statement, president Johnson announced: "The American League has decided to take up the vacant territory in Baltimore and Washington, enter Philadelphia, while a fourth Eastern city will be named later. (It eventually was Boston.) The Philadelphia franchise was given to Connie Mack and the Washington franchise to James Manning. Both men already are assured of affluent backers in their cities. I expect the Baltimore franchise to go to John McGraw and Wilbert Robinson, former stars of the Orioles."

Shortly before the meeting, Johnson invited McGraw and Robinson to come to Chicago for a talk. Ban quickly laid his cards on the table. "We've definitely decided to spread into the East," he said. "I know that you men have interested some Baltimore people in backing a new American Association club there. Well, there won't be an American Association. We've already got the jump on them. While they've been talking, we've been acting. We're already in Chicago, Philadelphia, Cleveland, Detroit, Washington, and Milwaukee. Now we are going into Baltimore, and we would like to have you two men in the American League. You both have a lot of contacts there. Well, bring the people who had offered backing for an American Association team into our league. If you can bring this about, there will be a substantial interest for both of you in the new venture."

Then, turning to McGraw, he added, "If you come in with us, Mr. McGraw, you no doubt will manage the American

92

League Orioles. However, there is one thing I must make clear to you at the very outset: I am going to run the American League as a clean league. Clean baseball will be one of the platforms we will wage our fight on. Many things have been going on in the National League that have disgusted patrons of the game. These things must stop. Furthermore, as a league president, I always back up my umpires. Now, I know of your reputation in the National League; you're a battler, and you've made it very tough for Nick Young's umpires."

"I always play hard, and play to win," said McGraw. "That also is the way I run my teams."

"Yes, John, I know you are an aggressive ball player and manager," added Johnson with less severity. "And, of your intense desire to win. I don't want to curb your zeal; it is desirable in a baseball man, but aggressiveness cannot be carried into rowdyism. You must understand now I will tolerate no rough stuff, nor the type of language you and your Oriole players have used in the past.

"I think we can get along," said McGraw in parting.

McGraw returned to Baltimore and talked it over with Harry Goldman, a young baseball enthusiast of some means, who had been heartbroken when Baltimore was dropped from the National League. Goldman, who was known as Judge, also had been interested in the proposed Baltimore American Association team. But his main interest was to see his beloved Baltimore back in the big league picture.

McGraw reported he was impressed with Johnson. "He's a strong man, and he has something on the ball," he said. "Just in talking to him, I can see that he already has big plans for his league." It, too, was apparent that Ban had taken the play from the American Association promoters, and, as he had said, actually had gotten the jump on them. McGraw, Robbie, and Goldman decided the best bet for Baltimore was to enter the American League, and at the next league meeting, McGraw represented the Monument City.

From then on, McGraw and Robbie became confirmed

93

American Leaguers. A new league and a new club in Baltimore would enable them to continue their Diamond Café connections, perhaps make their sports rendezvous even more profitable. A new Baltimore baseball company was formed with Sidney Frank, owner of the biggest block of stock, as president; Harry Goldman, secretary; and McGraw, manager. Frank had strong political connections, with a brother on the City Council.

Hanlon was the new club's first obstacle. The new Orioles had hoped to play at Union Park, the old National League park, vacated after the 1899 season. But, with the National-American League war already raging, Hanlon, who had a lease on Union Park, refused to surrender it, or sublease the park to Frank, Goldman, McGraw, and Robinson. Foxy Ned was still manager and a heavy stockholder in Brooklyn.

In Cleveland and Washington, the new American League clubs merely had to move into vacated National League parks. But, in Baltimore, the new American League stock company was confronted with the necessity of building a new park, and building it in a hurry. Goldman finally found a piece of property owned by Johns Hopkins University at Twenty-ninth Street and York Road which the university agreed to lease for baseball purposes. Fortunately, in those days, it didn't take a year or more to erect a structure worthy of housing a major league franchise. Grandstands and bleachers still were constructed of lumber; manual labor was cheap, and in Baltimore, Philadelphia, and Boston, new American League parks were constructed between late winter and the April openings. Ground for the new Oriole park on York Street was broken on Lincoln's Birthday, February 12, and the ball park was ready for its opening game, scheduled for April 24.

At the National League's annual meeting in December, 1900, it ignored a communication from Ban Johnson asking for a clarification of the American League's position, and requesting a new deal in baseball. Johnson took this to be a declaration of war, and ordered his raiders, John McGraw,

94

Clark Griffith, Jimmy McAleer, Connie Mack, George Stall- ings, and Hugh Duffy, to get busy.

The American League, in 1901, 1902 and 1903, was made up largely of players snatched from the National League, both reserve and contract jumpers. McGraw entered into this task of lining up players for the new Orioles with all the aggressiveness of his intensive nature. The early Boston Red Sox landed such big fish as Jimmy Collins, Cy Young, Lou Criger, and Chick Stahl, and the Athletics pulled in another prize in Napoleon Lajoie. McGraw concentrated largely on players who had been with him in Baltimore, especially on the 1899 club. Ball players were in a mood to sign with the new league, as most of them rebelled against the National League's $2,400 salary limit. Many good players had been working for as low as $1,500.

Raids on Hanlon's Brooklyn club netted most of the pitchers who had been with McGraw in 1899: Joe McGinnity, Harry Howell, and Jerry Nops. For a fourth regular on the staff, McGraw engaged the old Baltimore favorite, Frank Foreman, still a formidable competitor at the age of thirty-eight.

Robbie, a 1900 Cardinal teammate, of course, went with his old pal and business associate as first-string catcher. Other players grabbed from the St. Louis Nationals were Keister, who played shortstop on the 1901 Orioles, and outfielder-first baseman Turkey Mike Donlin, a hard-boiled, hard-hitting, roystering character who had started with St. Louis as a pitcher. Mike was tough as nails, but a natural hitter and a swashbuckling type of player.

Next to winning Joe McGinnity back from Brooklyn, McGraw's biggest prize was another Irish fighter, Roger Patrick Bresnahan, catcher and all-around player, who had been on the reserve list of the Chicago Cubs. McGraw first saw Bresnahan in 1897 when Roger, aged seventeen, was a pitcher for the Washington club. Roger, nicknamed the Duke, was born in Tralee, Ireland, later became an off-season de- tective in Toledo, and fitted into the best traditions of the

95

Orioles. Only twenty-one when he first joined McGraw, he was a versatile fellow. He pitched a few games, caught, and played a bang-up game at third base and the outfield. However, it was his ability as a catcher, especially his generalship behind the plate, along with his hitting and base running, which won him a plaque in the Hall of Fame at Cooperstown.

Perhaps McGraw's most amusing capture was second baseman Jimmy Williams from the Pirates. Barney Dreyfuss of Pittsburgh lost less players to the American League raiders than any of his fellow club owners, enabling him to win three war-year pennants, but he never forgave McGraw for the way he snatched Williams. Jimmy lived in Denver, and Dreyfuss sent him his train fare to Hot Springs, Arkansas, to start his training. McGraw met him on the train, and signed him to an Oriole contract. "I not only lose Williams," complained Dreyfuss, "but I pay half of his fare East, for that McGraw to steal him from me."

A raid on the Giants won hard-hitting outfielder, John Bentley "Cy" Seymour, a former pitcher and a later-day National League batting champion, and a foray on the Phillies gained a player with the same surname as that of McGraw, John Joseph Dunn. He wasn't much bigger than McGraw, and of the same aggressive type. He was a pitcher with a high-pitched voice, which later was to be heard in many a Baltimore baseball argument. In 1901, the Chesapeake city knew Jack Dunn largely as a sore-arm pitcher, but a versatile one who had the faculty of fitting in anywhere. While Jack's 1901 pitching record was three wins and three defeats, he participated in 96 games, hitting .247.

According to Jim Price, Jimmy Sheckard was the prize jumper of the National-American war, and actually made four jumps between Hanlon's Dodgers and McGraw's Orioles. His jumps mostly were made during the winter months, and he actually played only two games for the A. L. Orioles.

McGraw also took on the colorful old Oriole of the three-time champions, Steve Brodie. Jim Jackson, the starting

96

center fielder, was a former Philadelphila semi-pro. Perhaps for the laughs, McGraw hired the eccentric left-handed pitcher, Crazy Schmidt. His starting first baseman, Frank Foutz, a Baltimore boy, was a poor hitter; Frank was succeeded by Warren Hart, a .312 hitter, who couldn't field. Eventually Mike Donlin wound up at first base.

A 1901 Baltimore outfield reserve was George Rohe, who in 1906 was to win baseball immortality with the Hitless Wonder White Sox. As an ugly duckling substitute, filling in at third base, Rohe hit two decisive triples in key games, enabling the light-hitting White Sox to defeat the famous Cubs, winners of 116 National League games, in the 1906 World Series.

In view of the big build-up of the 1954 Orioles and extensive training trip by Jimmy Dykes' hopefuls, it is interesting to read the following account of the 1901 Orioles' first home exhibition game with Yale by the *Sporting News* correspondent, Frank Patterson. The game was played at Maryland Oval, the property of the Maryland Athletic Club.

The day was cold and windy. The game was played at the Maryland Oval, with few accommodations, and situated about five miles from the city, and car fare was 20 cents, and yet nearly 2,500 rooters were present and paid for the privilege of shivering in heavy overcoats for two hours to see the new team. . . . Club members were all privileged to see the game without paying, but nearly all of them paid, "just to help the club along a bit," as they explained it.

There is another reason why the friends of the club feel jubilant to a degree, and that is on account of the showing made by the team against as good a club as "Old Eli." The Orioles had not had any outdoor practice whatever. They had been working in the Hopkins University cage and were in fairly good condition, but the team had never even lined up together. Besides this, the weather had prevented McGinnity and Howell, who did the pitching, from using any speed or "letting out any." They were lobbing them over and took no chances with their arms. On the other hand, the

Yalensians had had a lot of practice, and their pitchers were young and not afraid to put on speed. They were no mean antagonists at any time, but nevertheless the new team simply toyed with the collegians, winning by a score of 10 to 3, with the game well in hand from the very first.

The Orioles were out of big league ball only one year, so the excitement on April 26, 1901, when American League ball was ushered in at Baltimore, was hardly as great as it was on April 15, 1954, after Baltimore had been out of the big league picture for fifty-two years. But, there was some similarity. There was no automobile parade, but there was a parade of the rival players—Orioles and Boston Puritans, league president Johnson, Oriole president Frank, and city dignitaries in horse-drawn carriages. At the new ball park, there was a huge floral horseshoe to bring luck to McGraw and the American League Orioles.

Actually the start of the season was delayed two days by rain, but the twice-delayed opening put no damper on the attendance or enthusiasm. The opening crowd was 11,000, considered quite good by Baltimore papers. Those who came were well rewarded as the Orioles stove in Jimmy Collins' Boston club, 10 to 6. Baltimore's line-up that day was John McGraw, third base; Mike Donlin, left field; Jimmy Williams, second base; Billy Keister, shortstop; Cy Seymour, right field; Jim Jackson, center field; Frank Foutz, first base; Wilbert Robinson, catcher; Joe McGinnity, pitcher. Not a bad line-up in any period of the game!

The Orioles rapped Win Kellum, the Boston pitcher, for eleven hits, including a pair of triples by Donlin, a brace of doubles each for McGraw and Jackson, and two doubles and a single for Keister.

The Birds still were feeling their oats next day, when they took old Cy Young, the Boston ace, to the cleaners. McGraw and his cohorts tore into the former Temple Cup star for three runs in the first inning, and they really belabored the 511-game winner in the third, rocking Cy for eight juicy runs.

98

BOSTON (A.L.)

	A.B.	R.	H.	O.	A.	E.
Dowd, L.F.	5	0	1	3	1	0
Hemphill, R.F.	4	0	0	2	1	0
Stahl, C.F.	5	0	1	2	1	0
Collins, 3B.	4	1	2	2	1	1
Freeman, 1B.	3	0	1	9	1	0
Parent, S.S.	3	0	0	0	3	0
Ferris, 2B.	4	1	0	2	3	0
Criger, C.	4	2	2	4	1	0
Kellum, P.	4	1	1	0	7	0
McLean*	1	1	1	0	0	0
	37	6	9	24	19	1

* Doubled for Kellum in 9th inning

BALTIMORE (A.L.)

	A.B.	R.	H.	O.	A.	E.
McGraw, 3B.	4	1	2	1	2	0
Donlin, L.F.	4	2	2	4	0	0
Williams, 2B.	3	1	0	1	2	1
Keister, S.S.	4	2	3	0	5	1
Seymour, R.F.	3	2	1	2	0	1
Jackson, C.F.	4	1	2	4	0	1
Foutz, 1B.	3	1	0	12	0	1
Robinson, C.	4	0	0	3	1	1
McGinnity, P.	4	0	1	0	3	0
	33	10	11	27	13	6

Boston	0 0 0 0 1 0 0 2 3	—	6
Baltimore	3 0 1 0 0 2 0 4 x	—	10

Two-base hits—McGraw 2, Jackson 2, Keister, Collins, Criger,
McLean. Three-base hits—Donlin 2, Keister. Stolen base—Seymour, Keister. Sacrifice—McGraw. Left on base—Boston 6;
Baltimore 4. Bases on balls—off McGinnity 5; off Kellum 4. Struck
out—by McGinnity 2; by Kellum 2. Umpire—Cantillon. Time of
game—one hour and 45 minutes. Attendance—10,371.

Fred Mitchell, later manager of the Braves and Cubs, took the rest of the thrashing as the Orioles prevailed, 17 to 6. Marylanders were saying, "Why these new Orioles are as good as the old ones ever were."

A week later, when the Orioles played a return engagement in Boston, McGraw ran into his first big hassle with Ban Johnson. McGinnity went into the ninth inning, leading by a score of 8 to 2, when the Puritans put on a furious rally. Iron Man Joe finally extinguished the flames after five Boston runs were in, giving Baltimore the game, 8 to 7. However, while the rally was on, McGraw flew into a frenzy over a decision by Umpire John Haskell. Mac jumped up and down, brought his spikes down on Haskell's toes, jostled the umpire and used a few epithets that Johnson had warned would not be tolerated in the American League. Haskell threw the sputtering McGraw out of the game, and Johnson suspended him for five days.

On the day McGraw's suspension went into effect, a Boston writer penned the following (typical of the manner in which the press outside of Baltimore liked to bait McGraw):

Boston drew 8,000 for its first Saturday game with Baltimore. This was a pretty good game, too, and the people talked about it because McGraw did not play, and they read in their newspapers that John J. Muggsy had been told to sit on the bench for five days.

This added to the interest and while it was felt that the Orioles wouldn't battle as stubbornly as if their manager and captain were playing, yet there was so much talk that everybody felt inclined to go see the menagerie even though the "great animal" [Muggsy] was not exhibited.

The storm over the argument with Umpire Haskell was only the beginning of a series of battles between the Orioles and president Johnson's office. There were other suspensions for McGraw, and punishment was meted out to Donlin, Bresnahan, Seymour, and lesser lights. The worst offense came in September, when Joe McGinnity sprayed an umpire with to-

100

bacco juice, shoved him, and gave him the full benefit of a vocabulary picked up in an Oklahoma blacksmith shop. Ban suspended McGinnity for the remainder of the season.

Several times while the Orioles were playing in Chicago, Johnson had the club's young manager on the carpet. "This league will not stand for such tactics," Johnson hammered away at McGraw. "Early in the season, you received my bulletin on conduct on the field. I took it up with you personally, item for item. Now, I must warn you, in all solemnity, that your misconduct, and that of your players, must stop."

"Your umpires always are picking on me, and on my team," snapped McGraw. "They always have rabbit ears when they umpire Oriole games. Why don't they hear some of the things other teams are saying about them?"

Johnson was having other disciplinary problems. In Detroit, George Stallings was as much of a disturber of the peace and decorum of the league as was McGraw, and even the White Sox manager, Clark Griffith (called "Ban's pet" by other managers), prolonged an argument so long in Chicago that the umpire forfeited the game against him.

"Yes, Mr. McGraw, I have problems in other cities," Ban replied. "For that reason it is all the more important that you co-operate with me, rather than constantly fight me."

In the heat of the 1901 campaign, Steve Brodie pulled one of his dillies. It was the subject of one of McGraw's better stories in later years, but it made Mac mad as a hornet when it happened. In a game with the Athletics, the Orioles trailed by one run in the late innings and needed two to win. Brodie was on second base with Bresnahan at bat, when Roger hit a ball into deep right center field. It was a sure triple, and possible homer.

Pausing at third base, Brodie became entranced with the hit and Bresnahan's chance to stretch it into a game-winning homer. "Come on, Rog; come on, boy," he coached. "You can make it." Steve coached Bresnahan so diligently that the runner sped past Brodie at third base, and slid into the home

101

plate ahead of the outfield relay. Then Ossie Schreckengost, the Athletic catcher, got the ball, and pressed it into Bresnahan's ribs. Roger was called out for passing another runner on the base line. Steve still was trying to figure it out when the wrath of McGraw descended upon him.

Incidentally, it was in 1901 that McGraw made his famous crack, "The Philadelphia Athletics will be the White Elephants of the American League." The Shibes and Connie Mack showed their scorn for McGraw's jibe by making the white elephant the symbol of their club. White Elephants went on their players' jackets, their stationery and decorations. And, now after a half-century, McGraw's remark came true.

Despite their early display of batting power, the 1901 American League Orioles had to be satisfied with fifth place. They managed to win three more games than they lost, finishing with 68-65, .511, but Griffith's White Sox, Collins' Boston Puritans, Stallings' Tigers, and Mack's White Elephants all came in ahead of McGraw's Birds. Between suspensions and injuries, Mac took part in only 73 games, hitting .352. The aggressive Dunn did most of the substituting at third, and while he held up well in the field he hit 100 points less than McGraw.

Donlin was McGraw's best hitter with .340; Billy Keister turned in a pleasing .328; Williams, the shanghaied Pirate, hit .321 and Cy Seymour, .302. Robbie just missed the .300 class with .298. Young Bresnahan was full of fire and enthusiasm, but hadn't yet hit his full stride, batting .262 in 86 games.

McGinnity was easily the class of the pitching staff with 26 victories and 19 defeats. If it hadn't been for Joe's late season explosion and suspension, he could have made it 30, as he usually worked Monday, Wednesday, and Saturday. Venerable Frank Foreman was the only other pitcher to go over .500 with 13 victories against 7 defeats. Harry Howell's record was 14-21 and that of Jerry Nops, 11-12.

In a way, the Orioles were the determining factor in Chicago winning the American League's first race as a major league. While the Birds fought the second-place Red Sox to a nine-nine split, they were doormats for Griffith's champion White Sox. It led a facetious Boston writer to comment: "If we (Boston) could only play Griffith every day, it would be easy. McGraw's truculent Orioles really were tough on Collins' team. The best Boston could do with the scrappy Marylanders was an even break in eighteen games, whereas Muggsy's Roughnecks became Little Lord Fauntleroys when they played Griffith, and won only four games from Chicago out of eighteen."

CHAPTER X

John McGraw Returns to National League

THE BASEBALL WAR went on full blast in the winter of 1901-02. Ban Johnson moved his Milwaukee club to St. Louis, and Jimmy McAleer, the new Brown manager, raided the Cardinals of their remaining stars. A move of the Milwaukee franchise to St. Louis 53 years ago may seem strange today, inasmuch as the 1953 Milwaukee Braves drew 1,826,397, approximately what the Browns drew in their last five seasons in the American League. But, in 1902, St. Louis was the fourth city in the country in population, and then regarded as a baseball stronghold.

In the back of Johnson's mind, there also was a plan to move one of his Eastern franchises to New York. He felt he had to be in the nation's foremost city to assure recognition as a real major. The club to be transferred would be Baltimore or Washington. Baltimore was larger, but Johnson always felt a sentimental yen to have a club in the capital city. McGraw knew of Johnson's long-range plans, made several secret trips to New York and built up useful contacts, including one with Andrew Freedman, the Giant owner hated and detested by most of his fellow owners. Freedman was first lieutenant to the powerful Tammany leader and New York boss, Richard Croker.

National League affairs then were in disorder over an issue known as Freedmanism. In 1901, the political leader had been unsuccessful in an attempt to turn the National League into a gigantic eight-club baseball syndicate, with New York getting the lion's share of the stock and all managers to be appointed by the league and to receive a standard salary of $5,000. In the National League's 1901 annual meeting, the clubs split four-four in an unsuccessful attempt to elect a president. The pro-Freedman clubs favored Nick Young, the old president; the reform clubs backed Al Spalding, the Chicago baseball pioneer. After twenty-five futile ballots, the anti-Freedman faction, taking advantage of a technicality, elected Spalding president. He seized the league's records, scores, books, and private papers, only to have Freedman go into court and get an injunction restraining Spalding from filling the presidential office. The league, again unable to elect a president, decided to entrust its affairs to a three-man Executive Committee consisting of John T. Brush of Cincinnati, chairman, A. H. Soden of Boston, and James Hart of Chicago.

A number of clubs were in favor of expelling Freedman as a bad influence on baseball, but he held the lease on the Coogan's Bluff property on which the Polo Grounds is located, and with his political influence Andy could keep any other club out of New York. During McGraw's visits, Freedman seriously considered leaving the National League, and probably would have come into the American if Johnson had sanctioned it. But, knowing of Freedman's record as a troublemaker, Ban was unwilling to handle this hot potato.

However, all of this was under the surface. There was no inkling in Baltimore of any likely shift of the city's franchise. Despite McGraw's interest in a possible New York American League club and his 1901 difficulties with Ban Johnson, he made every effort to field a championship Oriole club in 1902. There had been a shake-up in the Baltimore high command, with John J. Mahon, a Baltimore contractor who was high up in the Democratic party in Maryland, succeeding Sid Frank as the Oriole president. Mahon was the father-in-law of Joe Kelley, slashing left fielder of Hanlon's three-time champions.

Players were signing contracts with one league, and jumping a few days later when a better offer came from a club in the rival circuit. McGraw's biggest loss was Mike Donlin, the .340-hitting outfielder, who jumped to the Cincinnati Reds. Jack Dunn, whose Irish temper had clashed with McGraw's fiery nature in 1901, took a "hop, skip and jump" and landed with the Giants. Steve Brodie jumped to New York with "Dunnie."

Offsetting player losses to the National, McGraw pulled a few raids of his own, and further damaged Hanlon's team in Brooklyn, when he induced Joe Kelley to sign with his father-in-law's club. McGraw also had Sheckard for a few games, when Jim again had a change of heart and returned to Hanlon. Dan McGann, the young first baseman who blossomed into stardom under McGraw's management on the 1899 Orioles, was lured away from the Cardinals, and balancing the loss of Dunn and Brodie to New York, a counter-raid on the Giants yielded Al "Kip" Selbach, a runt outfielder and a fine lead-off man, and catcher Alex Smith. For some reason or other the popular Billy Keister was released to Washington, but McGraw filled the shortstop gap by obtaining Billy Gilbert from the disbanded Milwaukee club. Other American League clubs helped Baltimore's pitching staff; Comiskey of the White Sox permitted McGraw to have Tom Hughes, and the Tigers passed along Jack Cronin. With such 1901 holdovers as Mc-Graw, McGinnity, Howell, Robinson, Bresnahan, Williams, and Seymour, it gave Baltimore one of the league's strongest clubs on paper.

The 1902 American League race looked like a free-for-all. The Athletics, the eventual winners, were hit hard in the early season, losing the service of five ex-Phillies—the great Lajoie, Elmer Flick, a hard-hitting outfielder, and three pitchers, Bill Bernard, Chick Fraser, and Bill Duggleby—when the Pennsylvania Supreme Court upheld the validity of the reserve clause in Philadelphia National contracts. Griffith was making a determined effort to make it two straight in Chicago, and McAleer's St. Louis club showed up unexpectedly strong.

However, the Orioles kept up with the pack for two months, when a series of events in the late spring knocked the Birds out of the running and had a lasting effect on Baltimore baseball.

The Orioles were playing Detroit at home, May 24, when with Dick Harley on third and Dick Barrett on second and Tom Hughes pitching, the Tigers attempted a double steal. Bresnahan's throw to McGraw at third was quick and accurate; he had Harley by a good 15 feet. But the Detroit player slid in with his spikes high, and dented them deep into McGraw's left kneecap. Like a wounded tiger, McGraw sprang at Harley, and the two men rolled over on the ground, blood from McGraw's wound covering both players. Umpire Silk O'Loughlin, Baltimore pitcher Tom Hughes and other Orioles tore the men apart, but McGraw couldn't get up. As Hughes tried to give his manager a helping hand, John fell back on the ground. McGraw was badly injured, and rushed to the hospital. McGraw was out of action for a month, but he never completely recovered from this spiking. It slowed him on the bases and interfered with his ability to stoop quickly for a ground ball. It practically finished him as a regular player at the early age of twenty-nine.

Jim Price, who was a witness to the play, informed the author years ago that the spiking was not accidental. "There was a feud on between McGraw and Harley," he said. "McGraw had a sharp tongue, and could get under the skins of his opponents with his barbed taunts. Harley seemed to be smarting over something McGraw had said to him earlier in the game, and there is no doubt in my mind that he was out to get John. He came in with his spikes high and kicked out with one foot as he approached McGraw."

On June 26, the Athletics were playing Baltimore, and Connie Mack was pitching Rube Waddell, his eccentric left-hander, in Rube's first American League game. Mack personally had snatched the great Rube from the Los Angeles club. Waddell was to make Mack's first pennant possible by winning

107

twenty-three out of thirty games in three months, but Rube got off to a rocky start against the cocky Orioles.

"Waddell's got a lot of stuff, but he's an awful clown," McGraw told his players. "I know him from the National League. Kid the ears off him! Ride him unceasingly! Bunt on him! Never let up on him! When you have him talking back, he's licked."

Like a flock of angry mocking birds, the Orioles squawked at poor Rube. They brought up all of his crazy adventures of the past. They bunted toward first, bunted toward third; eventually they talked and bunted Rube silly. The great south-paw lost his first American League game, 7 to 3.

Two days later, June 28, McGraw, though still walking with a slight limp, made his first appearance at third base since the accident exactly five weeks before. It was to be an important date in Baltimore baseball. A few days before, in the Athletic series, he had appeared briefly as a pinch-hitter, but this was his first try at third base since the Harley spiking. The Orioles were playing Boston and were behind when the Birds put on a spirited seventh inning rally. In a rundown play, Tommy Connolly, the retired chief of American League umpires, called out Cy Seymour for allegedly failing to touch third base. McGraw insisted just as vehemently that Cy had touched the bag and called on Connolly to question Jim Johnstone, the base umpire, on the play.

"I don't need to consult Johnstone on a play that I saw with my own eyes," said Connolly.

"Your eyes, my eye! You're blinder than a bat if you say you saw Cy miss third base," yipped McGraw, and then he let Tommy have the full treatment. Connolly ordered the scrappy Baltimore chieftain out of the game; McGraw, still sputtering fire and brimstone, refused to go, and Connolly forfeited the game to Boston.

McGraw had been in earlier 1902 disputes with Ban Johnson's umpires, for which he had been fined and suspended for periods of three days. This time Johnson sent McGraw a

108

wire on June 29, "As of today, you are suspended indefinitely."
That wire closed John McGraw's historic and colorful career
as an active Oriole.

In early 1902, McGraw had married the Baltimore belle,
the comely Miss Blanche Sindall. Now, at his home, John
sputtered, raged, and brooded. Seriously injured, and out of
the game for five weeks, he was indefinitely suspended after
the very first game in which he had attempted to play. Furthermore, Ban had thrown the book at him in the form of an
indefinite suspension. He felt he was being persecuted by Johnson, that Ban had it in for him, and that the league no longer
was big enough to hold both men. Also, that he had been
given a very shabby deal. He had won Baltimore away from
the American Association crowd in the winter of 1900-01,
had lured such stars as Robinson, McGinnity, Seymour, Donlin, Kelley, McGann away from the National League. Now,
the club owed him back salary and other money he had advanced for player salaries. Johnson knew all of this, and still
was kicking him around.

While McGraw was convalescing from the Harley spiking,
he had paid another visit to New York. Again, it was on the
business of moving the Orioles to New York. He met Frank
Farrell, a lesser Tammany chief than Freedman, but quite influential. He owned a string of race horses and was the former
owner of a New York gambling house. He was interested in
backing an American League club in New York, and eventually became the first owner of the New York Highlanders,
later called the Yankees.

As McGraw was sitting out his indefinite suspension, he was
visited by Andy Freedman's team secretary, Fred Knowles.
"Would McGraw be interested in managing the New York
Giants?" asked the emissary.

McGraw promised to give the offer due consideration. He
was interested. Anything to get away from Ban Johnson. And
in New York, there was a golden opportunity! Furthermore,

109

he had learned that Johnson would bypass him in the event that the Baltimore franchise was shifted to New York. McGraw told Knowles he could report back to Freedman that he would give the offer a lot of thought and would give Andy definite word within a few days.

In McGraw's book, *My Thirty Years in Baseball,* ghosted by Bozeman Bulger, well-known New York writer of a quarter-century ago, McGraw reported the 1902 Baltimore club was losing money daily, and that he had advanced the Orioles between $6,000 and $7,000 of his own money to meet salaries, saying, "Nobody else kicked in."

He requested Oriole president Mahon to call a meeting of the board of directors, and put the matter squarely before them. In McGraw's own words, as reported in his book, he told them: "Gentlemen, here is the situation. I have advanced nearly $7,000 to keep the club going. The company is in debt to me that much personally. Now, I think I should be paid that money back or should be given my unconditional release. It's not up to me to carry the club. We've got to have a showdown. You can do either one thing or the other."

He said the directors discussed the matter at some length; no one seemed willing to reimburse him, and at the end of the discussion it was decided to give him his unconditional release. Then McGraw added: "I was free to do as I pleased. I did not jump, as has been often said, and neither did I deceive the stockholders in any manner whatever. That transaction also is a matter of record."

Knowles, acting for Freedman, again came to see McGraw in Baltimore. He offered McGraw a four-year contract, calling for $11,000 a year, under which the young manager would be supreme boss of the Giants. McGraw accepted the New York post July 7, but did not formally take over the Giant command until July 19.

Writing of the same meeting in which McGraw asked for a showdown, *Sporting News* correspondent Frank Patterson re-

110

ported as follows in his Baltimore news letter in the periodical's July 12 issue:

The Baltimore Baseball Club met today to take formal action on John McGraw's request for his release. There were present: President John J. Mahon; Vice-President Sydney Frank; Mr. Theodore L. Straus; Attorney Conway W. Sams; Secretary Harry S. Goldman; Messrs. Miles S. Brinkley, Joseph J. Kelley, Wilbert Robinson and McGraw.

The following statement was made:

"The club has formally granted Mr. McGraw the release he asked for. In view of the fact he was not in harmony with the president of the organization, of which the Baltimore club is a part, it was not to the advantage of our club to retain him. The meeting was perfectly harmonious, and there is still the utmost good feeling on both sides. Mr. McGraw has now no interest of any kind in the Baltimore club; he has sold his stock amounting to $6,500 to Mr. Mahon. No director has yet been elected to succeed Mr. McGraw, but Messrs. Kelley and Robinson will succeed him as joint managers, with equal authority. The Baltimore club will receive no bonus from the New York Club for the release of Mr. McGraw, as has been reported."

McGraw said: "I realize the fact that I was only a dead loss to the Baltimore club to stay here, as I would not play in the American League as long as President Johnson is president. I appreciate the kindliness which has prompted the Baltimore club to give me the release I asked for, and I wish to assure them publicly that in consideration of their kindness I shall not tamper with any of the Baltimore club's players. I also wish to affirm the statement that the Baltimore club received not a dollar from any source for my release."

While McGraw will not state the salary he will receive from the New York club, it is understood that the inducement offered him to return to the National League is $10,000 a year.

Joe Kelley, upon whom the greater part of the responsibility of the Baltimore team will now devolve, says that he still considers the club a good business proposition, but the impression among those here interested in the game is that McGraw's break is a great

111

victory for the National League and a severe blow to the American organization.

It is feared among the followers of the game in this city that the withdrawal of McGraw will cause a drop in the interest of the game here and eventually the disruption of the Baltimore club.

In the meantime, hell broke loose in Baltimore and all over the big league baseball belt. McGraw was castigated by Ban Johnson, American League club officials, and writers favorable to the American League. Such terms as traitor, renegade, and Benedict Arnold were used freely in discussing the ex-Oriole manager and new director of the Giants. Patterson, the *Sporting News* correspondent, reported that McGraw was pilloried even more in the press outside of Baltimore than in the Monument City. The Baltimore writer who jumped hardest on him was Joe Cumming of the *Baltimore News,* who wrote:

The trouble has been that he [McGraw] could not reconcile his own temperament to the strict government of the American League. He rebelled against authority; he declined to uphold the rules which he himself helped, or at least, should have helped to make, and became absorbed in the idea that the president of the American League, and his umpires, had one desire—to make it unpleasant for him. Such a belief could have but one result—unpleasantness for the club with which he was connected, the loss of his services and the ultimate retirement of himself.

It is possible that the heat engendered by McGraw's decision to leave the Orioles and the American League, the vicious name calling and the general bitterness were factors in worsening the situation. It will be noted that in McGraw's statement after the directors' meeting, July 8, he was quoted as saying "I shall not tamper with any of the Baltimore club's players." But, by the July 19 issue of *Sporting News,* correspondent Frank Patterson told some of the Orioles' new woes: "With McGraw in the role of Benedict Arnold; with Kelley declaring himself ready to go to Cincinnati if offered enough; with Robbie disgusted and announcing his retirement from

112

baseball; with Mahon, the chief stockholder, sore at President Johnson; with the fans disgusted and swearing off from baseball, and the team disorganized and dissipating—the outlook in Baltimore is not what might be termed promising."

About the time this was penned, the situation grew from bad to worse. Oriole stars suddenly started jumping right and left. McGraw took with him to New York pitchers Joe McGinnity and Jack Cronin, catcher Roger Bresnahan, and first baseman Dan McGann. Joe Kelley, supposedly the new co-manager, and Cy Seymour jumped to the Cincinnati Reds. Kelley became Cincinnati manager in 1903. Oriole shortstop Billy Gilbert joined the Giants at the end of the 1902 season, and became McGraw's New York second baseman.

No doubt, when McGraw first decided to ask the Orioles for his release, he did not intend to wreck the team he was leaving. But these were bitter war times, and John T. Brush, chairman of the National League's executive committee, saw a golden opportunity to strike a knockout blow at his American League foes. He also hated Johnson, who in his days as a Cincinnati baseball writer frequently attacked and belittled Brush as a tightwad and skinflint. Brush and McGraw, acting for Freedman, bought 201 shares of the Orioles, a majority holding, from Mahon for $50,000. Prior to that McGraw had swapped his half interest in the Diamond Café to Wilbert Robinson for Robbie's Oriole stock. It enabled Mahon, and some smaller stockholders, to get back the money they had put into the venture.

It was because of this sale that McGraw was to tell the author years later: "McGinnity, McGann, Kelley, Seymour and the others did not jump. Brush and Freedman purchased a majority interest in the Orioles, taking over the contracts of the players, and they were free to send these men to their respective clubs."

In another conversation long after the events just described, McGraw told me exactly why he had jumped the American League in July, 1902, though he never liked the word "jump."

113

The author mentioned the conversation in an earlier book, *The Baseball Story*, published in 1950. Prior to this conversation I had made several references to McGraw's early American League connections in my New York newspaper column. I was seated next to McGraw at a baseball dinner; there had been a little drinking, and he was in a mood to talk. And he chose the subject of his own accord.

"Do you want to know why I left Baltimore, and the American League, in 1902?" he asked. "Well, I'll give you the real story. The move to shift the Orioles to New York had been contemplated for some time. In fact, I did much of the ground work, built up the contacts, scouted around for grounds, and was to get a piece of the club. Naturally, I assumed I would be manager. Then I suddenly learned that I no longer figured in Johnson's New York plans and that he was preparing to ditch me at the end of the 1902 season. So, I acted fast. If he planned to ditch me, I ditched him first, and beat him to New York by nearly a year."

A story printed in the *New York Sun* by Joe Vila, the best-informed New York sports writer at the turn of the century, in middle July, 1902, confirms McGraw's later-day remarks to the author on how close he came to entering New York as an American Leaguer. Vila wrote as follows:

If a scheme, hatched several weeks ago, had gone through, John J. McGraw would not have signed a contract to manage Freedman's New Yorks, but would have been at the helm of a new baseball club representing this city in the American League. McGraw, who has been a failure as a manager in Baltimore, concluded two months ago that baseball in that city, whether under the auspices of the National or American League, was a failure.

Last winter he got to work to secure what he believed would be a team capable of winning the American League championship. He engaged a corps of players whose salaries totaled $50,000. He notified the Baltimore public that unless his team was liberally supported, these salaries and other heavy expenses could not be paid. But the Baltimore team, as managed by McGraw, was a loser almost from the start.

114

Rows with the umpire on the field were frequent and Ban Johnson, in an effort to cleanse the sport, was compelled to suspend McGraw and other players on frequent occasions. These penalties did not stop McGraw, however, until recently when, as an excuse to Baltimore for fulfilling his engagement with Freedman, he gave it out that he would no longer stand the persecution of Johnson, who he said was trying to wreck the Baltimore team in order to transfer it to New York for the benefit of the American League.

As a matter of fact, McGraw himself planned to bring the Baltimore club, lock, stock and barrel, to this city more than a month ago. On June 4, at the Gravesend race track, McGraw was informed that there was a vacant plot on Manhattan Island, bounded on the west by First Avenue, on the north by 113th Street, on the south by 111th Street and on the east by the East River. The plot, with 112th Street closed, is larger than the Polo Grounds, and when McGraw heard of it he immediately consulted with Frank Farrell, known as the "pool room king," who owns race horses and not long ago was willing to pay $218,000 for the Empire City track in Yonkers.

In the presence of the Sun reporter, McGraw told Farrell about the plot, and it was agreed that if the grounds were available, Farrell would lease it. But upon investigating matters, it was discovered that the ground had been condemned by the city for a public park.

About the same time, Hughie Fullerton of Chicago, the best-known baseball writer in the Midwest, wrote:

The American League has successfully weathered one of the worst storms it is likely to have. Comiskey [the White Sox owner] thinks that the league is lucky in getting rid of the Baltimore traitors. He has known for a long time that McGraw was seeking to sell out the league and that Brush and Freedman were planning a raid which they hoped would dismantle the league. The American League, thanks to the honest stockholders in the Baltimore club, was kept informed of the intentions and plans of McGraw and, not being caught napping, Johnson was ready to put in a team at a moment's notice.

As noted from these July, 1902, excerpts, there was an inclination to be pretty severe with McGraw. But the Vila story justified, in some measure, McGraw's resentment—and perhaps spirit of revenge—when John learned that after doing all the spade work in New York, he was to be dumped. It is the author's belief that it was during McGraw's indefinite suspension of June 29 that Johnson advised him that he no longer was being considered in the future New York American League picture. And, then the hot-headed Irishman from Truxton hit the boiling point, and reacted as he did.

The jumping of McGinnity, McGann, Bresnahan, Cronin, Kelley and Seymour left the Orioles in a bad way, and brought on the real crisis. The club then was carrying only fourteen players, and with Wilbert Robinson in Hudson, Mass., for the funeral of his mother, there weren't enough players available to field a team. At first, it was believed that Robbie's sympathies were with McGraw and the seceders, but *Sporting News* accounts of the time tell of friction between the two old pals and that Robbie scarcely spoke to McGraw because of John's actions. Later, however, they resumed their old comradeship and Robbie served as coach under McGraw on the Giants before the friendship snapped for good in 1913.

Ban Johnson, breathing fire, resentment, indignation, and scorn for McGraw, came on the scene to see what could be salvaged from the situation. A game scheduled with St. Louis on July 17 had to be forfeited to the Browns. Johnson held a meeting of the minority stockholders, still headed by loyal Baltimore big league advocates, Harry Goldman and Sydney Frank, and announced he was taking over the franchise to keep the club alive and protect the rights of these minority stockholders.

He obtained a statement of loyalty from Wilbert Robinson, back from the funeral, threw his support behind Robbie as manager and named Al Selbach as team captain. Johnson sent SOS messages to other American League clubs for players. Chicago contributed pitcher John Katoll, who had been

116

severely disciplined by Johnson for a 1901 outbreak, and out-fielder Herm McFarland; Detroit's gifts were first baseman Frank Dillon and Harry Arndt, another infielder; Cleveland sent along outfielder Jack Thoney, an early speed boy; the Boston club contributed pitcher George Prestiss, and the Athletics, pitcher Lew Wiltse, whose younger left-handed brother, George "Hooks" Wiltse, soon would star for McGraw in New York.

From time to time, Robbie also picked up a bunch of minor leaguers, free agents and semi-pros: Tom Jones, later a crack first baseman with the Browns and Tigers, Ike Butler, Bob Lawson, Andy Oyler, Abe Yeager, Jack Burns, I. L. Mathison, Bill Mellor, Ernie Courtney, Rees, Heiseman, and Shields. Even Big City Tim Jordan, later Baltimore International first baseman and a National League home-run champion in Brooklyn, got into one game as an outfielder.

The makeshift club, with Harry Howell pitching, won its first game from the Browns, 5 to 4, but that was too good to last. At the time McGraw and the others left, the Orioles were running fifth, had a percentage around .500, and still were in the running. However, Uncle Robbie's team of ugly ducklings and humpty dumpties quickly settled in the celler; Baltimore finished last with 50 victories, 88 defeats, and a percentage of .362.

There have been worse tailenders in baseball. At home, the Birds split six games with the champion Athletics, but in Philadelphia, they won only three and lost ten. Some late season Athletic games were shifted from Baltimore to Philadelphia. Against second-place St. Louis, the Orioles had a truly horrible record, two victories and eighteen defeats. They made a crazy showing against Cleveland; in Baltimore they defeated the Indians eight games to two, but in Cleveland they lost eight and won only one. Only against the Detroit Tigers were the 1902 Birds consistent, getting five-five splits in each Oriole Park and Detroit.

117

An examination of the individual records of some of the 1902 Orioles gives an idea of the line-up scrambling poor Uncle Robbie had to do in order to field nine men. While Harry Howell had a 9-14 pitching average, he appeared in 96 games, also playing first base, second base, third base, shortstop, and outfield. Catcher Alex Smith was another jack-of-all-trades, as he shifted from catcher to first, to second, to third, and the outfield. It was the same with Wiltse, pitcher, first base, second base, outfield.

Late in 1902, when the baseball war still was on, Baltimore fans again found themselves outside the major leagues. At the request of president Johnson, the Baltimore American League franchise was transferred officially to New York. Johnson and Farrell, the New York owner, made a cash settlement with Goldman, Frank, and other minority stockholders who had stuck after McGraw, Mahon, and Kelley withdrew. Clark Griffith, manager of the Chicago White Sox, was put in charge of what was termed an all-star New York squad, including Willie Keeler, who jumped from Brooklyn. Griffith's post was the job McGraw once had hankered for. The only players retained from the 1902 tailend Orioles were pitchers Harry Howell and Lew Wiltse, second baseman Jimmy Williams, outfielder Hermus McFarland, and infielder Courtney.

Baltimore fans have been unjustly maligned for their failure to give their early American League club better support. In each 1901 and 1902, the club drew a little better than 100,000, not too bad for that period. Had the Orioles been able to rent old Union Park, it would have been easy, but the expense of building and carrying their own park, along with the high war salaries, put a heavy burden on the stock company's treasury. And, after the wholesale jumping of July, 1902, the fans knew there was little in it for them—that their club would be transferred whenever Ban Johnson willed it. They were in the unhappy position of the St. Louis Brown fans of 1953—every game was like a wake.

Wilbert (Uncle Robbie) Robinson, catcher of Hanlon's great Oriole team and McGraw's successor as manager of the American League Orioles in 1902.

John McGraw as a rookie with the Orioles in 1892.

Baltimore Sun Papers

McGraw in 1895 as the scrappy third baseman of the Orioles, champions that year.

Baltimore Sun Papers

Baltimore Orioles, National League Champions in 1894, '95, '96. Top row: Joe Quinn, John McMahon, Charles Esper, George Hemming, Frank Bowerman, William Clarke, James Donnelly. Middle row: Walter (Steve) Brodie, Bill Hoffer, Joe Kelley, Manager Ned Hanlon, Wilbert Robinson, Hughie Jennings, Henry Reitz. Bottom row: Jack Doyle, John J. McGraw, Willie Keeler, Doc Pond, and Sam, the mascot.

Hughie Jennings, great shortstop for the old Orioles. He hit .397 in 1896.

Wee Willie Keeler, who hit .432 for 1897 Orioles.

Jack Dunn, president-manager of seven straight Oriole winners, 1919-1925.

Urban Shocker, whose pitching helped the Browns to their second-place finish in 1922.

St. Louis Post-Dispatch

Kenny Williams, slugging left-fielder and leading home run hitter for the 1922 Browns.

St. Louis Post-Dispatch

Gorgeous George Sisler, one of the great first basemen of all time, who twice hit over .400 for the Browns.

Dan Howley, who led the Browns to first division finishes in 1928 and 1929.

Another great Brownie first baseman, George McQuinn. He hit .438 in the 1944 World Series.

St. Louis Post-Dispatch

Luke Sewell, manager of the 1944 Browns, American League Champions.

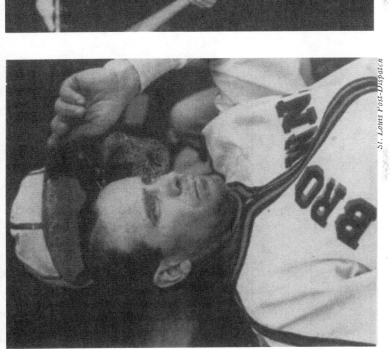

St. Louis Post-Dispatch

Chet Laabs, whose two home runs on the last day of the 1944 season clinched the pennant for the Browns.

The Orioles' pitching ace in 1954. Bob Turley, since traded to the Yankees in the Million Dollar Deal.

Another Oriole star in '54, shortstop Billy Hunter, also traded to New York.

Baltimore News-Post

Vern Stephens being greeted by Bob Kennedy after homering against the Yankees at Memorial Stadium. Vern led 1954 Orioles in home runs and runs batted in.

Paul Richards, then managing the White Sox, greets Oriole manager Jimmy Dykes before the Orioles' home opener in 1954. By 1955 Richards would have Dykes' job.

Vice President Nixon throws out the first ball at Memorial Stadium as Baltimore officially re-enters American League, April 15, 1954.

Shaking hands after the Browns' franchise was awarded to Baltimore on September 29, 1953, are, left to right: Clarence Miles, president of the new Orioles; Will Harridge, president of the American League; Mayor Thomas D'Alesandro of Baltimore; and Bill Veeck, former owner of the Browns.

Baltimore News-Post

48,000 fans fill Baltimore's Memorial Stadium to celebrate Orioles' return to the majors, April 15, 1954.

Memorial float hailing the old and the new Orioles in the 1954 opening day parade, with Vice President Nixon in the center.

In Mrs. McGraw's interesting book *The Real McGraw,* edited by Arthur Mann, it is said that John McGraw kept Ban Johnson informed of all of his dickerings with Andy Freedman and the Giants, and that McGraw was permitted to leave Baltimore as part of a deal whereby the American League was permitted entry into New York, also that the alleged hatred between McGraw and Johnson was largely newspaper talk and that there was no real animosity between the two men.

The author has the utmost respect and esteem for Mrs. McGraw, a gracious lady whom he has known for four decades, also for Arthur Mann, a friend, a splendid writer, and student of baseball. It would be pleasant to go along with such a contention, but unfortunately the incidents of this chapter, from what I was told by such older writers as Jim Price, Joe Vila, Bill Hanna, and Hughie Fullerton, do not substantiate it. I do not doubt Mrs. McGraw felt she gave the correct version. She was a bride of only a few months when her husband took her from her native Baltimore to New York. As related they were saying bitter things about John in Baltimore, and elsewhere, in the summer of 1902. McGraw usually was close-mouthed about his personal affairs, but no doubt he tried to soften the situation for his bride by telling her that things were not exactly as they seemed, that Johnson had known all along what he was doing, and that Ban did not hate him as every one insisted.

However, the theory of a deal does not hold up well in view of what happened in January, 1903, after committees of National and American League club owners concluded peace terms in Cincinnati. One of the conditions was that the American League be permitted to enter New York, provided it agreed to stay out of Pittsburgh. John T. Brush, who by this time had purchased the Giants from Freedman, along with Ebbets of Brooklyn, filed a minority report, protesting strongly against the peace agreement. Brush actually went into court, and by injunction sought to block the peace terms, especially the stipulation that granted permission for the American League to come into New York. It was not until Johnson threatened to renew the war and six fellow National League owners put every possible pressure on Brush that he called off his legal action.

In the first decade of the New York Americans, then termed the Highlanders, there was a cold war between the two New York clubs. The Giants' official family, and writers friendly to them, disdainfully referred to the Highlanders as the Invaders. It wasn't until the Polo Grounds wooden stands burned to the ground in 1911, and Frank Farrell offered Brush the loan of his Highlander park, that Brush finally softened in his attitude toward the Invaders.

The hatred between Johnson and McGraw was not cooked up by the writers of that era. They merely wrote of what they knew. The author did not come on the New York sports scene until 1911, nine years after McGraw left Baltimore, but the bitter feeling between McGraw and Johnson frequently came up in conversations with baseball men and sports writers. It was regarded as baseball's No. 1 hatred.

An incident still stands firmly in mind. It took place around 1911 or 1912. The day after the American League's annual meeting, Ban Johnson had a practice of holding court in the bar room of New York's Walcott Hotel, while he and his party awaited the time to leave on the Twentieth Century for Chicago. My sports editor, Jim Price, assigned me to these sessions, in case somebody let something slip over a highball or a glass of beer that might be the germ of a story. Charley Comiskey, some other Western club owners, Frank Farrell, and such New York writers as Joe Vila, Bill MacBeth, and George Tidden usually attended these sessions. Ban loved to pontificate on baseball and other subjects, but frequently there was a sense of levity to his remarks.

On this occasion, talk was far from serious; Ban was in a merry mood, and peals of ribald laughter rang out of the room. All was *gemüttlichkeit* and good fellowship! Then one of the

120

writers, MacBeth, made a remark mentioning John McGraw. Perhaps MacBeth, with a few drinks under his belt, did it to get a rise out of Ban; MacBeth was noted as a prankster.

A dark cloud swept across Johnson's face; he grew stern and severe, and said sharply: "This had been a nice party until now, Bill. Don't ever mention that man's name in my presence again." A few moments later he arose, saying stiffly, "Well, I've got to be getting upstairs." All the fun had left him.

It was the same with McGraw. No one mentioned Ban Johnson's name in his presence. If the name came up, he would say with the sarcasm for which he was noted, "That so and so!"

Such 1902 American League managers as Connie Mack, Jim McAleer, and Clark Griffith had pleasant relations with McGraw when they later met in World Series play. Comiskey, who was quoted as being glad the league was rid of "the Baltimore traitors" in 1902, held no grudge, and in the winter of 1913-14, he and McGraw made a round-the-world baseball trip with their respective teams. But Johnson never forgot or forgave the Baltimore incident of 1902. Both Johnson and John carried their hatred for each other to the grave.

CHAPTER XI

Orioles Land Berth in International League

THERE STILL was a chance for Baltimore to get major league baseball after the American League pulled out of the Chesapeake town. Ned Hanlon wasn't satisfied with conditions in Brooklyn. His pennant winners of 1899 and 1900 had drawn only fair crowds. Brooklyn also was hit hard by the American League war, losing such valuable players as Joe McGinnity, Willie Keeler, Joe Kelley, Harry Howell, Bill Donovan, Frank Kitson, Jim McGuire, Duke Farrell, and Addie Joss, a draftee from Toledo. Nevertheless, Ned had kept the Brooklyns, then called Hanlon's Superbas, in the first division during the war years, finishing third in 1901 and second in 1902. But, the 1902 runner-up came home twenty-seven and a half games behind the champion Pirates. It meant little interest in the race and little business at the gate.

"We're not doing anything here; we might as well go back to Baltimore," Hanlon told Ebbets, his associate. "They're sore down there, about the American League running out, and will welcome back National League baseball."

However, Ebbets, a New Yorker, who had been in Brooklyn baseball since his early twenties, couldn't see it. He argued: "No, Ned, I can't go with you on that. Some day Brooklyn will be as big, and important, as Manhattan; one can only guess the future possibilities of this borough. I still have faith in Brooklyn."

There then began a battle between Hanlon and Ebbets for

control of the Brooklyn franchise, the former intending to move it to Baltimore, the latter fighting to stay in Brooklyn. Ebbets succeeded in scraping together enough money to buy out the stock held by Ferdinand Abell. Ned and Charley then engaged in a lively tussle for Harry Von Der Horst's stock. The Baltimore brewer was quite ill; the bitter baseball war had taken quite a toll on his health and finances. He announced he was ready to sell and get out of baseball. Hanlon tried to get some Baltimore money to buy his stock, but couldn't raise enough. Ebbets, broke after buying out Abell, couldn't raise the money either, but he induced a Brooklyn furniture dealer, Henry W. Medicus, to buy the Von Der Horst interest. That insured the retention of the franchise in Brooklyn, and Baltimore then had to wait a long time before getting back into the big league picture.

Though Hanlon remained in Brooklyn as manager of the Superbas, he got back into Baltimore baseball in 1903. Failing in his efforts to win a place for Baltimore in the National League, Ned did the next best thing; he acquired a franchise in the old Eastern League, which changed its name to the International League in 1911. It was the oldest minor league and the strongest loop outside of the majors.

Hanlon and Sidney Frank, the 1901 president of the American League Orioles, purchased the Montreal franchise. Montreal remained out of the league only half a season, for in mid-season, 1903, Montreal interests purchased the Springfield, Mass., franchise and moved it to Montreal.

Hanlon and Frank also purchased Oriole Park from the American League. Considerable money was due on it, and they picked it up at a bargain. Wilbert Robinson and Hughie Jennings started in command of these new Birds, and the Reach Guide for 1904 attributed the Orioles' fourth place finish to "the spirited management of the club by Hughie Jennings in the second half of the season." The Baltimore news letter in the *Sporting News* of July 11, 1903, has an intimate account of the change, and has Steve Brodie still bobbing up in the Baltimore scene.

Robbie has retired from the management of the local club in disgust, and Hugh Jennings, once the star of stars on the diamond and marvelous shortstop and run-getter for the champion Orioles in their palmiest days, has become the manager and is playing.

Think of Hugh Jennings in a minor league! Verily, times have changed and, by the way, Walter Brodie, after wearing even Robinson's patience to the breaking point, left here and now is with Toronto and in the games here last week the veteran outfielder was hitting like a fiend and fielding as only he knows how. Steve truly is a physical marvel.

Robinson, first as playing manager and then as a pampered private, still caught 75 games and hit .266 at the age of 39. In 1904, Wilbert again started the season as acting manager, as Jennings was completing his studies at Cornell Law School and did not report to the club until May. However, from then on Hughie put in full time at his Oriole managerial job, and made such a success of it that he was called to Detroit as manager in 1907, and celebrated with three quick American League flags. It was at Baltimore that Hughie introduced his famous cry of "Ee-yah" on the coaching lines, while standing on his right foot, kicking out with his left, and his arms widely extended.

Jennings' Baltimore teams couldn't win a pennant, but Hughie had strong aggressive fighting clubs, that always were in the thick of the contention. In 1904, the "Ee-yah" man's Orioles finished a good second to George Stallings' Buffalo Bisons, but the real humdinger of a race came in 1905. It was something like the 1897 finish between Hanlon's National League Orioles and the Boston Beaneaters. This time another New England team, Jack Dunn's Providence Clam Diggers, beat out the Birds by a half-game, the closest race in the loop up to that time. Providence won by two points, with a record of 83-47, .638, against 82-47, .636, for the Birds. As Jack Dunn then raised his excited high-pitched voice against Jen-

124

nings' "Ee-yah," who then would have believed that Dunn soon would become the darling of the Baltimore fans? Baltimore fans then enjoyed ribbing him; they would imitate "Dunnie's" voice, and call out, "Now pipe down, Jack, before you get your pipes all jammed up."

For the greater part of the season, Jennings had no fear of Dunn, or his Providence Diggers. Jersey City, which in 1903, had a stratospheric percentage of .742, was the club to beat. Up until Labor Day, the Birds and the Jerseys—then known as the Skeeters—bobbed in and out of first place. Then Providence came strong in September, and Jennings concluded: "Dunnie is getting too close for comfort. We'll really have to give it all we have to stay in front of him."

The Birds gave Hughie all they had, but just missed staying in front. In the last week of the season, Providence dislodged the Skeeters, came abreast Baltimore on next to the last day of the season, and won out on the very last day, September 24, with a victory over Rochester. An unplayed game with Buffalo cost the Orioles the pennant. Hughie muttered mournfully: "The hell of it is that I had to lose to that wild-eyed Dunn by the margin of a rained-out game we couldn't play off."

Hughie's last Oriole club, his team of 1906, finished a good third behind Buffalo and Jersey City. Baltimore fans were getting used to the International League brand of ball. They still chafed at being in the minors, but admitted Hughie and his boys always hustled and put on a good show. And they saw some interesting players, Tom Jones, Tim Jordan, and Hunter at first base; Charley Laudenslager, Lou Castro, and Mullen at second; Phil Lewis, Jennings, and Neal at shortstop; Steve Griffin, Larry Quinlan, and Mowery at third; Tom Dowd, John Kelly, Steve Brodie, Jack Hayden, Walter McCredie, Herm McFarland, and Tom O'Hara, outfield; Wilbert Robinson, Hugh Ahearn (sometimes just called Hearne), and Bill Byers, catchers; Merle Adkins, Del Mason and Fred Burchell, pitchers.

125

Jennings, his arm much improved, played his old shortstop position, also second and third. Though in his late thirties, Hughie still was lively as a cricket, playing 92 games in 1904, 56 (all at shortstop) on the near champion of 1905, and 75 in 1906. Robbie retired at the age of forty after the 1904 season; he had disposed of the Diamond Café and gone into the butcher business in Baltimore. Castro, who had played with the Athletics, was the son of a Colombian diplomat, the first of the Central-South American Latins to play big league ball. And Baltimore, as in the past, had its physician-pitcher, for Adkins off the diamond was Dr. Merle Theron Adkins, product of the University of Wisconsin.

Baltimore owner Ned Hanlon sold first baseman Tim Jordan and shortstop Phil Lewis, a Cornell alumnus, to Brooklyn manager Ned Hanlon's team. In Brooklyn, Big Tim led the National League home-run hitters in 1906 and 1908, and Lewis hung up some kind of a record in reverse, five errors in one game at shortstop. Pitcher Burchell went to the Red Sox and moundsman Mason to the Redlegs.

CHAPTER XII

Start of the Dunn Dynasty

FOLLOWING THE departure of Jennings for Detroit at the end of the 1906 season, Hanlon scanned the list of available managerial material. And again he came up with one of his happy hunches. Following Jack Dunn's hard-won pennant in Providence in 1905, his club slipped to seventh in 1906. As is usual in such a case, there was friction, criticism, and recriminations. Jack wanted to get away from Rhode Island. Hanlon wanted a manager. It was that easy. "How'd you like to run our club in Baltimore?" asked Foxy Ned. "If the salary is right, I'd like to switch," said Jack.

So, one morning Baltimore fans awakened to learn the man they had raged against in 1905 was the new flight leader of the Birds. But only an Assyrian astrologist and seer could have predicted how high Jack's Birds would soar. And that the Dunn dynasty would run the Baltimore baseball show for 46 years.

John Joseph Dunn, soon to be known as the McGraw of the minors, was the same player who was with McGraw on the Baltimore Americans in 1901, and jumped to the Giants, where McGraw again caught up with him in July, 1902. Dunn was born in Meadville, Pa., on October 6, 1872, making him less than a year older than McGraw. After pitching independent ball in Bayonne, N.J., Dunn served his minor league apprenticeship with Binghamton and Toronto. He used the latter club as his springboard to the majors, landing with the Dodgers in 1897. Two years later "Dunnie" contributed twenty-one victories to Ned Hanlon's first Brooklyn pennant.

Jack's arm started to go bad for pitching in 1900 and Hanlon traded him to the Phillies. It was from that club that he jumped briefly to the American League.

Jack always was a fair hitter and an all-around baseball man. Though too short to play first base, he was at home in any other infield position. As proof of his versatility, in 1902 he pitched, played second base, shortstop, third base, and the outfield for the Giants. After McGraw moved to New York, he retained Dunn for infield utility chores, and Jack played on McGraw's first Giant champions, the club of 1904. The next season "Dunnie," as he invariably was called in his later years, left New York for his first managerial post in Providence.

Dunn resembled McGraw in many ways. Both men had an inherent Irish shrewdness, for Jack was as keen as a steel trap. Never a great ball player, he was a master strategist and had a remarkable sense for recognizing talent in the rough. Furthermore, Dunn knew how to bring along his kids and develop them into stars. He had the same Irish terrier truculence that got McGraw into so many arguments. Jack, too, was easily riled and ready to fight at the drop of a hat. His cuss words, delivered in his high-pitched voice, were a legend in baseball. Often he let loose on his own players, but reserved some of his finest taunts for umpires and opponents. When Jack exchanged compliments with George Stallings, of Buffalo and later of Rochester, one could smell the sulphur and brimstone a mile away. "Dunnie" carried out the traditions of the old fighting Orioles of the nineties, but he was a managerial natural, and soon became the dominant figure among International League managers as was McGraw in the National League.

There was nothing scintillating about Dunn's start as Baltimore skipper in 1907. He yipped a lot, frequently shouted his outraged indignation to the high heavens, was thrown out of a number of ball games, but wound up in sixth place.

128

Even so, he finished only one game under the .500 mark. But Jack hit pay dirt early, and won Baltimore's first International League flag in 1908. It wasn't one of Jack's better clubs, but it had enough to beat out "Dunnie's" old team, the Providence Clam Diggers, led by Hughie Duffy, .593 to .581. His leading hitter among the Oriole regulars was outfielder O'Hara with .282.

Jack really had to jockey about his talent to win this flag. He had few full-time regulars, and his first Baltimore championship was due largely to the superlative pitching of Doc Adkins. The good physician-pitcher from Wisconsin carried the staff with twenty-nine victories and twelve defeats. Doc also was the workhorse of the league with 326 innings pitched in a 140-game season. Frank "Rube" Dessau, later with Brooklyn, and "Mac" McCloskey helped out with records of 15-13 and 15-14, respectively. A home-grown left-handed butcher boy, Charles "Butch" Schmidt, won five games out of six. Dunn later was to shift big "Butch" Schmidt to first base and sell him to the Boston Braves where "Butch" became the clean-up hitter of George Stallings' miracle World's Champions of 1914.

Dunn, at the age of 36, still was good enough to play 92 games, mostly at second base, and hit .245. Connie Mack let Jack have his tall former Philadelphia high school shortstop, Jack Knight, and McGraw sent Dunn his former utility man, Sammy Strang, who once was undecided whether to try for a career in grand opera or play professional baseball.

However, the most interesting player among Dunn's 1908 champions was Wilbert Robinson, who at 44 was lured out of his butcher shop to help out the Oriole catching. The other catchers still were Bill Byers and Hugh Ahearn, alias Hearne. The man who sixteen years before had lashed out seven hits in a nine-inning Oriole National League game, still had a little of his batting skill left, whacking out 22 hits in his 30 games. A paragraph by J. M. Cummings of the *Baltimore*

News indicated Robbie wasn't just a fat old fuddyduddy puttering around, but contributed his full share to the pennant:

The Orioles' tried and true brace of catchers—Byers and Hearne, were reinforced by the genial veteran, Wilbert Robinson. It was very much like old times to have Robbie in Oriole uniform again and he soon showed that he had lost none of his cunning, nor had age slowed his foot, palsied his arm, or dimmed his eye. Robbie played, if anything, a better game than in the year of his "retirement"—1904. He and Hearne and Byers made a trio of backstops that no other team in the Eastern League and few in the major leagues could match.

Just a real old Oriole!

Following a third-place finish in 1909, Dunn made the move which was to bring him fame, fortune, affluence, and make him a permanent resident of Baltimore. Though Jack later was a good spender, during his playing and early managerial career he had carefully stowed away a good part of his baseball earnings. He also had made profitable investments. With the aid of his own capital, and money he borrowed, he purchased the Baltimore franchise from Ned Hanlon for $70,000 in the winter of 1909-10, and by the season of 1910 Dunn was owner, president, manager, and part-time second baseman of what many then considered was the best minor league franchise in baseball. Dunn now was free to buy, sell, trade, and consult no one but himself.

In the first four years of Dunn's ownership, he always had been promising first-division clubs; he was in the race but he couldn't lead the flock first under the wire. It was third in 1910, second in 1911, fourth in 1912, and third in 1913.

During this period, Baltimore clubs were fed a steady player supply by the Athletics, who then had their greatest club, four champions in a five year period and World's Champions in 1910, 1911, and 1913. In fact, the Shibes and Connie Mack of the Athletics had a pretty good block of Oriole stock, acquired at the time that Dunn gained control.

130

In 1910, it was announced that the Athletics had purchased Clarence "Lefty" Russell, a Baltimore home bred, who had a 1910 Oriole pitching record of 24-14, for $12,000. Quite a furore was raised over this sum in both Baltimore and Phildelphia, as it supposedly was $1,000 more than the $11,000 that the Giants paid for Rube Marquard in 1908, the previous top price for a minor league star. However, the $12,000 deal probably was on paper, as Mack already had sent to Baltimore two capable pitchers, Rube Vickers and Jimmy Dygert, and Maurice Rath, who like Jack Knight was a former Philadelphia high school infielder. Unfortunately, "Lefty" Russell never was worth anything near $12,000, as he was a total flop in Phillie. As for Vickers, Dunn worked him as early Baltimore managers had employed Bobbie Mathews and Matt Kilroy. In 1910, Rube won 25 games and lost 24, and in 1911, he won 32 and lost 14, fifty-seven victories in two years.

Near the end of the 1912 season, Dunn sold Mack his two crack young outfielders, Eddie Murphy and Jimmy Walsh. Eddie was 1912 International batting champion with .361, and succeeded Danny Murphy as Athletic right fielder on the Philadelphia champions of 1913-14. However, the Mack-Dunn axis worked both ways; having a lot of good pitchers, Mack permitted Bob Shawkey, a crack Athletic pitching prospect, to browse in Oriole Park in 1912 and 1913. After "Dunnie" sold Schmidt to the Braves, Mack sent along his extra first baseman, Ben Houser; also a talented Dixie shortstop, Claude Derrick, Mack's former infield utility player; and a wild left-handed pitcher from Texas, Daring Dave Danforth. In 1911, Dunn used Cy Seymour in center field. Cy was one of the American League Oriole jumpers of July, 1902, who three years later interrupted Hans Wagner's batting championship monopoly for a year, winning the National League batting crown in 1905. Old Cy, at 38, still could swish his bat, hitting .296 for Dunn in 112 games.

In 1913, "Dunnie" enriched the Oriole treasury by the

sale of two home-bred ballplaying brothers, third baseman Fritz Maisel and outfielder George Maisel, who came from the suburban town of Catonsville. Jack picked up a $12,000 check from the Yankees for little Fritzie. He wasn't much of a hitter, but a flying Mercury on the base paths. At the time of his sale in August, he had 44 steals in 111 games with the Birds. In his remaining 51 New York games he stole 25 more, 69 for the season. In 1914, Fritz's first full season with the Yankees he led the American League in stolen bases with 74. He did it, too, on a batting average of .239. That season, Ty Cobb, Eddie Collins, and Tris Speaker, the three top hitters in the league and all great base runners, stole 35, 58, and 42 bases, respectively. George Maisel, two and a half years younger than Fritz, was sold to the St. Louis Browns. He later played a little with the Tigers, and then bobbed up in the National League with the Cubs.

CHAPTER XIII

Babe Ruth and the Federal League

TWO INTERESTING history-making events happened in Baltimore baseball in 1914. A 19-year old Baltimore-born youngster from St. Mary's Industrial School, George Herman "Babe" Ruth, signed with Dunn's Baltimore Orioles, and the Federal League, terming itself a third major loop, entered a team in Baltimore. Both events had a terrific impact on American professional baseball, but inasmuch as the Federal League promised to return Baltimore to the bigtime, the advent of the Baltimore Terrapins completely overshadowed the early sensational play of Ruth, Baltimore's Hall of Fame immortal, who was destined to revolutionize baseball.

Perhaps these two events should be handled separately, but they interlocked so closely, and the Federal League had such a big bearing on the mid-season disposal of Ruth that Babe and the Feds are treated in the same chapter.

Ruth, second only to Ty Cobb among all-time baseball greats, was born over his father's saloon at 426 Camden Street, February 6, 1895, the year of the great Orioles' second pennant. George Herman was of German descent; there have been reports that Ruth's first International League contract was signed, "George H. Ehrhardt," but Babe always insisted his father's name was Ruth. Perhaps he changed the spelling from the more German name of Roth. Babe's mother's name was Kate Schanberg. Ruth was a tough kid, brought up in a tough neighborhood. When he was seven his parents placed him in St. Mary's Industrial School, outside of Baltimore. It has been referred to as an orphanage, also as a reform school. Actually, it was a Roman Catholic training school for orphans, delinquents, runaways, incorrigibles, and boys whose homes were broken up by divorce, desertion, or other causes.

For years, it generally was believed that Ruth was in St. Mary's from the age of seven until he played professional baseball. However, the records of St. Mary's show that Babe was in and out of the school several times, once being out for as long as three years, but misconduct invariably overtook him and he was sent back.

At St. Mary's, he was taught the trade of tailor and shirt-maker. But the tough kid also loved to play baseball, and became quite proficient at it. At first, he was a left-handed catcher, using a left-handed mitt on his right hand. Though skinny as a youngster, young Ruth quickly grew to six feet and could hit baseballs for tremendous distances. Once, when he burst into uproarious laughter as one after another of his pitchers was having his ears pinned back, Brother Matthias, the coach, commented sharply: "If you think it is so funny, George, go in and pitch. Let's see what you can do." Ruth checked the rally; blotted out the opponents in the remaining innings, and fared so well that from that time on he was a pitcher with an alive jumping fast ball.

Brother Matthias was Ruth's fairy godfather, and he had a salutary effect on Babe all of his life. He recognized Ruth's inherent talent, and through him and Brother Gilbert, one of the higher-ups at the school, word was passed along to Dunn of the great prospect at St. Mary's. Early in 1914, Dunn signed the kid to a contract for $600, which Babe thought was all the money in the world. As Ruth still was a minor, Dunn had to sign a court order making himself accountable for Ruth's conduct until George was twenty-one. It led to reports that Jack legally adopted the St. Mary's boy. Some trace his nickname to the fact that he was Dunn's adopted babe. However, years ago a man, who as a boy had been in St. Mary's with Ruth, told the author the nickname started shortly after Ruth came to the school in 1902. The homesick boy cried a lot; older boys teased him and called him "Babe." It stuck and became the most famous of all baseball nicknames.

A few weeks after Ruth signed what he considered his fabulous contract, he accompanied Dunn's Orioles on their 1914 training jaunt to Fayetteville, N. C. As Ruth never had been out of Baltimore before, he was one of the greenest kids ever taken on a training trip. He stuffed himself with food to the bursting point, almost had his head torn off in an elevator, and fell for every prank the older players rigged for him. Perhaps to get him away from ribbing older players, Dunn roomed him with Rodger Pippen, then a young baseball writer on the *Baltimore News* and now sports editor of the *Baltimore News-Post*. Rodger contributed the box-score in which Babe hit his first home run in professional baseball to Ruth's book, *The Babe Ruth Story*. It was a scrub game between two of Dunn's squads at Fayetteville, the Buzzards and Sparrows. Babe played shortstop and pitched for the Buzzards; Pippen played center field for the same side.

However, Ruth's pitching, rather than his hitting, made the national headlines. In pre-season exhibition games in Carolina and Baltimore, against the World's Champion Athletics, the National League champion Giants, and the Phillies, young Ruth breezed through such hitters as Frank Baker, Eddie Collins, Larry Doyle, Red Murray and Sherry Magee as though they were schoolboy opponents at St. Mary's. He hung up an imposing string of early shutout innings. There was a show in New York called: "Along Came Ruth." Copyreaders would put that heading over games in which the young southpaw from St. Mary's repelled the vaunted big leaguers.

McGraw was so impressed with young Ruth's pitching that he contacted Dunn after a Giant-Oriole exhibition and said: "Jack, that young left-hander you had out there today looked awfully good. Whenever you're ready to put Ruth on the market, I want you to give me first crack at him." McGraw

135

always insisted Jack had agreed, but "Dunnie" then was having many worries and didn't pay too much attention to McGraw's remarks.

In an effort to fight off the Federal League invasion, Jack put together a club he felt certain would hold the city against the opposition. He enrolled a team of ex-big leaguers and players destined for major league stardom. Gleichmann was at first base; Neal Ball at second; Claude Derrick at shortstop; and Ezra Midkiff at third. Ball had played for the Yankees, Indians, and Red Sox; with Cleveland he made baseball's first authenticated unassisted triple play. Derrick had been Mack's utility infielder and also played with the Yankees; Midkiff was the Yankees' 1913 regular third baseman.

In the outfield, Dunn had two former Yankees, Birdie Cree and Bert Daniels, and a little speed boy, George Twomley. Jack had two hustling young catchers in Ben Egan and Jim "Wicky" McAvoy. Both had been with the Athletics. The pitching staff was headed by young Ruth; Ernie Shore, a Wake Forest collegian with a 1912 trial under McGraw; Ensign Cottrell, sent to the Orioles by Connie Mack; Dave Danforth; and Allan Russell, a former Baltimore Sunday School Leaguer and younger right-handed brother of Clarence "Lefty" Russell. Allan, a spitballer, later pitched for the Yankees, Red Sox, and Washington.

Many regarded it as the greatest minor league club up to that time. Dunn was proud of it, and said: "With a team like that our fans won't be interested in those Federal League frauds." But even though young Ruth, the local kid, was winning nearly every time out, and the Orioles were spread-eagling the International League, Baltimore fans turned their back on Jack to root for the "major league" Terrapins.

Here's how the Federal League came about: An ill-fated attempt was made in 1912 to launch an outlaw United States League with cities entirely in the East: Baltimore, Washington, New York, Brooklyn, Philadelphia, Newark, Richmond, and Reading, Pa. Mayor Whitman of Reading was president, and he hoped the league eventually would blossom into a full major. The United States League folded after a month, but made another brief attempt to get going in 1913. A. N. Elrod was president of the Baltimore club.

In 1913, the independent Federal League started in the Midwest as a six-club league, taking in five big league cities, Chicago, St. Louis, Cleveland, Pittsburgh, Cincinnati, and Indianapolis. The Cincinnati club, which played its games at Covington, Kentucky, was shifted to Kansas City in midseason. It lasted the full season. The Federals had a few big names; the great Cy Young was manager at Cleveland and Deacon Phillippe, a Pirate World Series hero, was in command in Pittsburgh.

By the winter of 1913-14, an enterprising Chicago stationer, James A. Gilmore, was elected president of the Federal League. He had all of the enthusiasm, perseverance, and brass of Ban Johnson in 1901. He, too, promptly expanded Eastward, taking in the best of the defunct United States League teams. His 1914 line-up was Baltimore, Brooklyn, Buffalo, and Pittsburgh in the East, and Chicago, St. Louis, Indianapolis and Kansas City in the West. Gilmore enlisted some wealthy men in his organization. The Ward brothers, baking millionaires, backed the club in Brooklyn; Charles Weeghman, owner of a chain of Chicago restaurants, took over the Whales of Chicago's North Side; Otto Stifel, a brewer, and Phil deCatesby Ball, wealthy manufacturer of ice-making plants, were the angels in St. Louis. Harry Sinclair, the oil multimillionaire, sponsored the 1915 Newark club, with the eventual idea of moving to New York. With Sinclair in, the Federals had bigger financial resources than the existing major leagues.

In the Monument City, 600 enthusiastic Baltimoreans, interested in seeing the city back on the big league map, raised $160,000 to finance the Terrapins, or "Terps" as they often were called. Carroll W. Rasin, a business man, was president; Judge Harry Goldman, secretary of the American League

137

Orioles of 1901-02, was vitally interested, as was Ned Hanlon, who owned the ground on which the new Federal League park was built and had a big piece of the Terrapins. Stuart S. Janney, a prominent Baltimore attorney, also was active in the Terrapin picture.

The Federal League early showed its disrespect for the reserve and ten-day release clauses in major and minor league contracts, and Gilmore, again following the 1901 precepts of Ban Johnson, encouraged wholesale raids on the National and American Leagues, as well as the two larger minor leagues, the International and American Association. Managers were largely stars who jumped from the major leagues. In Baltimore, the team boss was Otto Knabe, formerly crack second baseman of the Phillies; in Chicago, it was Joe Tinker; in Brooklyn, Lee Magee; in Kansas City, George Stovall; in St. Louis, Mordecai Brown and Fielder Jones.

Jumping to the Terrapins from the Phillies with Knabe were Mickey Doolan, a great fielding shortstop, and third baseman Runt Walsh. It knocked a terrific hole in the Phillie infield and sent that club reeling from second in 1913 to sixth in 1914. Pitcher Jack Quinn and outfielder Guy Zinn were won in raids on Stallings' Boston Braves, and center fielder Benny Meyer jumped from Brooklyn. The rest of Otto's players were taken largely from the International League and American Association but were men who had played in the big leagues, pitchers Frank "Piano Legs" Smith and Irving "Kaiser" Wilhelm, catcher Fred Jacklitsch, first baseman Harry Swacina, and outfielder George Simmons.

The Federal League made it even tougher for Dunn by going into business directly across the street from Dunn's International League Park. The new Federal League park was located at 29th Street and York Road, later known as Green-mount Avenue. It was on the northwest corner; Dunn's park was on the southwest corner. But the two organizations were anything but neighborly.

Dunn had a cruel eye-opener when the Federal League

138

opened its season April 13. The Terps were given permission to open a day before the rest of the league, also a day before the National and American openings. So Baltimore had the national spotlight all to itself that day. The author's managing editor on the old *New York Press,* James Murphy, was a Baltimore man; he thought the event of sufficient importance to send me down from New York to cover Baltimore's return to the big leagues. Baltimore newspapers got out special baseball supplements, telling of Baltimore's past baseball glories, the city's pride and joy in returning to big league ball, much as they did on April 15, 1954. The sellout crowd swamped the wooden grandstand and bleachers and massed behind outfield ropes. And, everybody had a good time; Baltimore, with Jack Quinn pitching, defeated Buffalo, 3 to 2.

Dunn opened a few days later to about 5,000, but from then on it got worse for Jack, instead of better. Though Knabe's Terps fell apart in 1915, they were contenders all the way in 1914, finishing third, only four and a half games behind the champion Indianapolis club. Jack raved and ranted; he shouted he had a far better club than the Federal League intruders, but Baltimore just wouldn't buy it. The city had become major league conscious, and no longer was interested in anything with a minor league label. Dunn's attractions were clubs such as Providence, Jersey City, and Toronto; the visitors at the Federal League park wore such lettering as Chicago, Brooklyn, St. Louis, and Pittsburgh on their shirt fronts. And, if the Feds weren't a full major league, they showed such players as Tinker, Hal Chase, Lee Magee, Benny Kauff, Russ Ford, Tom Seaton, Les Mann, Eddie Roush, Max Flack, Ed Konetchy, Rebel Oakes, Otey Crandall, and other big league jumpers.

It might have been better for Dunn if his club hadn't been so darn good. In the early season, the Orioles were making a shambles of the International League race, leading by as much as ten games. This was reduced somewhat in early July, when Baltimore's lead over second-place Rochester was four and a half games. But, it generally was conceded the second half of the I.L. race would be played largely for exercise. Then came an Oriole home crowd of less than 50, and Jack Dunn really got scared. He saw the investment of a lifetime going down the drain. He was paying practically major league salaries inflated by a new baseball war, and despite money advanced by Joe Lannin of the Red Sox and Connie Mack, he was daily going deeper and deeper into the hole. Only desperate measures would enable him to salvage something from the unhappy and worsening situation, and get him out from under his big payroll.

He began to peddle his top-ranking players right and left. Babe Ruth, Ernie Shore, and catcher Ben Egan went in a package deal to the Red Sox for $8,500; Claude Derrick, Bert Daniels, and George Twomley were sold to the Reds at $5,000 for each player; Birdie Cree, the loop's batting leader, was sold back to the Yankees for $5,000 and outfielder Bill Holden; pitcher Ensign Cottrell was sold to the Braves and Ezra Midkiff to the Louisville Colonels.

The Baltimore correspondent to *Sporting News* wrote rather bitterly in the issue of July 16, 1914:

No one is inclined to blame Dunn . . . for anything he has done. The most sensational sales of ball players ever recorded in the history of the game, the spectacle of the breaking up of the greatest team ever gathered together outside of the "fat fours" of the present major leagues, the countrywide holding up of Baltimore to ridicule—none of this seems to concern Baltimore fans a particle. Such a situation only indicates how dead is the interest in International League ball here.

Convinced that the case is hopeless here and advised presumably by the powers that be that if he wanted financial aid the proper thing to do would be to realize on his assets first, Dunn took the advice from higher up and began to unload. He had put all he had in the ball team and it was up to him to get some of it back.

In breaking up the $8,500 which Dunn received for Ruth, Shore, and Egan, Babe's price tag supposedly was $2,900, that of Ernie Shore $2,100, and catcher Egan, the one who didn't stick, $3,500. Before discussing the ridiculous figures for Ruth and Shore, let us glimpse a little of Babe's Oriole activities while Dunn was hopelessly bucking the Terps.

Following Ruth's great exhibition showing, Babe pitched his first International League game, April 22, 1914, when he defeated Buffalo, 6 to 0. Oddly enough, Joe McCarthy, later Ruth's manager in New York, played second base for Buffalo, and Paul Krichell, for many years head scout of the Yankees, caught for the Bisons. Even though Babe was playing to empty stands, his pitching was the sensation of the league. Dunn was broke, but he played fair with Babe; after one month, he doubled his salary to $1,200, and after the second month, he raised it to $1,800. Babe used part of the raise to buy a red motorcycle that he raced through Baltimore's downtown streets.

In the meantime, the Feds were hot on young Ruth's trail, offering him a $10,000 bonus to sign, and a $10,000 contract. Babe later said: "It was a lot of money to stick under the nose of a nineteen-year-old kid; it was a big temptation, but I talked it over with 'Dunnie,' and he told me I owed it to him to stick." But Dunn, in a way, was Ruth's legal guardian, and Babe couldn't have signed a Federal League contract without his consent.

When Jack decided to break up his team and sell Ruth, he gave Connie Mack first choice. He seemed to forget the early season conversation with McGraw. McGraw didn't forget, and yelled in New York that he had been doublecrossed by Dunn, one of his old players, whom he once had befriended.

At the time that Dunn offered Ruth to Mack, the tall New Englander was winning his fourth pennant in five years, but he was vexed by the conduct of his stars. Some threatened to jump to the Feds; others forced him to tear up contracts in mid-season and high-pressured him into signing others with higher salaries. He was winning another one-sided race, and the Athletic treasury was empty.

"Jack, you have a great young pitcher in Ruth," Mack told

141

Dunn. "But, I can't give you what he is worth. My players have me broke. Why don't you go to Joe Lannin. He's still got a lot of money. See what he'll give you for Ruth."

Lannin, the owner of the Red Sox and the Providence Clam Diggers, was the angel of the International League during the Federal League strife. Not only did he carry his own club, Providence, but also the distressed Buffalo Bisons, while he helped other clubs, including Baltimore. The bargain price for Ruth, Shore, and Egan no doubt was the result of earlier Lannin advances and repayment for the Boston man's efforts in keeping the International League alive.

The Ruth sale was completed July 8. Babe stayed with the Red Sox for a month, during which he won two games and lost one. Lannin then sent Ruth to Providence to help Bill Donovan win the International League pennant. Babe turned the trick with a late season display of near-shutout pitching. Even though he missed a month of International League ball, Ruth's record with Baltimore and Providence was twenty-two victories and nine defeats. His batting ability hadn't yet developed as he hit .231 and walloped only one homer in 46 games. How he later developed into a brilliant left-handed pitcher with the Red Sox, and then the home-run king of the Yankees, the man of many records who changed baseball from the inside baseball of Hanlon's old Orioles to a sluggers' orgy, is known to every baseball fan. Baltimore always will retain a warm spot in its heart for the obstreperous boy from the waterfront.

In Boston, right-hander Ernie Shore also quickly developed into one of the great twirling heroes of the game, a World Series star in 1915 and 1916, and one of the six big-league pitchers to hurl a perfect game. Oddly enough, his fellow ex-Oriole, Ruth, got an assist on it. On June 23, 1917, Babe, the starting pitcher, walked the first Washington batsman, Eddie Foster. Babe was so angry at Umpire Owens' call that he punched the umpire in the jaw, and naturally was tossed out of the game. Shore came in; Foster was nailed stealing, and tall Ernie got the next 26 men.

As for Jack Dunn's Orioles, they went into a complete eclipse after the July, 1914, break-up of the team. Jack called in young minor leaguers and semi-pros to fill the gaps in his line-up. Even Jack Dunn, Jr., who had played baseball for Baltimore City College, gave a helping hand, appearing in 89 games. The boss's boy played a beautiful fielding game, but didn't have much authority at bat. Where Birdie Cree, the early season center fielder, hit .356, Junior, who played the position in the second half, hit a poorly .173. Thanks to the reservoir of early victories, the club did not fall completely out of the standing, finishing sixth with 72 victories and 77 defeats. At the end of the season, Dunn had enough; he turned the city over to the Feds and retreated with his International League franchise and leftovers to Richmond.

Dunn ran into fresh difficulties in the old Confederate capital. Richmond was in the Virginia League, and that circuit promptly demanded $15,000 for its territorial rights. Both Dunn, hard up for ready cash, and Ed Barrow, International League president, termed the price outrageous. They finally compromised on $12,500, with "Dunnie" paying $2,500 and the league, $10,000.

The 1915 season was a tough one for the 600 backers of the Baltimore Terrapins. Following a satisfactory third-place club in 1914, Otto Knabe felt he had insured a pennant by snatching Chief Bender, the great Indian pitcher, from the Athletics. But, with the late Chief, the Feds were a lark and Baltimore a good place to have fun in. From an Athletic record of 21-10 in 1913 and 17-3 in 1914, Bender plummeted to an unbelievable 4-16 with the 1915 Terrapins. The Terps tumbled with him and hit absolute bottom. Despite the club's fine early attendances in 1914, the Baltimore Federals showed a two-year loss of $64,343.

In the winter of 1915-16, with America's entry into World War I getting closer and closer, the Feds made peace with

143

organized baseball. Chicago's Weeghman was permitted to buy the Cubs and move them to his new park on Chicago's North Side (Wrigley Field of today); Phil Ball bought the Browns and merged them with his St. Louis Federals; and substantial cash settlements were made to the Ward brothers of Brooklyn, Sinclair of Newark, and the Pittsburgh Feds. Sinclair, who had taken over bankrupt clubs in Buffalo and Kansas City, also was permitted to sell the cream of the Federal League stars to the highest bidders among National and American League clubs. In giving out the statement of the peace terms, the major league and Federal negotiators added: "The Baltimore Federal League club will be taken care of through amalgamation with the Baltimore International League club."

Jack Dunn squealed bloody murder. As soon as it became apparent the Federal League would not be in the field in 1916, Dunn announced his return to Baltimore. "After what I've been through, I'm not amalgamating with anybody," Jack shouted. "Nobody is horning into my club."

Ed Barrow, the International League's fighting chief, gave out a similar bellicose statement from New York. "If the National and American Leagues want to make peace with the Federals, that's all right with me," said Barrow, "even though I think the Feds were licked anyway. And, if they want to take care of the Baltimore Federals, that's also well and good. But, they won't take care of them at our expense, or at the expense of one of our clubs. We were no party to this peace agreement."

The big leagues had no way of enforcing this phase of the peace treaty. Everybody was taken care of but the Baltimore club, and its directors and stockholders. They decidedly were left out on a limb.

Out of this unhappy situation grew the most famous litigation in all baseball history, a Sherman anti-trust suit by the Baltimore Federal directors against the major leagues for $300,000. As the law provided for triple damages, the Baltimore directors stood to win $900,000, a lot of money forty years ago. Several times they had their hands on it. They accused the big leagues, and their minor league accomplices, of being a gigantic baseball monopoly, and charged the reserve clause was a violation of the basic rights of an American citizen. The major leagues had a battery of crack attorneys, topped by George Wharton Pepper, later U. S. Senator from Pennsylvania. Major Stuart S. Janney, William L. Marbury, and Charles A. Douglas, three high-ranking Baltimore lawyers, represented the directors.

The case bounced around the nation's courts for six years. In the lower courts, first one side and then the other got the verdict, until it finally reached the Supreme Court. The nation's highest tribunal put off its ruling until 1922, when it sided with organized baseball, and upheld baseball's reserve clause. William Howard Taft was the Chief Justice, but the great liberal, Oliver Wendell Holmes, wrote the unanimous decision, ruling that the conduct of organized baseball was not "chattel slavery," as contended by the Baltimore attorneys, and that while professional baseball was played for money, it was primarily a sport; that the games are played for personal effort and therefore, nothing is produced; that baseball is not a commodity and that the trust laws are not violated by mere travel between the states to play a schedule.

As late as 1952, the Supreme Court, with an entire line-up of new Justices, again upheld the finding of Taft, Holmes, Brandeis, et al., of thirty years before, ruling "that Congress had no intention of including the business of baseball within the scope of the federal anti-trust laws."

CHAPTER XIV

Jack Dunn's Seven Straight Winners

FOLLOWING DUNN'S return from Richmond, he scored partial successes as Baltimore fans, awakened from the Federal major league dream, gradually were weaned back to International League baseball. It was fourth for Jack in 1916, and third in each of the war years, 1917 and 1918. In the latter year, the International League was the only minor circuit to go to the Labor Day deadline, permitted by the War Department. During these difficult war seasons, Dunn managed to stay in the black by judicious deals with the majors. Near the close of the 1917 season, he received a nice wad of Ruppert's New York Yankee greenbacks for pitcher Herb Thormahlen, second baseman Wilson "Chick" Fewster, and outfielder William Harmong Lamar. Turner Barber, a .352-hitting outfielder, was sold to the Cubs for another substantial sum.

Thormahlen, a slim left-hander, had a 25-12 record with the 1917 Birds when sold. Fewster and Lamar both were Maryland products. Chick was a Baltimore boy, who was on the threshold of stardom when he was almost killed by a pitched ball hurled by Jeff Pfeffer, Brooklyn pitcher, at the Yankees' 1920 training camp at Jacksonville. Fewster never was the same player after that. Lamar came from Rockville, where a grandfather was one of Maryland's most distinguished jurists. Bill later played for the Red Sox, Dodgers, and Athletics, but his nickname, "Good Time" Lamar tells the story of why he never made greater use of his inherent talent.

146

On Dunn's return to Baltimore, Jack took over the larger Federal League Park, across the streets from his old grounds. It was larger and more up-to-date than the original American League Park, hastily erected by Sid Frank, Harry Goldman, and McGraw in 1901. The Baltimore Fed directors were in bitter legal warfare with the major leagues, but they had no further use for their ball park, and were glad to have Dunn take it off their hands.

Following the close of World War I, the National Association, the governing body of the minors, was in a rebellious mood against the majors. At a meeting in New York in January, 1919, a few months after the Armistice, it took a most important step, one that was far-reaching for Baltimore baseball and the personal fortunes of Jack Dunn. It withdrew from the National Agreement with the majors. It meant the minor leagues operated without a player draft, and, therefore, were under no compulsion to sell players to the majors. When the minors eventually entered a new National Agreement, the three then Class AA leagues, the International, Pacific Coast and American Association, and two smaller leagues, the Western and Three-I, reserved the right to continue operations under their post-war draft-free status.

From the start, Jack Dunn had been in the vanguard among the non-draft men. As the controversy grew in intensity, he became a vociferous, impassionate—even belligerent—champion of the non-draft leagues. And no one in the minors took greater advantage of this draft-free operation than "Dunnie."

It meant if he now developed a Ruth, an Ernie Shore, a Turner Barber, or a Herb Thormahlen, there was no need of selling him for fear of losing the player for the then $7,500 draft price. Dunn also grimly remembered the Federal League war, which for a season had driven him out of Baltimore. The Feds did it by claiming major league status, a league from which no players could be drafted by the older major leagues. Jack couldn't promise Baltimore fans major league ball, but he promised them something nearly as good. "I'll give Baltimore a major league team, even though it still operates in the International League," he said. "Nobody is drafting my players, and I'm not selling. We'll keep our good players right here in Baltimore. And I am hoping the other International League clubs will follow a similar policy, so that the entire caliber of the league will be raised."

Free from the draft shackles, Dunn's success no doubt exceeded his fondest expectations. Beginning with 1919, his Orioles ran off a string of seven successive championships, the longest pennant run in the history of organized baseball. Most of these flags were won by top-heavy percentages, and only in 1920, when the Toronto Maple Leafs were tough to shake off, were the Orioles extended to win. In each of the seven years, the club won 100 or more victories, going as high as 119 in 1921 and 117 in 1924. The Orioles' brilliant seven-year pennant winning record follows:

Year	Won	Lost	Per.	Games Ahead
1919	100	49	.671	8
1920	109	44	.712	1½
1921*	119	47	.717	10
1922	115	52	.689	10
1923	111	53	.677	11
1924	117	48	.709	19
1925	105	61	.633	4

* Beginning with 1921, the International League played a 168-game schedule.

The amazing thing about the club is that Dunn changed it as he went along. Of the regulars, only third baseman Fritz Maisel, reclaimed from the St. Louis Browns, and shortstop Joe Boley, whose legal name was John Bolinsky, played on all seven championship teams. It wasn't until Jack had won four straight pennants that he finally gave in, and sold one of his stars, Jack Bentley, to the majors. And, then it was necessary; his one-sided races were killing interest in the league, and his

148

young stars coming up, forced him to dispose of some big-name players, and netted him a fortune as he did so. And, strangely enough, after the big names, Jack Bentley, Max Bishop, Lefty Grove, disappeared from the Oriole line-up, the club won as consistently as before. Furthermore, these Orioles were a gang of International League record-smashers in much the same way as were the Yankees in the majors during the period of Babe Ruth and Lou Gehrig.

The Orioles did not fare as well in Junior World Series competition as might have been expected. Invariably, they went into the post-season games with the champions of the American Association a heavy favorite, but only managed to break even in six series. They did not play a series in 1919. Unlike the great Yankees of the American League, Dunn's famous Orioles were not clean sweep artists in these post-season contests. With the exception of 1920 and 1921, their Junior World Series were terrific battles right down to the last out. The Orioles vanquished St. Paul, five games to one, in 1920, but lost to Joe McCarthy's Louisville Colonels, five games to three, in 1921. Baltimore again had St. Paul's number in 1922, winning five games to two, but Kansas City wore down the Birds in the full nine games in 1923 with a five to four verdict. In 1924, St. Paul finally got some measure of revenge for earlier defeats, defeating Dunn's team, five games to four, with a tenth contest resulting in a tie. The Orioles knocked off McCarthy's Louisville club, five games to three, in 1925, the fall before Marse Joe moved to the Chicago Cubs.

As the result of their failure to do better in these Junior World Series, some Baltimoreans, and other critics, rank Dunn's later champions below the fine club of 1914, which Jack dismantled during the Federal League war. Others place it below the Newark club of 1937, which had such later-day Yankee stars as Charley Keller, Joe Gordon, Spud Chandler, Buddy Rosar, Atley Donald, and Steve Sundra. However, the writer has no hesitancy in placing Dunn's clubs of 1921-22-23 at the very top of the all-time minor league parade. These

149

Orioles could have put up a strong fight for fourth place in either the National or American Leagues.

The 1919 club had Jack Bentley on first; Max Bishop at second; Joe Boley at shortstop; and Fritz Maisel at third. The outfield was made up of Otis Lawry, Merwin Jacobson, and John Honig. Ben Egan, sold to the Red Sox in 1914 in the package deal with Ruth and Shore, and Wade Lefler were the catchers, and the pitching staff was headed by James "Rube" Parnham, Harry Frank, Harry Seibold, and Rudy Kneisch.

The infield had a decided Maryland flavor. Jack Bentley, scion of an old Sandy Springs Quaker family, was a former Washington southpaw pitching rookie. With the exception of Ruth, and possibly Red Ruffing, Bentley was baseball's hardest hitting pitcher. Though Max Bishop was born in Waynesboro, Pa., he grew up in Baltimore and was a product of Baltimore City College. The little guy attended there in short pants. In 1918, Dunn signed the sprightly kid when Max was in his Junior year. Bishop recommended Boley, a Polish boy from the Pennsylvania anthracite country, who had played summer independent ball with Max. The two became a noted second base combination. Maisel, as related before, is a native of Catonsville, Md. Fritzie played a lot of brilliant ball after returning to the Birds; the pint-sized third baseman was a stockholder in the club and deputy manager whenever Dunn was absent. In recent years, Maisel has been a fire chief in Baltimore County.

Otis Lawry, the left fielder, was the 1919 I. L. batting champion with .364. He came from Maine and had put in several seasons with the Athletics as a part-time second base-man. Otis used to drive umpires wild by trying to umpire strikes and balls from left field. Jacobson, third in batting with .351, had had brief trials with the Giants and Cubs. Long lanky Rube Parnham, a horse for work, led the pitchers with twenty-eight victories against twelve defeats, but a little Jewish chap, Harry Frank, playing his first season of pro ball, was the marvel of the staff, winning twenty-four games out of thirty. Seibold, like Parnham, had been up with the Athletics. In Philadelphia, Seibold was regarded the better pitcher. It is interesting to note that in the 1920 Reach Baseball Guide, the names of Jack Dunn, Sr. and Jack Dunn, Jr. appear among the names of Oriole players who participated in less than fifteen games.

By 1920, the year Dunn barely nosed out Dan Howley's Toronto Maple Leafs by a game and a half, Bentley did considerable pitching, winning sixteen games and losing three. When he wasn't busy on the mound, he played first base and was good enough to hit .371. This year Merv Jacobson was was the loop batting leader with .404. Bill Holden replaced Honig in right field, while Lena Styles was added to the catching staff. Lefler, one of the other catchers, played first base when Bentley pitched.

There were two important acquisitions to the pitching staff that year, Robert Moses "Lefty" Grove and Johnny Ogden. In the International League, Grove was known as Groves. "The writers there put that final 's' on my name. It didn't belong," claimed Lefty. Hughie Bradley says that when the tall southpaw joined the Orioles, he reported as Groves. Grove was a tall hillbilly from Lonaconing in the Maryland Cumberlands. He had been signed by Jack Dunn, Jr., and always was one of Jack Senior's favorite ball players. Wilbert Robinson, then manager in Brooklyn, also had had a tip on Grove, and sent Joe McGinnity to look him over, but Dunn offered more. Bob was a real country boy, and Rube Parnham, a sort of Oriole Dizzy Dean, loved to play tricks on him. Rube would lie in bed by the hour thinking up schemes to take Grove places and then stick Lefty with the check. Early in his baseball career, Robert Moses had a mountaineer's suspicion and distrust for strangers, but he mellowed in later years and became a delightful companion. Dunn started him with the Martinsburg team of the Blue Ridge League in 1920, but with Toronto pressing him, he called Bob to Baltimore in midseason. Grove let go his fire ball so effectively that he won twelve

151

games out of fourteen and struck out 88 batsmen in 123 innings, a pretty good sample of what was to come.

Johnny Ogden, a right-hander from Swarthmore College, also became one of Dunn's "pets." But he earned his manager's high esteem, winning twenty-seven games in 1920 and losing only nine. Johnny really took in the slack, as Parnham, whose career had its majestic peaks and dizzy dips, was incapacitated much of the season and appeared in only fifteen games. Even so, he was credited with five victories against no defeats. Harry Frank kept up his good work with a 25-12 performance.

The season of 1921 was the season of records. The club set an International League record with its 119 victories. Jack Bentley had the highest batting average in this century, .412, made the most hits in I. L. history, 246, and hung up the loop's highest pitching percentage, .923, the result of winning twelve games and losing one. Ogden was particularly brilliant, winning thirty-one games and losing eight, while young Grove, in his first full season, won twenty-five and lost ten. They already were comparing his speed with that of the Athletic immortal, Rube Waddell. And another Baltimore boy was added to the caste that season, Alphonse Thomas Thomas, Jr., better known as Tommy Thomas. He was a bargain waiver pick-up from Buffalo, but in his first season with the Birds, he proved his worth by winning twenty-four games and losing only ten.

As Dunn won his fourth straight flag in 1922, pressure was put on him to sell some of his stars. Every now and then, Jack had to deny that his shortstop-second base combination, Boley and Bishop, would go to the Athletics. "I've said again and again I'm not selling any players," he shouted. But, at the close of the season, Dunn finally succumbed and announced the sale of Jack Bentley, the clubbing pitcher-first baseman, to the Giants for $65,000 and three lesser players. Clayton Sheedy was Bentley's first base replacement, and the Orioles went right on winning. A year later, after Pennant No. 5 of

152

the string, little Max Bishop when to the Athletics for $50,000.

The 1923 season, in many ways, was the most eventful of the five pennant-winning campaigns. It saw Lefty Grove establish both the International League strike-out and base on balls records with 330 and 186, respectively. Big Mose really was cutting loose with his fire ball, and became the most talked of pitcher in the minors. Dunn received offers for him from practically all of the sixteen major league clubs. Jack merely said: "He's pitching for me." Grove won twenty-seven games that season and lost ten. Even so, he wasn't the most sensational of "Dunnie's" pitchers. Big Jim Parnham bounced back with a fantastic season, winning thirty-three games and losing seven. What's more, he won his last twenty games for the longest winning streak in the International League. A useful Maryland pick-up in 1923 was Dick "Twichy" Porter from Princess Anne, a versatile fellow who played either second base or the outfield and soon became another fine major league prospect.

Parnham, the unbeatable of 1923, seesawed down to mediocrity in 1924, and slumped from 33-7 to 6-5. Nevertheless, the Orioles continued blithefully along their winning way. At the end of the Swarthmore College season, Dunn signed another great young right-hander, handsome George Earnshaw, a Social Registerite nonetheless. George posted seven victories without a defeat as his introduction to I. L. ball, while Grove won twenty-six and lost six.

In the fall of 1924, "Dunnie" finally capitulated on the matter of his prize left-hander, and agreed to give Grove his chance in the majors. As in 1914, when he gave Connie Mack first choice on Babe Ruth, he also gave Connie, his old friend and benefactor, first consideration in the Grove negotiations. The Athletics didn't get him for any bargain, but Dunn gave them a chance to match the figures of some of the other bidders. The A's landed the prize for $100,600, the biggest price Dunn received for a player, and one which stood out even more when contrasted with the ridiculous sum for which Babe Ruth was disposed of ten years before. The Athletics paid

153

for Grove in ten annual payments of $10,000; the $600 was for carrying charges.

Next to Ruth, Grove proved the International Orioles' most brilliant graduate. He won 300 games for the Athletics and Red Sox; Grove and Eddie Plank, an earlier Athletic southpaw great, are the lone left-handers in the majors' 300 victory class. How many games the Cumberland mountaineer might have won had Dunn sold him earlier to the majors is mere conjecture, but Lefty was ready for the big leagues after his big 1921 season. In four and a half seasons with the Orioles, he won 108 games and lost 36 for a percentage of .750 and struck out 1118 batsmen.

With Grove gone, many thought the great Dunn pennant run finally had reached its end. They would have been surer had they known that Parnham, the 33-7 beauty of 1923, would be idle all season. But, as in the past, others carried the load and at the finish of the 1925 season Baltimore ambled in four games ahead of second place Toronto. Tommy Thomas was super-brilliant in that seventh pennant-winning year, winning thirty-two and losing twelve. Johnny Ogden worked a little harder and won twenty-eight, while losing eleven. And Earnshaw proved he soon would be among the game's elect with a brilliant 29-11 record.

Gradually, in these latter championship years, Dunn had been bringing some old-timers to his club: such former big league outfielders as Jimmy Walsh, an earlier Oriole; Maurice Archdeacon, the speedboy; Tilly Walker, who tied Ruth in American League homers in 1918; and Sherry Magee, old time Phillie slugger; and catchers Lew McCarty, former Dodger and Giants, and Red McKee, an ex-Tiger.

With the winning of the seventh pennant, Dunn disposed of another star to the majors. The hard-working and beloved Tommy Thomas was sold to the White Sox for another $50,000 and Archdeacon, who had been with Dunn on option. From the time "Dunnie" had sold Bentley in 1922,

154

he banked $300,000 from the sales of Bentley, Bishop, Grove, Thomas, and lesser players.

On these seven straight winners, there was comedy and tragedy. The big tragedy in Jack Dunn's life came when his son, Jack, Junior, died on March 18, 1923, while the Orioles were training for their fifth straight flag. Young Dunn succumbed to pneumonia at the early age of 27. He was the apple of his father's eye; Jack reared his boy in the baseball business and hoped he eventually would succeed him as owner-president. The young man was secretary-business manager at the time of his death. At the very time that Jack, Junior, was buried, his son, Jack III, almost died of mastoiditis. Only a delicate but highly successful operation saved the life of Dunn's grandson. Dunn never recovered from his son's death, and if there were humorous incidents after that, they were largely forced, or the result of Jack's effort to forget.

Yet, life had to go on and baseball had to go on. Some of the club's most amusing incidents revolved around Hugh Bradley, then a fun-loving young Baltimore baseball writer. Hughie has a high-pitched voice which sounded much like Dunn's voice. In Rochester, the visitors' clubhouse was next to the home club's dressing quarters. Some of the Rochester players heard Hughie's high-pitched tones on the other side, and thought at first it was Dunn. So, they cooked up a prank with fellow gay blades on the Orioles to have Bradley come into the clubhouse and bawl out George Stallings, the Rochester manager, at a time when George was addressing his players on the other side of the wooden partition.

"That Stallings is a mess," said Hughie, raising his voice. "I've been around for a long time, but Stallings is absolutely the dumbest manager I've ever met. You'd think he'd learn something, but the older he gets, the more stupid he becomes. He ought to get wise to himself, and get out before they throw him out." After saying his piece, Bradley quickly departed.

Stallings, a fiery Georgian, rushed around to the door of

155

the Baltimore clubhouse, breathing vengeance. "Where's Dunn, that dirty so-and-so; I'm going to bust him right in the mouth," he roared. Of course, Jack wasn't there, and when Stallings eventually caught up with Dunn and blistered him with a fresh verbal barrage, Dunn was lost for words and could only mutter: "What's wrong, George? What ails you? I never said a thing behind your back that I wouldn't say to your face."

But if Hughie liked to play pranks on Jack, Jack was just as fond of playing them on Hughie. And some of the humor was rather rough. At the end of a day's practice while the club was training at Eustace, Fla., Bradley lolled on his bed and dozed off into a pleasant late afternoon nap when he was rudely awakened by something that felt like Niagara Falls rolling over him. Jack Dunn had emptied a pitcher of ice water all over the sleeping sports writer. Hughie screamed in his high tones, and Dunn yelled a few tones higher. Each called the other everything under the sun. The hotel manager got into the argument, and then there were three shrieking. It ended by the hotel man ordering Dunn to take his club out of the hotel. "And, I want you out this afternoon," he demanded. The Orioles had a $5,000 guarantee to train in Eustace, and it took all the persuasive powers of Butch Schmidt, Oriole vice-president and road secretary, to patch up the dispute and permit the Orioles to roost at the Fountain Inn for the remainder of their Eustace stay.

In another escapade while the club was training in Eustace, Dunn tried to give Bradley a thrill by suddenly turning his car into the Orlando County Fair track, intended for trotting races, and with his accelerator down to the floorboard, whizzed Hughie on several wild laps around the track. The more Hughie protested, the faster Jack drove his gasoline-propelled trotter.

Jack was a fighter, and a hard loser—even a bad loser. And, in the tradition of the Orioles of Hanlon, McGraw, Kelley and Jennings, umpires were his natural enemies. Furthermore,

156

when his team was the Juggernaut of the International League, he held tremendous power over umpires. If an umpire particularly displeased him, he soon was out of the league.

The late Bill McGowan, former senior American League umpire, was having a tough time in a Sunday Baltimore-Syracuse double-header. He became involved in a big rhubarb with Harry McCurdy, the Syracuse catcher. Bill thumbed the backstop out of the game, but just as Harry was going through an exit, he made a parting remark to McGowan. The barb must have hit a particularly tender spot, as Bill darted through a runway and made a flying leap at McCurdy, swinging rights and lefts. Baltimore policemen at the game arrested McGowan for assault. Dunn immediately called up John Conway Toole, the league president, in New York.

"Are you trying to get McGowan out of jail?" someone asked.

"Out of jail, hell," snapped Jack. "I'm trying to get him out of the league."

Dunn at the time was getting by with Sunday baseball through a subterfuge. Maryland hadn't yet legalized Sunday baseball, and "Dunnie" had a scheme whereby he sold score-cards at admission prices. He was getting a lot of opposition from clergymen and others opposed to Sunday baseball, and the McGowan-McCurdy row didn't help. It is a matter of record that after McGowan umpired four seasons in the International League, he fell back to the Southern Association in 1923. It was from the latter circuit that he graduated to the American League.

On another occasion, when George Magerkurth, the heavy-weight umpire, was a newcomer in the league, Jack baited "Maje" from the visitors' bench in Reading. Dunn was in mufti, and Magerkurth, walking over to the bench, said, "You can't sit there, Mr. Dunn, you're not in uniform."

"Don't tell me where I can or can't be sitting," yelled Jack.

"But, you gotta get out of there," insisted "Maje," and when

Dunn made no sign of moving, the umpire pulled out his watch.

Whereupon, "Dunnie," à la Joe Kelley, slapped the watch out of Magerkurth's hand, but unlike the Kelley incident, it wasn't Dunn's watch.

The Orioles survived the loss of Bentley, Bishop, and Grove, but the departure of Tommy Thomas was the sale which finally ended baseball's longest pennant run. The 1926 Orioles still made a fight for it, reached 101 victories, but this time Dan Howley's Toronto Maple Leafs stacked up 109. At the end of this season, Joe Boley, the great little shortstop, at long last was put on the block. After playing eight seasons for the Birds, he went to the Athletics for $50,000, to rejoin his old pal, Max Bishop, and help make up the keystone combination of the Athletic champions of 1929, 1930, and 1931.

Perhaps Boley had been the sparkplug that had applied a magic spark to the club that won 877 games in eight years. With Joe gone, the Orioles descended to mediocrity. Dunn procured Everett Scott, the once famous shortstop of the Red Sox and Yankees, to plug the gap, but by that time the once wizardy "Scottie" was playing shortstop standing on a quarter. The Birds finished fifth with .509 in 1927 and were tied with Montreal for fifth in 1928 with an even .500. There had been more sales. Johnny Ogden was sold to the St. Louis Browns in 1927 after having won 213 games, the most ever won by an International League pitcher. Earnshaw was a long holdout in 1928, and was disgruntled when he reported a month late. In June of that year, Dunn sold him to the Athletics, where he became another pitching immortal.

Not only Baltimore, but the entire nation, was shocked on October 22, 1928, when news came of the sudden passing of the great Oriole leader at the early age of 56. At Towson, a Baltimore suburb where Jack was exercising his hunting dogs, he suffered a heart attack and fell from his horse. Death was instantaneous, shocking his legion of friends and admirers.

Many baseball men had had arguments and disagreements with him, but all agreed he was one of the truly great. Jack was an expert shot and his bird dogs were as much a source of pride with him as were his outstanding ball players. Once he traded a ball player for a hunting dog and claimed he got all the better of the deal.

The death of Jack Dunn ended the golden era of Oriole International League baseball. Jack's widow, Mary Dunn, inherited the club and Charles H. Knapp, the Oriole attorney, was elected president. When John Conway Toole, president of the International League, died the following February, Knapp also was elected president of the loop. Charley filled this dual role for a number of years.

When Jack Dunn died, the International League still was free of the draft, a baseball condition which had made Dunn's pennants and success, artistic and financial, possible. Most of the other non-draft leagues of the early 1920's had returned to the draft status, but the International, with Dunn and Toole leading the fight, had stubbornly held out. It brought Jack in violent conflict with the new baseball Commissioner, Judge Landis, a strong pro-draft man.

In a speech in New York, before the sale of Grove to the Athletics, Landis said with much fervor: "No one should be permitted to build a brick wall around a player. In a non-draft league, a minor league club owner may hold a player to eternity. This is not right. I insist it is an un-American practice. In this country, everybody's boy should have his chance to rise in whatever livelihood he selects. Wherever a non-draft minor league operates, a young ball player does not get his rightful opportunity to advance to the top in baseball."

Dunn took these remarks as a direct slap on himself. "What's wrong with my stars playing in Baltimore if I pay them as much as they could get elsewhere?" he demanded. "You never heard of Grove kicking about any brick wall being erected about him, did you? After every good season, I gave Lefty a substantial raise. I can name a half-dozen big league

159

clubs where players aren't treated nearly as well as I treat the Orioles. And, I'm just as good an American as Judge Landis!"

The sale of Grove, Tommy Thomas, and the others did not lessen the tension between Jack and the Commissioner. The Judge wanted the draft on all minor leagues; Jack Dunn felt restoration to the International League would be giving up his life blood. He did pay splendid salaries. Grove was getting $10,000 when he moved up to the Athletics, and Boley had a $10,000 contract after serving eight seasons with the Orioles. When the Birds were playing in the old International League strongholds of Newark and Jersey City, Jack used to put up his club at the swank McAlpin Hotel in New York. The Jersey clubs raised such a rumpus that Dunn was forced by the league to house his team in less expensive north New Jersey hotels.

Yes, Jack Dunn was a big leaguer all his life, even though he operated for years in a top minor league.

CHAPTER XV

George Weiss Shows His Early Genius

CHARLEY KNAPP was running the affairs of the Orioles late in 1928, when George Martin Weiss, president-owner of the New Haven club of the Eastern League, stopped by in Baltimore to consult the club on some spring exhibition games. Weiss, the present genius behind the Yankee baseball empire, already had acquired a reputation as a shrewd operator. His interest in baseball went back to his undergraduate days at Yale, when he promoted a semi-pro club in New Haven. George had irked Jack Dunn considerably in 1922, when prior to the Junior World Series between Baltimore and St. Paul, Weiss's New Haven Eastern League champions had beaten the great Orioles, two games to one. Jack claimed the New Haven victory "ruined my show."

While Knapp and Weiss were talking over spring exhibitions, Charley suddenly asked the New Englander: "How'd you like to take over here, George? I don't have the time to run this thing. I know you could do it, and I think you'd find it quite an opportunity."

Weiss promised to think it over, and eventually accepted the post of Baltimore general manager, retaining his New Haven club for the time being.

"The affairs of the Baltimore club were in general confusion when I took over," reported Weiss. "Little had been done since Jack Dunn's death. They were standing by waiting for somebody to buy the club. Clark Griffith of Washington was inter-

161

ested for a while; he was seeking a minor league farm, but lost interest in Baltimore and purchased the Chattanooga club instead.

"Even though Dunn had made a lot of money selling ball players, the club treasury was empty when I took over. So, one of the first things I did was to get some money for operations. I sold Dick Porter, the International League batting champion in 1927, to the Cleveland club for $40,000. That gave us some money to work with. I also increased the admission prices that Dunn had lowered in 1927 and 1928, after Jack had dropped from the heights. I appointed Fritz Maisel manager, and we were ready to go. While we won no pennants, we had one of the greatest slugging teams in the minors, and in my three years in Baltimore, I sold $250,000's worth of ball players. The empty treasury was in pretty healthy condition when I left."

In Weiss's three years as Oriole general manager, he had one second and two thirds, also the greatest home run slugger of minor league baseball, Joe Hauser, who hit 63 home runs, three above Ruth's fabulous major league mark, in 1930. In that season Hauser also hit for 443 total bases and drove in 175 runs. Joe's home runs and total bases of 1930 give the Orioles two more all-time highs in the International League record book.

However, the remarkable thing about George's three-year Oriole administration was the cash he received for some rather ordinary Oriole players. That is, they proved ordinary when they tried their luck in the majors. Weiss doesn't exaggerate when he says no other minor league club owner or general manager, not even Dunn, sold a quarter of a million dollar's worth of players in such a short time. By this time, with Jack Dunn's strident voice stilled by death, the International League again had consented to operate as a draft-league, and Weiss usually made his sales before his Oriole players were subject to the draft. Players he sold during the period of 1929-30-31 included pitchers Jim Weaver and Monte Weaver;

catchers Al Bool, Pinky Hargraves, and Tom Padden; infielders Johnny Neun, Joe Hauser, and Jim Stroner; and outfielders Dick Porter, Vince Barton, George Leopp, Ralph Boyle, Johnny Gill, and Denny Southern. Some of these players found their way back to Baltimore.

The word, Oriole, still was a wonder word in baseball, and club presidents shopping in Weiss's Baltimore emporium, still were hopeful of picking up another Grove, Earnshaw, Bishop, Boley, or Thomas. Weiss's best customers were the Pittsburgh Pirates, Washington Senators, and Boston Braves. But of George's extensive sales, only Dick Porter, catchers Tommy Padden, and Pinky Hargraves, and pitchers Monte Weaver and Jim Weaver proved real big-league caliber.

Johnny Neun, a Baltimore boy, already had made his way into the record books before playing for his home-town team in 1929. While playing for Detroit, Johnny made an unassisted triple play at first base—a most rare play for a first baseman, and stole five bases in one game against the club which now employs him as a scout and minor league director, the New York Yankees. After holding Neun one season, Weiss sold him at a tidy profit to the Boston Braves.

It was a sample of Weiss's successful operations. He usually made his deals with the majors for cash and players. Then he'd immediately prime the throw-in for a return to the big league market. For instance, catcher Eugene "Pinky" Hargraves came from Washington in a deal early in the 1931 season. After Pinky hit .340 for the Birds, he was put back in the showcase and the Braves eagerly snapped him up. In the same season, Denny Southern, a former .300 hitter with the Phillies, came from Pittsburgh as a throw-in. Denny hit .327 for the Birds, and Uncle Robbie of Brooklyn did a little shopping in Weiss's Baltimore emporium. But Southern was anything but a bargain, and again faded from the big leagues after hitting only .161 for the 1932 Dodgers. But George had gotten his price.

It is interesting to note that when Weiss disposed of Joe Hauser, his big home-run man, the best offer came from the

163

St. Paul club of the American Association. After Hauser had made a promising start with the Athletics, Joe developed a trick knee and big league clubs were leary of him. But Joe went on a new home run rampage in the American Association, and set a homer record for the higher minors of 69.

Weiss's smart deals and able operation of the Orioles naturally attracted attention to the young man from Yale. One especially interested was Col. Jake Ruppert, wealthy president of the New York Yankees, who was just putting in a new farm system. After looking over the minor league field, Ruppert concluded Weiss was just the man to run it. It generally was believed that the late Ed Barrow, then Yankee business manager, recommended Weiss to Ruppert for the job of farm director. But, it just didn't happen that way. Barrow and Weiss did not click too well at the time, and the Baltimore man was hand-picked by the New York brewer. He signed Weiss at a secret conference on New Year's eve, December 31, 1931. The first Barrow knew of it was on New Year's Day, when Ruppert called him up, and said: "I've just got you a new farm director, George Weiss. I hope you fellows can get along."

With Weiss gone, Charley Knapp named Henry Dawson, who later ran the Yankee club in Norfolk, as general manager. The 1932 Orioles might have won their ninth International League pennant but for the wizardry Weiss immediately worked in Newark. George directed the Bears to the 1932 I. L. pennant, and the belting Birds had to be satisfied with the runner-up position. But it was a memorable season for the Orioles, especially for Russell "Buzz" Arlett, an outfielder Weiss had procured from the Phillies before he switched to the Yankees.

Arlett, a rather cumbersome fielder, already had won honors as a slugger in the Pacific Coast League before being acquired by Philadelphia. Buzz was a switch hitter, and really showed Baltimore how he could put wood to the ball. This was none of the finesse of the early Orioles, but real power in the raw.

164

Buzzy quickly made Baltimore fans forget Joe Hauser. Arlett hit .339 in 1932, banged out 54 homers, scored 141 runs, and drove in 144. Even so, he missed 21 Baltimore games.

Buzz also made the International League record books with a bang that season. In the 71-year history of the International League, under one name or another, there have been only five occurrences that a batter knocked out four home runs in one game. Arlett did it twice, within a period of five weeks, in 1932. He put on his first four-homer show in Reading on June 1.

On July 4, the Orioles were playing Reading a holiday double-header at Oriole Park, and Buzz thought he should show the home folks just how he had performed that four-homer trick. He celebrated the nation's birthday with real fireworks. In the first game, he exploded four homers in consecutive times at bat, and belted in nine runs as Baltimore won, 21 to 10. Arlett hit the second of these homers batting right-handed, and the other three left-handed. Just to make it a real day, Buzz hit a fifth homer and double in the second game, which Baltimore won, 9 to 8.

Buzzy still was "bustin' out all over" in 1933, when he was down to 39 homers but banged in 146 more runs. Frank McGowan, a talented outfielder who played some splendid baseball for Baltimore, was playing manager that year; he finished a good third, but from then on the club deteriorated until it had a temporary upsurge during World War II. However, night ball, a natural for the Chesapeake seaport, had come to Baltimore, and the novelty of seeing baseball and the players under the arcs kept the turnstiles clicking.

In 1934, Johnny Ogden, Dunn's old pitching star, succeeded Dawson as general manager and remained until 1939. His manager was Guy Sturdy, a former Brown infielder, who had played for St. Louis when Johnny pitched for the Browns. The Ogden-Sturdy combination started in low gear, as the Birds tumbled to eighth place for the first time in their International League history. They then made a partial recovery, advancing to fifth in 1935 and running fourth the next two years. Charles Knapp, who had remained a helpful and faithful adviser to Mrs. Dunn, died in July, 1936.

The club got off to a miserable start in 1937. Though Sturdy seemingly had some pretty good material, the club couldn't win for trying. On May 19, they were a pitiable last with four victories and eighteen defeats and a woeful percentage of .182. "I guess something's got to be done; we can't go on this way any longer, Guy," Johnny Ogden told his manager. Sturdy was out, and Clyde "Bucky" Crouse, a former White Sox catcher obtained in a deal with Buffalo, was installed as manager. The midstream shift of managers worked for one season. Under Crouse the club played well over .500 ball the rest of the way, and finished fourth, qualifying for the Shaughnessy play-offs, which the new capable International League president, Frank Joseph Shaughnessy, had installed a few years before.

Crouse's good 1937 season was just a temporary shot in the arm; from then on the Birds really hit the skids. The proud Orioles that had won seven straight pennants now struggled through a six-year period in which only one club, the team of 1940, stuck its head out of the second division. Crouse crashed to the cellar in 1938, and then he was out. In an effort to drum up business, the great name of Rogers Hornsby had been added to the team's payroll. The tempestuous Texan was engaged as coach and utility infielder. Hornsby was at the low point of his career; he had been fired by the Browns as manager in midseason, 1937, was in bad with several other big league clubs, and was in Judge Landis' doghouse. The old warrior, then 42, was glad to find a friendly haven in Baltimore, but the player with a major league lifetime average of .358 collected only two hits in 27 times at bat with the 1938 Birds and hit a feeble .074. Even so, it was the start of Rogers' partial comeback.

Joe Engle, Clark Griffith's picturesque club president in Chattanooga, called Hornsby to Tennessee in midseason, 1938, to tackle the job of manager of the Lookouts, and Baltimore

166

did not stand in his way. The Orioles then rehired Hornsby as manager in 1939, but after a sixth placer the former batting king moved to Oklahoma City. Johnny Ogden also moved out at the end of this season, giving way to another old Oriole pitcher, native son Tommy Thomas. At first, Tommy was hired only as manager, while an advisory committee directed the affairs of the club. But, by 1942, Tommy combined the roles of general manager and field manager. Thomas remained with the club for a decade. His first club in 1940 managed to stagger home fourth, but in the early war years, the Birds were at their worst, seventh in '41, fifth in '42, and sixth in '43. However, with much war industry in Baltimore and a lot of new people flocking to the Monument City, the Birds fared satisfactorily at the gate. Mrs. Mary Dunn, Jack's widow, died in February, 1943, and willed the club to Jack III, who was such a sick baby at the time of his father's death in 1923. Young Jack became the new president of the club.

In 1944, Baltimore profitted by the war upheaval in the player ranks much as did the St. Louis Browns in the American League. The Browns won their only American League championship that year with a team of 4-F's, returned Servicemen, and those who according to the wartime ballad were either too young or too old. The Orioles bobbed up with a similar type team in minor league ball. As the Browns leaped from sixth place to a pennant, so did the Orioles, winning their ninth and last International League flag to the intense pleasure of a lot of enthusiastic war workers and older citizenry.

As the 1944 Browns clinched their American League flag on the last Sunday of the regular season, so did the Orioles. In fact, they made it even closer. At the end of a dingdong race, the Orioles led George Weiss's Newark club by one point, .553 to .552, one of the lowest percentages ever to win a pennant. Where Jack Dunn once lost a flag by inability to play off a rained-out game, in 1944 two unplayed games represented the Orioles' margin of victory. Newark actually won one more game. The two rivals closed as follows: Baltimore, 84-68, .553; Newark, 85-69, .552.

This 1944 team was a frail champion compared with Jack Dunn's great pennant winners or the strong team he broke up in midseason, 1914. There were frequent shifts in Tommy Thomas' line-up, but for most of the season the club lined up with Bob Latshaw on first; Blas Monaco at second; Fred Pfieffer at short; Francis Skaff at third; Howie Moss, Felix Mackiewicz, and Stan Benjamin in the outfield; and Sherman Lollar behind the plate. The pitching staff was made up of Charles Embree (19-10); Ambrose Palica (14-10); Frank Rochevot (6-1); Rollie Van Slate (7-12); Hal Kleine (5-4); and Johnny Podgajny (3-3). The club then had a working agreement with Cleveland, and Lollar, Bob Lemon, then an infielder, Mackiewicz, Embree, and Kleine were Cleveland property.

This club went far in the 1944 post-season play-offs. In the I. L.'s Governor's Cup Series, the Birds had to battle hard all the way, knocking off first the fourth-place Bisons and then the second-place Newark Bears in stubbornly contested four-to-three victories. In the Junior World Series, they had it a little easier, winning over an old foe, Louisville, by a four-to-two margin for the International League's first victory in six years.

One of the reasons the 1944 Orioles did so well in the league season and the play-offs was the ability of little Blas Monaco to extract bases on balls from rival pitchers. Blas was a steady .294 hitter, but that only told half of it. They just couldn't keep him off the bases. He had an eye like Willie Keeler's and walked 167 times for another entry into the International League record book and scored 135 runs.

The old wooden stands at Oriole Park, the Federal League park built on Ned Hanlon's acres in 1914, was burned to the ground on July 4 of that war year. Young Jack Dunn received the city's permission to move into the new Baltimore Stadium at 33rd Street, Ellerslie Avenue and Ednor Road, a stadium which was constructed primarily for football. It then had no roof, which made it pleasant for night ball, and Jack Dunn III still is proud of the fact that his club drew 52,000 paid for a Junior World Series game on the same day that the Cardinals and Browns, playing the big World Series in St. Louis, played to 31,630. The Orioles drew 349,778 in the regular season and 157,667 more for their play-offs. A number of big league clubs looked at these attendance figures with considerable envy. It is small wonder that the *Sporting News* handed its plaque for minor league executive of the year to Alphonse Thomas.

During the busy war season, Herb Armstrong joined Thomas as Oriole business manager, after having served on a part-time basis in 1933. Herb remained continuously on the job after that, and moved without a hitch into the present Baltimore American League organization. Armstrong had been a minor league player, and was a former mathematics teacher and athletic coach at Baltimore's McDonough School. For years, Herb has been highly respected in Baltimore and the boys he taught and coached form a loyal legion.

Following the war pennant, the club slipped to fourth in 1945, and was put out of the Shaughnessy play-offs, four games to three, by the champion Montreal Royals. Sherm Lollar was magnificent that season; he hit .364, caught most of the club's games, and won the International League's most valuable player award. He moved up to Cleveland, but soon was traded to the Yankees and became a member of their 1947 World's Champions. In 1946, Baltimore gave the slugging first baseman, Eddie Robinson, his final tune-up for the Indians. This 1946 Oriole club finished third, but succumbed to the second-place Syracuse Chiefs in the play-offs. It also drew 607,352 fans, high for the International Orioles.

Then came another dizzy drop, to sixth in 1947, the cellar in 1948, and seventh in 1949. Cleveland helped little in the way of players, and faithful Tommy Thomas, hero of 1944 but now plagued with a bad ball club, resigned in May, 1949.

Young Jack Dunn sadly accepted the resignation, and following his grandfather's precept took a seat on the bench and managed the club for the remainder of the unhappy season.

In the same year, the club changed its major league affiliation from Cleveland to the St. Louis Browns. The next two years, they received such St. Louis players as first baseman Hank Arft, pitcher Bill Kennedy, and infielder Eddie Pellagrini, and obtained an experienced catcher, Clyde Kluttz, from Pittsburgh. Bob Young, born and bred in Baltimore, started his career with the Cardinal organization, but in 1949 Rochester traded him to Baltimore. Young subsequently moved up to St. Louis, only to return to his old home town when the Brown franchise was shifted in 1953.

Nick Cullop, former left-handed pitcher and first-base slugging star, became manager in 1950 and immediately celebrated by lifting the Birds to third place and placing them in their last Junior World Series. Nick's club was especially hot in the I. L. Governor's Cup Series, knocking off the second place Montreal Royals, four to three, and the champion Rochester Red Wings, four to two. However, the Cardinals' other Class AAA farm, Columbus, Ohio, avenged Rochester's defeat by downing the Birds in the little World Series, four games to one. Showing Baltimore's baseball appetite, the first three games in the city's stadium drew 20,468, 17,679, and 21,287, respectively, as contrasted with 3,200 and 3,827 for the fourth and fifth games in Columbus. This 1950 Oriole club had a remarkable knack for winning the close ones. From July 30 on, they participated in eight straight one-run decisions, winning seven of them— from scores of 8 to 7 and 6 to 5 all the way down to 2 to 1 and 1 to 0.

By 1951, young Dunn gave up his association with the Browns, and made a new one with the Phillies. Discussing the Orioles' major league hook-ups during this period, C. M. "Abe" Gibbs, capable veteran Baltimore sports writer, commented: "Under Bill Veeck of the Indians, they were no good; the DeWitts of the Browns were more inclined to be helpful, but when the Orioles made an affiliation with the Phillies, under the eminent Bob Carpenter, they found they were dealing with real folks."

Working with the Phillies, the Orioles received such pitchers as Bob Miller, John Thompson, Howard Fox, Bob Greenwood, Ron Mronzinski, and Jack Sanford; catchers Stan Lopata and Joe Lonnett; second basemen Mike Goliat and Putsy Caballero; and outfielders Jack Mayo, Stan Hollmig, and Danny Schell. In 1953, they were given shortstop Ted Kazanski, the Phillies' $80,000 bonus beauty, to ready him for the major league team in Philadelphia, but trouble developed on the Phillie infield and Ted was called up after playing only 60 Oriole games. Many felt the Detroit lad wasn't ready for the jump, and his .290 International League average shrivelled to .217 with the Quakers. In early 1954, he couldn't buy, borrow, or steal a hit, and had to be benched. When Kazanski was called in, the Phillies sent Jack "Lucky" Lohrke to the Birds.

Even though the Phillies tried to be helpful, the Orioles' last three years in the International League were inglorious, sixth in 1951 and 1952 and fourth in 1953. But in the 1953 Shaughnessy play-offs, their last series in the International League, the Birds showed some of the fight and tenacity of the old Orioles, extending the champion Rochester Red Wings to the full seven games before they yielded. The last Baltimore International League manager was little Don Heffner, Oriole second baseman in the early 1930's, who was sold to the New York Yankees. Don, a grand little guy and acute baseball man, was traded by New York to the Browns and built up his managerial reputation while managing the Browns' farm club in San Antonio.

CHAPTER XVI

In the Bigtime Again

DURING THE half-century career of the International League Orioles many Baltimoreans continued to hope—and pray—that sooner or later the big Chesapeake Bay city would be back on the big league map. We have told how Ned Hanlon battled Charley Ebbets in the early century in his effort to move the Brooklyn franchise to Baltimore. The backers of the Baltimore Feds of 1914 and 1915, including Hanlon, were spurred on by an intense desire to see Baltimore returned to baseball's bigtime. They resented implications that Baltimore was a "minor league town." Dunn's effort to give Baltimore a draft-free team was prompted by the same considerations.

When the Phillies had their doleful tailenders under William Baker and Gerry Nugent in the 1920's and 1930's, sports-minded Marylanders looked upon the Quakers as a club which possibly might be shifted to Baltimore. This especially was true after the Phillies gave up old Baker Bowl and became tenants of the Macks and Shibes at Connie Mack Stadium. The Phillie club then had few assets outside of a National League franchise. Thomas D'Alesandro, Jr., first as a private citizen, then as a Congressman and later as Baltimore's mayor, became a constant aggressive advocate of big league ball for Baltimore. But the major leagues then seemed frozen to the sixteen clubs that made up their set-up as though there were something sacred about it. There had been no changes since the early Baltimore Americans were shifted to New York in 1903. Despite weak franchise and poorly patronized teams, the majors had remained wedded to the old order.

Then, during the training season of 1953, a colorful, picturesque, unpredictable character, Bill Veeck, president of the St. Louis Browns, started a series of moves which broke the log jam. Though later developments thrust the dynamic Veeck, called the "Sport Shirt," to the sidelines, Veeck actually was the boy who directly was responsible for the return of big league ball to both Baltimore and Milwaukee.

Actually, the series of events started with Fred Saigh, former Cardinal owner, who got into difficulties with Uncle Sam over income tax payments. Fred was sentenced to fifteen months in the federal penitentiary on January 28, 1953, but the United States Marshal in St. Louis gave him until the following May 4 "to put his affairs in order." It was apparent to Saigh that his continuation in baseball would embarrass the game, and part of his task of putting his affairs in order was to sell the Cardinals to Augustus A. Busch, Jr., president and the big works in St. Louis' large brewery, Anheuser-Busch, Inc.

That's when Bill Veeck, who had acquired the Browns in midseason of 1951, became alarmed. "I could fight a little guy like Fred Saigh," he said, "but how can I fight $30,-000,000?"

Veeck had been a successful operator of the Milwaukee American Association club before heading a syndicate which bought the Cleveland Indians in 1946. Milwaukee, like Baltimore, had long been interested in returning to big league ball. Veeck knew Milwaukee and well-heeled Milwaukee brewers who were willing to put up big money to procure a big league franchise for Wisconsin. He started negotiations to move the Browns to Milwaukee, negotiations which he made only a farcical effort to conceal.

The "Sport Shirt" had made considerable progress in his negotiations when Louis R. Perini, the wealthy contractor who owned both the Boston Braves and the Milwaukee

173

American Association Brewers, also became alarmed. He announced he would not give his consent to Veeck invading his minor league territory.

Perini immediately recognized he had put himself in a tight squeeze. His seventh place Boston National League club of 1952 had drawn a pitiable 281,278; Milwaukee, which had won the 1952 American Association flag, easily doubled the Boston attendance. But, as the man accused of blocking big league ball for Milwaukee, Lou realized his name would become Mudd in Wisconsin. Perini already had the problem of depressed attendance in Boston; now he was threatened with virtual boycott for his crack minor league club in Milwaukee.

Furthermore, while Perini's team was training in Bradenton for at least one more season in Boston, Lou also had been keeping Milwaukee in the back of his mind as a possible place to shift his unappreciated Braves. Had he permitted Veeck to come into Milwaukee, he would have given up his ace in the hole. He responded quickly and made a snap decision to move his Boston Braves to Milwaukee immediately and shift this Milwaukee A. A. team to Toledo, which in 1952 had become vacant territory.

In the meantime, Veeck, realizing he was blocked in Milwaukee, turned his attention to Baltimore. For some time Mayor D'Alesandro had been·looking upon the Browns as the big league club most likely to be shifted. The two already had built up contacts. The Mayor told Bill he would be doubly welcome, and that he would see that the capacity of Memorial Stadium would be increased to fulfill all major league requirements. Baltimore writers with young Jack Dunn's team in Florida got hold of the story, and soon all Baltimore was thrilled at the coming of big league ball to the city.

However, the two franchise changes first had to be voted upon and ratified at historic meetings of the two major leagues called for Florida in middle March, a month before the start of the 1953 season. The chances of the shift of the Browns to Baltimore being approved seemed better than that of the shift

174

of the Braves to Milwaukee. Six out of eight American League clubs could approve the transfer of a franchise. In the National League, it required unanimous consent. And there was considerable sentiment for Boston, which with Chicago, was one of the two 1876 charter members continuously active in the senior loop.

The American League met first, at the Tampa Terrace Hotel in Tampa, March 16. Three top-ranking Baltimoreans also attended: Mayor Tom D'Alesandro, Thomas Biddison, city solicitor, and William Callahan, chairman of the Baltimore Stadium committee. Veeck and the Baltimore delegation thought everything was in the bag, and that the meeting would be a cut-and-dried affair. However, Veeck, his Baltimore associates, and expectant Baltimore fans were in for a shocking surprise. After a stormy meeting, it was announced that Veeck's request to move his St. Louis franchise to Baltimore was rejected five votes to two as American League president Will Harridge gave out the bad news for Baltimore in the form of a statement: "The American League clubs have decided it is not advisable to transfer the St. Louis club for the 1953 season. The league decided that the numerous problems involved preclude the transfer of the franchise by reason of the short period of time before the opening of the season."

To make the American League action still more bitter for Tom D'Alesandro, Baltimore writers and fans was the action of the National League in St. Petersburg two days later, when the parent major league unanimously granted its consent for Perini to move his Boston franchise to Milwaukee. Milwaukee was in, but Baltimore still was out.

In the American League vote in Tampa, Veeck had only two clubs supporting him in the final showdown. No announcement of how the clubs voted was made, but it generally was understood that Frank Lane, general manager of the Chicago White Sox, and Hank Greenberg, general manager of the Cleveland Indians, were Veeck's only supporters. The Yankees led the fight on Veeck and on the Baltimore shift.

175

Baltimore got little satisfaction when it learned that the adverse vote was anti-Veeck, rather than anti-Baltimore. While trying to lift up his Browns by the boot straps, the "Sport Shirt" had championed the "Have Not" clubs against the "Haves." He had made an effort to cut in on the TV sugar of Brown games in New York, Boston, and Cleveland. And, by lack of tact, he had stirred up other antagonisms. Some didn't like Veeck's Barnum and Bailey type of operations, and some just didn't like Bill. The Browns also had made St. Louis commitments for 1953, which unfulfilled might have broughts suits and embarrassment to the league. Commissioner Ford Frick also was reported to have been of the opinion that it was too close to the 1953 league season to consider franchise changes. Will Harridge did hold out some hope for Baltimore, when he remarked: "The action of the American League in Tampa was for the 1953 season, and does not preclude the matter from coming up again at a later date." Baltimore held to this ray of hope, and several times during 1953 Mayor D'Alesandro headed parties to see the Browns, the expected future Orioles, play their games.

Events in St. Louis soon foretold that 1953 would be the last season for the American League Browns. On the eve of the season, Bill Veeck sold Sportsman's Park, the American League park since 1903, to Gussie Busch of the Cardinals for $900,000 and became Busch's tenant. But Veeck needed this money to pay off heavy obligations, and soon had to sell ball players and his Arizona ranch to meet current expenses. Applications for the franchise came not only from Baltimore, but from Los Angeles, San Francisco, Montreal, Toronto, Minneapolis-St. Paul, Kansas City, and Houston. Veeck personally investigated the Los Angeles and San Francisco bids, but as the season drew to its close, he still was of the opinion that a move to Baltimore was his best bet. It was the one city that had a big league ball field ready.

On September 27, the Sunday before the World Series, Harridge called upon his club owners to meet in New York and consider Veeck's second request to shift his franchise to Baltimore. And again it resulted in a slap in the face for Veeck. Also, seemingly for Baltimore. This time the measure was voted down, four to four. Clubs voting against the move were New York, Philadelphia, Boston, and Cleveland. The latter club shifted from its Tampa position, when it supported Veeck. Del Webb, half-owner of the Yankees, raised the most powerful voice against the move. Webb comes from Phoenix, Arizona, but has extensive interests in Los Angeles and elsewhere in California. He favored a Brown shift to Los Angeles and requested a 30-day delay to give the Los Angeles people a better chance to line up their proposition.

Baltimore was not only aghast, but by this time very angry. Many felt the proud city was being given the run-around, and editorial writers joined their brethren on the sports side in expressing their indignation, with the New York club being their special target.

However, all was not lost. Things were stirring under the surface. The untiring Baltimore delegation, headed by Mayor D'Alesandro and attorney Clarence W. Miles, representing the money of some of Baltimore's outstanding business lights, did not desist. They kept on swinging. They called on Ford Frick, Commissioner of baseball. They insisted Baltimore simply had to have that franchise. Soon a tip went out of New York that the American League had nothing against Baltimore, if the brash Veeck was eliminated from the picture. On the 28th, president Will Harridge announced that the St. Louis Brown situation had to be settled immediately and he called an emergency meeting of his league for September 29, the day before the World Series.

With some 500 reporters in New York for the World Series, "the Baltimore Story" stole the headlines from the approaching Yankee-Brooklyn Series. For, happy days, Baltimore finally was in! After twice blocking Veeck's efforts to move from the Mississippi to the Chesapeake, the league approved the Baltimore shift after an aggressive group of Baltimore business men, headed by attorney Miles, purchased 79 percent of the Browns, the Veeck interest, for $2,475,000. The Baltimore interests acquired 206,250 shares, which were purchased for $12 a share. That was a lot of money for a paper franchise and a tailend team, but the sale did include the Browns' top minor league farm, the San Antonio club of the Texas League, where the Browns owned an up-to-date park and valuable real estate.

Of course, the new owners immediately announced the nickname of their club would be the Orioles, the time-honored name of Baltimore teams, good, bad, and indifferent, through the years.

Phil Wrigley, owner of the Chicago Cubs and Los Angeles Angels, gave the Baltimore shift a valuable assist when he announced earlier in the day he would not stand for any draft of his Los Angeles territory and would have to be handsomely compensated if he ever moved out of that city. Jerry Hoffberger, president of the National Brewery, helped matters by giving Clark Griffith of Washington a new TV-radio contract. That won the Washington club's vote. Del Webb of the Yankee was appeased, when the American League amended its constitution to permit the league to operate as a ten-club loop any time it so desired.

All along, Jack Dunn III, who inherited the International League Orioles from his grandmother, said he would do nothing to hinder the shift of a major league franchise to Baltimore should one become available. He was a born-and-bred Baltimore boy, and wanted big league ball in his home town the same as any one else. Yet, young Jack has done quite well with the new organization. He received $350,000 for his Baltimore minor league Orioles, and a ten-year contract at $25,000 annually as an officer in the new American League club. This was the same arrangement Veeck had worked out with young Jack when he expected to move into Baltimore in 1953. Jack III now is employed as road secretary of the club. The International League also received an indemnity of

178

$48,749.61 for surrendering its Baltimore territory. The "Int" team was moved to Richmond, where it now is a farm for the Orioles.

It was a happy group of Baltimoreans when the American League finally decided to permit Baltimore to return to its fold after an absence of over half a century. Mayor D'Alesandro, his long battle rewarded after seemingly discouraging setbacks, danced a jig around Clarence Miles. For the benefit of the photographers, His Honor raised his hands over his head as does a boxer when he is proclaimed the winner. An enthusiastic crowd greeted the new "big leaguers" at the Camden Street station when they returned to Baltimore. Mayor D'Alesandro and Miles promptly announced work would be rushed to increase the baseball capacity of Memorial Stadium from 31,000 to 46,500, with the new capacity ready for the opening of the 1954 season.

Yet, the man above all others responsible for Memorial Stadium was Rodger Pippin, the veteran sports editor of the *Baltimore News-Post* and *Sunday American* and the chap who roomed with Babe Ruth on Babe's 1914 Oriole training trip. Without Rodger's zealous and untiring campaigning, there would have been no Memorial Stadium. And without the available stadium, there would have been no place to house the transplanted Browns and no big league ball for Baltimore.

Pippin was at it a long time. After Oriole Park burned to the ground in July, 1944, the baseball club moved into the earlier stadium, erected primarily for football. At first, it was considered a temporary move, but young Jack Dunn didn't wish to build in war and post-war times, so Pippin suggested a roof be built over the old stadium with the city taking the cost out of the rental paid by the International Orioles. He interested Governor McKeldin, then Mayor of Baltimore, but engineers reported back to the Mayor that it would not be practical to erect a roof over the old stadium.

Then Pippin launched a campaign in his *News-Post* column

to have the city erect a new, bigger, and better stadium on the same site. Through his zeal and diligent efforts, he had a measure authorizing a loan of $2,500,000 for the erection of a new stadium placed on the primary ballot of May 6, 1947. Despite strong opposition, some of it in high places, the Baltimore voters approved the stadium loan.

As a result of rising building costs and material delays, the original $2,500,000 stretched only far enough to build a single decker seating 30,000. With his eye on a major league Oriole team of the future, Pippin again started to beat the tomtoms for a two-deck grandstand. With an endless stream of columns, Rodger plugged for a 50,000-seat modern stadium, one measuring up to all big league requirements and something he considered worthy of a big metropolitan city such as Baltimore. Again the additional cost was criticized, but Rodger and his newspaper again were instrumental in having a second $2,500,000 stadium loan put on the November, 1950, ballot. This, too, was authorized by the Baltimore voters, and Rodger Pippin truly may be termed the Godfather of Memorial Stadium. Some of the money authorized by the 1950 voters was still in the city's till when Baltimore got back into the American League and was used in completing the stadium construction job.

There was talk in St. Louis of suits by disgruntled fans and Brown stockholders but everything became official October 29, when Clarence Miles handed a $1,475,000 check to Sidney K. Schiff, attorney and stockholder of the BBC Corporation, which had held the Veeck interests in the Browns. Schiff immediately took $300,000 of the money to repay a loan the Browns owed to the American League. A million dollars still was owed the old Brown owners.

It was natural that the aggressive Clarence Miles, who never quit in his fight to bring big league baseball to his beloved home town, should be elected president of the new Orioles. James Keelty, Jr., a prominent Baltimore realtor, was named

180

vice-president, and Clyde Y. Morris, Miles' law partner, was chosen secretary-treasurer. The other directors rank high in Baltimore's business Who's Who: George M. Bunker, president of the Glenn L. Martin Co.; John M. Willis, president-general manager of Bethlehem Steel's Baltimore shipbuilding division; Thomas S. Nichols, president of the Mathieson Chemical Co.; Harold I. Fink, hotel manager; Howard Jones, manufacturer; Joseph A. Iglehart, investment banker; Zanvvl Krieger, attorney; W. Wallace Lanahan, Jr., investment broker. All have heavy sugar in the new Orioles.

Bill DeWitt, before Veeck the No. 1 man in the Browns, came along as vice-president in charge of minor league operations, but Bill shifted to the Yankees during the 1954 season. James McLaughlin, DeWitt's former assistant in St. Louis, was named Director of Minor League Clubs. Herbert Armstrong, business manager of Dunn's International League Orioles, continued in the same capacity with the new team, and his son, Dick Armstrong, came from the Athletics to serve as Director of Public Relations.

In looking for a general manager, Clarence Miles first decided on Frank Lane, the aggressive go-getter of the Chicago White Sox. Mrs. Grace Comiskey, president of the Sox, would not give Lane his release to accept a very handsome offer, but Frank received a five-year extension of his Chicago contract as a result of the Baltimore offer.

Failing to get Lane, Miles next turned to the Philadelphia Athletics, and got permission from the Macks to deal with Arthur H. Ehlers, the Philadelphia general manager. Ehlers was signed to a three-year contract on October 26. Art seemed a natural for the Baltimore job, as he is a born and reared Baltimorean. He let out his first cry in the Chesapeake city, January 22, 1896, and had a brief fling at professional ball before serving overseas and getting gassed in World War I. Art has been active in baseball for many years, used to run the Pocomoke City club in the Eastern Shore League, was half owner and general manager of Reading in the Interstate

181

League, and served five years as president of the same loop. Next he put in a hitch as promotional director of the National Association (the governing body of the minors) before joining the Athletics as farm director in 1947. Three years later he moved up to the post of general manager with the same team.

Miles and Art Ehlers, the new general manager, inherited quite a managerial problem. They already had two former Brown managers on their hands, Rogers Hornsby, the Oriole of 1937 and 1939, and Marty Marion, the 1953 chief of the Browns. If Hornsby had retained his old hitting art and Marion the fielding skill that won him the sobriquet of "Mr. Shortstop," it would have helped considerably. But Hornsby, fired by the tempestuous Veeck as manager in July, 1952, after Bill had signed him to a three-year iron-bound contract, had $18,000 coming to him on the third year of this document. Marion had a holdover managerial contract for 1954, calling for something around $35,000. Ehlers called Marion to Baltimore; Art supposedly didn't think too much of Marty's low estimate of the team, thought it was a "defeatist complex," and decided to buy Marion off. Oddly enough, Lane, the man who nearly became Oriole general manager, then signed Marion as a coach for the White Sox.

The Athletics fired aggressive, cigar-smoking Jimmy Dykes as manager shortly after Ehlers accepted the Baltimore post. Jamie, too, had a holdover contract. The Macks gave out the story Jimmy played too much golf and didn't give enough attention to baseball. However, the feeling in Philadelphia was that Ehlers already had sent feelers in Jimmy's direction before the firing. Anyway, on Armistice Day, November 11, Ehlers signed Dykes to a new contract as 1954 Oriole pilot. It generally was understood the Athletics paid $10,000 of Jimmy's $25,000 salary as a sort of settlement on Dykes' holdover Athletic contract.

182

CHAPTER XVII

Browns in American League Since 1902

AND WHAT ABOUT the club the Orioles inherited, the St. Louis Browns? Actually, they had a sad heritage, only one pennant and eleven first-division clubs in 52 years. Twelve Brown clubs finished seventh and ten more wound up in the cellar. Five of the first-division clubs came in the six seasons between 1920 and 1925, the years Jack Dunn had his pennant trust in the International League.

The modern American League Browns couldn't even claim to be descendants of Von Der Ahe's and Comiskey's fabulous St. Louis Browns of the old major American Association, four straight winners in 1885-86-87-88. This Brown club was taken into the National League in 1892, at the same time that the Baltimore A. A. Orioles were admitted to the twelve-club National League. Actually, the present-day Cardinals are lineal descendants of the original Browns.

It may seem paradoxical today that the American League Browns started as the Milwaukee Brewers of 1901. Ban Johnson, first American League president, was a sagacious man, but he couldn't look forward a half-century and visualize a Milwaukee club averaging close to 2,000,000 a season for the years of 1953 and 1954. In 1902, St. Louis was the fourth city in the nation, and rated highly as a ball town. During the latter stages of the National-American baseball war, Johnson thought it a smart move to enter St. Louis and fight the Robinson interests there. So, he shifted his early Milwaukee club to the banks of "Ol' Man River." The new club took over Sportsman's Park, the old home of Von Der Ahe's Browns. The old nickname, "Browns," also was kicking around since the St. Louis Nationals abandoned it in the late nineties, so Johnson and Jimmy McAleer, the new St. Louis American manager, appropriated it, and hung it on their new team.

The 1902 Browns first were backed by a group of St. Louis sportsmen headed by Ralph Orthwein, but after one season Ralph sold the new franchise to Robert Lee Hedges, a Cincinnati carriage manufacturer. Johnson had known Hedges during Ban's baseball writing days in Cincinnati. Hedges was a smart early operator, knew how to get 100 cents out of a dollar, and whether his clubs were up or down, Robert Lee almost invariably showed a profit.

The club Ban Johnson shifted to St. Louis in 1902 had been a tailender in Milwaukee the season before. It was almost the same situation as the shift of the 1953 St. Louis Browns to Baltimore in 1954. And, how Baltimore wishes the same happy climb could have been brought about! In one season, this transferred club leaped from eighth to second. However, Clarence Miles, Art Ehlers, and Jimmy Dykes were in no position to raid the St. Louis Cardinals of such stars as Stan Musial, Red Schoendienst, and Harvey Hendrix as were Johnson, Orthwein, and McAleer 52 years before when they took the cream of the St. Louis National League's war-torn team.

Obtaining a first division team in 1902 was quite simple, even though it baffled McGraw in Baltimore. You went into the rival camp with pockets stuffed with greenbacks. In wholesale raids on the Cardinals, the Browns obtained Jesse Burkett, who batted .400 three times; Rhoderick "Bobbie" Wallace, a shortstop then considered second only to the great Hans Wagner; pitchers Jack Powell, Jack Harper, and Willie Sudhoff; and two other outfielders in addition to Burkett, Emmett Heidrick and Billy Maloney. Another ace pitcher, Frank "Red" Donahue, a 22-11 performer in 1902, was snared from

184

the Phillies. With this aggregation of filched talent, Jimmy McAleer ran second to the Athletics the season Connie Mack brought his first of nine pennants to Philadelphia.

The runner-up finish of 1902 was not an augury of good things to come. Only one other second-place club followed in the next 51 years. McAleer's club tumbled into the second division in 1903 and hit bottom for the first time in 1905. Brownie fans got some measure of comfort in 1906 when their outfielder, George Stone, beat out the great Nap Lajoie for the American League's batting title.

If the Browns suffered five successive second-division teams after their first second placer, Hedges prospered. The Cardinals, ruined by the war, were considerably worse, and the Browns became St. Louis' favorite ball club. Hedges did so well that by 1908 he increased the capacity of Sportsman's Park to 18,000, considered a big park for that period.

Hedges' enlarged park was nicely timed. In 1908, the American League had a freak race, with all of its strength massed in the West. Hedges and McAleer pulled a great deal for St. Louis when they purchased the playful left-handed star, Rube Waddell, from the Philadelphia Athletics. Connie Mack had tired of Rube's shenanigans after the left-hander blew the 1907 pennant for the A's. Waddell was the same zany in St. Louis that he had been in Philadelphia: he chased fire engines, tended bar, rang strangers' door bells, imitated a circus barker, and wrestled with admiring bar flies. But he had one more good season, winning nineteen games, losing fourteen, and striking out 232 batsmen. Rube's high spot in 1908 was the first game in which he faced his old team, the Athletics, in Philadelphia on July 29. Rube was out to show Mack what a blunder he had made by striking out sixteen of his erstwhile teammates, which stood as an American League record until Bob Feller knocked it out of the book.

With the aid of Waddell, Bill Dinneen, and Barney Pelty, one of the early Jewish players, the Browns fought abreast with the Tigers, Clevelands, and White Sox until Labor Day.

St. Louis slumped in September, leaving it up to the remaining three clubs to battle it out to the finish line. McAleer's team couldn't win, but they knocked out Nap Lajoie's Cleveland Naps. With only two days of the schedule left, the Naps could assure themselves of the pennant by taking three games from the Browns, a double-header and single game. But, Bill Dinneen stopped them in one game of the twin bill, and Detroit defeated the White Sox for the flag on the last day of the season. Cleveland lost the pennant by four points, as the fourth-place Browns finished eight games off the pace.

McAleer's second baseman was Jimmy Williams, the infielder John McGraw had snatched from Barney Dreyfuss' Pirates when "Mac" was manager of the American League Orioles. St. Louis had a Texan pitcher-outfielder-pinch hitter in 1908 named Dode Criss. Dode batted .341 for 64 games against .324 for Ty Cobb, who played the full season. Many St. Louisans angered at Ban Johnson when he named Cobb, rather than Criss, the batting champion. St. Louisans then took their Brown baseball most seriously, and any one suggesting the Browns be moved out of town would have been considered daffy. They finished a close second to the White Sox in American League attendance, 636,096 for the Sox to 618,947 for the Browns.

However, this fourth-place finish had to satisfy Brown fans for a full decade. The club skidded to seventh the following year, and it was 1920 before the Missouri club again saw the light of the first division. McAleer left after 1909 to pilot Washington, and was followed by a succession of managers, Jack O'Connor, Bobbie Wallace, George Stovall, Branch Rickey, Fielder Jones, and Jimmy Burke. The careers of O'Connor and Stovall came to turbulent ends, the former for trying to help Lajoie win a batting championship and the latter for squirting tobacco juice in the face of one of Ban Johnson's umpires.

O'Connor was involved in a lively rhubarb at the end of the 1910 season. An automobile company was offering cars to

186

the batting champions of the two majors, and young Ty Cobb and Lajoie were coming down the American League home stretch neck and neck. Cobb was most unpopular with fellow players at the time, with 90 percent rooting for Lajoie to beat out Ty. The Browns wound up the 1910 season at home, playing Cleveland a double-header. O'Connor went to such extremes to have Lajoie win that he had a kid third baseman, Johnny "Red" Corriden, play back on the outfield grass for King Larry. As a result, Lajoie closed with eight hits, six of them safe bunts. And Larry, by that time thirty-five, never was a particularly fast base-runner. A seventh Lajoie hit was a ball fumbled by shortstop Wallace; the scorer first recorded it as a Wallace error but a few minutes later changed it to a hit.

One set of unofficial averages had Lajoie the batting champion and car winner; another set had Cobb the winner by a fraction. The official averages eventually gave it to Cobb, .385 to .384. But, the manner in which Corriden played Lajoie and other shenanigans at Sportsman's Park on that final day raised a smell like a pig sty. It also developed that the St. Louis official scorer had been offered an expensive suit of clothes if he gave Lajoie the benefit of the doubt on all questionable hits. Ban Johnson held an immediate investigation to which he summoned O'Connor, Harry Howell, a pitcher-coach, Corriden, and the umpires. Howell, a former National and American Oriole, got into the act with frequent trips to the press box asking how Lajoie's doubtful hits were being scored. Johnson absolved Corriden as a kid who only was obeying instructions, but ordered the Browns to fire O'Connor and Howell, even though Jack's contract ran into 1911. O'Connor later brought suit in the civil courts, was awarded his 1911 Brown salary, with which he started a St. Louis saloon. Jack never got back into baseball, but Howell later was employed as a minor league umpire.

Stovall's expectorating job in 1913 brought Wesley Branch Rickey, who then didn't use tobacco and never took a drink, to the fore. Third baseman Jimmy Austin followed Stovall briefly as a fill-in manager, and then Lee Hedges named Rickey. It started Branch up the ladder on his way to baseball fame and fortune. Rickey wasn't a newcomer to St. Louis baseball. As a young college catcher from Ohio Wesleyan, he had joined the Browns late in the season of 1905. Just the opposite from the swearing, badgering O'Connor-Stovall type, Branch's worst cuss word was Judas Priest; he didn't even play ball on Sunday in a town which derived much of its revenue from big Sunday crowds. Perhaps that's why Hedges traded Branch to New York despite a .284 batting average and fair promise as a catcher in 1906. Rickey lasted only one season with the early Yankees, and next became baseball coach at Michigan, where he also studied law. His health broke down from overstudy and overwork, and he went to Montana and briefly put out his law shingle. But baseball soon lured him back. Hedges remembered Rickey as a young man with ideas; he invited Branch to return to St. Louis as presidential assistant. From that job, he moved on to the Brown management. Because Branch wouldn't manage the club on Sunday—wouldn't even go near the ball park on the Sabbath—outfielder Burt Shotton, who won pennants in recent years in Brooklyn, became Rickey's Sunday manager.

Rickey managed the Browns for the latter half of 1913 and in 1914 and 1915; the enthusiastic collegian tried a lot of new ideas and experiments as his clubs finished eighth, fifth, and sixth. Rickey's coaching years in Michigan paid off when he signed one of his Michigan boys, George Sisler, a fellow Ohian of Swiss descent, to a Brown contract in 1915. Pittsburgh also claimed the crack collegian. As a high school boy in Akron, Ohio, George foolishly had signed a contract with his Akron home town team. Though Sisler never reported to Akron, that club sold his contract to the Columbus American Association club, and Columbus, in turn, sold the contract to the Pittsburgh Pirates. After Sisler was graduated from Michigan, Barney Dreyfuss, Pirate president, insisted the player re-

188

port to his team. It started one of baseball's greatest rows. It finally was put up to the old three-man National Commission; president Ban Johnson voted to send Sisler to the Browns; National League president John K. Tener favored Dreyfuss' claim; and Garry Herrmann, commission chairman, sided with Johnson. Dreyfuss was so infuriated that he started a lengthy campaign to unseat Herrmann from the chairmanship, which reached success in 1920.

The signing of Sisler, nicknamed "the Sizzler," was the greatest thing that ever happened to the Browns. Though George did some early pitching, played the outfield, and even took a whirl at third base—a strange position for a left-hander —he eventually settled at first base, and became one of the super-stars of baseball. Sisler and Lou Gehrig of the Yankees usually are the men selected for first base on mythical All-Star All-Time teams. Gorgeous George was one of baseball's greatest hitters, a fielder whose brilliancy was compared to that of Hal Chase, and a top-ranking base runner. Sisler's star would have twinkled even more brilliantly in the baseball heavens but for a sinus and eye affliction, which kept him on the sidelines for an entire season and handicapped him severely in his later career. Even so, Sisler left the big leagues with a lifetime batting average of .340.

The Browns acquired a new owner, cantankerous, irascible, blustery Philip deCatesby Ball, shortly after the arrival of Sisler. Phil Ball, millionaire manufacturer of ice-making machinery and cold storage plants, and brewer Otto Stifel, backed the St. Louis Terriers during the Federal League years of 1914 and 1915. In 1915, the Terriers, managed by Fielder Jones of old Chicago White Sox Hitless Wonder fame, lost the Federal League pennant to Chicago by one point. It gave Ball the yen to stay in baseball. Among the terms of the major-Federal League peace agreement was that Ball should be permitted to buy the Browns. He purchased the club from Bob Hedges on December 18, 1915, for $425,000. Phil moved into Sportsman's Park, merged the best of his Federal League runner-up with the 1915 Browns, put the club in charge of his Fed manager, Jones, and kicked Branch Rickey upstairs as business manager. Though Branch had a five-year contract, he left the club a year later to accept the Cardinal presidency under a syndicate of new owners. It infuriated Ball; he tried to stop Branch by court proceedings and never forgave the man from Ohio Wesleyan. Ban Johnson later retaliated by inducing Miller Huggins, successful Cardinal manager, to leave St. Louis for the better-salaried managerial berth on the New York Yankees.

Ball was a character. He bought the Browns largely as a personal hobby. With the exception of a few years, he lost money constantly, but it never bothered him. When Rickey left the club, Ban Johnson told him, "Don't worry; I'll get you a better man as business manager, Bob Quinn of Columbus." Quinn came in, and did a really fine job. But, he got nowhere trying to save Ball money. When an early rain chilled the outlook for any patronage, Quinn called off a game with the Red Sox at 2:30. Ball arrived at the ball park at 2:45, being driven there post-haste by his Negro chauffeur. When Ball saw no action on the field, he went into a high dudgeon and stormed into Bob Quinn's office.

"What's the reason for this? Why isn't there a game?" he demanded.

"Oh, there were only a few hundred fans in the stands," hemmed and hawed Quinn. "A double-header later on will be more profitable."

The truculent Ball shook his fist. "Bob Quinn, let me tell you something," he roared. "I worked myself to a frazzle at the office so I could see this game, and if you want to keep your job, don't ever do anything like this to me again."

He feuded with his managers and ball players. Once he openly accused his second base pair, second baseman Del Pratt and shortstop Johnny Lavan, of not giving the Browns

190

their best. They brought legal action against Bill for intimating they were "laying down." Both players soon were traded.

During the war season of 1918, the Browns, leading the Senators, 4 to 0, blew in the ninth as Washington batted out five runs to win, 5 to 4. After the game, Ball was in one of his crabbiest moods, and Fielder Jones, his manager, threatened to quit.

"So, you want to quit," shouted Ball. "You haven't an ounce of courage. Get out of my office; I wouldn't take you back if you'd work for nothing. I want men who like to tackle a tough job. Quinn, get me a new manager." Bob engaged Jimmy Burke, former big league third baseman, and product of St. Louis' famed Kerry Patch, in the early century a breeding spot for big leaguers.

However, despite Ball's truculence and quirks, he was intensely loyal. Though a former Federal Leaguer, he stuck to American League president Ban Johnson through thick and thin, in Johnson's fight with the National League, in Ban's battles with his own clubowners and later with Commissioner Landis. In fact, Ball was the only one of the sixteen major league club presidents who refused to sign the contract with Judge Landis in late 1920. Bob Quinn, as vice-president, signed for the Browns.

When Sam Breadon, at that time president of the run-down Cardinals, first asked Ball to let him come into Sportsman's Park as a tenant, Ball ordered him out of the office. "Are you crazy, Sam?" he exploded. "I wouldn't let Branch Rickey [by then Cardinal vice-president-general manager] put one foot inside my ball park. Now, get out yourself."

After being repulsed a second time, the persistent Breadon made a third attempt. He begged Ball to hold back his temper for a few minutes and listen. "I was a poor boy—a very poor boy—in New York," he began. "I came here to St. Louis, nearly starved at first, but eventually made some money in the automobile business. I got into the Cardinals with that fan group—soon got in over my head—and much of my money is

191

in the club. We're heavily in debt, and our only chance to salvage what we put into it is to sell the Cardinals' real estate for $200,000, get out of debt, and move to Sportsman's Park. You're a rich man, Mr. Ball; money doesn't mean anything to you, but I'm about to go broke, and only you can save me."

Ball gulped. "Sam, I didn't know you were hooked so bad," he said. "I admire your frankness, and what's more I admire a fighter, a man that doesn't quit easily. Get your lawyer to draw up a contract, insert a rental figure you think is fair, and I'll sign it. Even if it includes having that Rickey around the place."

Ball often had much to criticize, but in 1917, he felt he got some of his investment back when on May 5 and 6, two Brownie pitchers, left-hander Ernie Koob and right-hander Bob Groom, pitched no-hitters against the powerful White Sox, 1917 World's Champions, on successive days. "No matter what they do to us this season, that's a Brownie mark that will stay in the books a long time," Phil exulted.

CHAPTER XVIII

1922 Pennant Lost by a Single Game

AFTER having only two first-division clubs in eighteen seasons, the Browns started to act like a real big league club in 1920, when Jimmy Burke finished fourth, and Phil Ball really enjoyed many of his games. Johnson had told Phil that Bob Quinn was better—and smarter—than Rickey. Maybe that was too high praise, but in those days Bob was sharp as a steel trap. With a smart deal here and a replacement there, he gradually was building up the club.

During the war season of 1918, Quinn swung a deal with the Yankees that was a dilly: he got pitchers Urban Shocker and Nick Cullop, catcher Les Nunamaker, infielders Joe Gedeon and Fritz Maisel (the Dunn Oriole), and $15,000 for second baseman Del Pratt, Ball's problem ball player, and the veteran Hall of Fame southpaw pitcher, Eddie Plank, who had jumped the Athletics in 1915 to join Ball's old St. Louis Feds. Plank never reported to the Yanks.

Shocker wasn't included in the original deal. The pitcher named was Ray Fisher, but when Ray went into the Army, Quinn demanded Shocker, then a promising Yankee young- ster. When Miller Huggins demurred, Quinn sent his ulti- matum, "Shocker or no deal." Huggins yielded. Shocker, a sturdy spitballer, soon became half of the Brown pitching staff. In 1920, he won twenty games and lost ten, which he jacked up to 27-12 in 1921, when the Browns ran third. In the latter season, Lee Fohl, a Quinn favorite, succeeded Burke as manager.

Sisler was sizzling more and more with each season, and in 1920 he reached .400 for the first time, hitting .407 to give the Brown their first batting champion since Stone. Ty Cobb had won twelve out of thirteen batting championships between the years 1907 and 1919, but in 1920 Gorgeous George left him far behind. Sisler cracked out 257 hits, which still stands as tops for all big leaguers. He scored 137 runs and drove in 122, stole 42 bases and his 19 home runs were second to Babe Ruth's majestic 54. It was about this time that Rogers Hornsby was perennial batting champion of the National League, and St. Louis fans never tired of discussing the respective merits of George and Rog.

After Sisler fell back to .371 in 1921, he rebounded with a vengeance in 1922, and soared to a phenomenal .420 to win his second batting championship. The late Bob Quinn once said: "Ty Cobb was the greatest ball player of all time, but in 1922 George Sisler was greater than any ball player ever was in one individual season." The writer, who covered New York baseball during the 1922 dizzy Yankee-Brown pennant race, subscribes to that statement. If Sisler hadn't injured a shoulder late in the season, forcing his absence from twelve games and to play others under a handicap, there is no telling what heights he might have reached. Even so, in 142 games, he knocked out 246 hits, scored 134 runs, and stole 51 bases. George also hit safely in 41 consecutive games, the best record since Willie Keeler's 44 straight games with the 1897 Orioles and the American League record until Joe DiMaggio's brilliant 56 straight games of 1941.

Sisler's great play, along with superlative pitching by Shocker, who worked 348 innings, made it possible for the Browns to put up a serious challenge for the 1922 pennant. They battled the Yankees, 1921 champions, right down to the finishing post and finally were nosed out by one game, the Browns closing with a record of 93-61, .604, against New

194

York's 94-60, .610. St. Louis loved it, as 712,918 fans paid their way into Sportsman's Park for the best Browns' all-time attendance. Considering there then was no night ball, nor artificial Sunday double-headers, that was a lot of people for hot St. Louis day games. The club made $350,000 and Ball was liberal with bonuses. He gave Shocker a $5,000 bonus in midseason, and after the players lost the pennant, he gave them $20,000 to split among themselves. Bob Quinn also received a tidy bonus for his efforts.

There were other splendid players on the club in addition to Sisler and Shocker. Most of the regulars hit better than .300. The tall lanky left fielder, Ken Williams, a $4,500 bargain from Portland, Oregon, batted .332, smacked out 39 homers, drove in 155 runs, and stole 37 bases. Center fielder Baby Doll Bill Jacobson, a husky Iowa farm boy once passed up by McGraw of the Giants, hit .317 and covered acres of ground. In right field was Johnny Tobin, a St. Louis home-bred, and one of the lone survivors of the St. Louis Feds. He hit .329, and was one of the league's best lead-off men. Marty McManus, at second, hit .312, and was a fighting aggressive Irishman, the "take charge" guy of the infield. Hank Severeid did practically all the catching, taking part in 134 games and hitting .321. The other catcher was Pat Collins. Wallie Gerber was a slick-fielding shortstop but only average hitter, while third base was handled by Frank Ellerbe and Kid Foster.

Urban Shocker was greater than a 24-17 record would indicate. He was the pitcher who invariably was sent after the key games. He appeared in twelve games against the rival Yanks, ten of them starting assignments, and if his New York record was only four victories and seven defeats, Urban was in some terrific ball games. Elam Vangilder (19-13) and Dixie Davis (11-6) were Fohl's only other outstanding pitchers. A young collegiate southpaw, Hub Pruett, now a practicing physician in St. Louis, could make a sucker out of Babe Ruth, but his seasonal record was only seven-seven.

195

Pitchers with such movie names as Beverly Bayne and Daring Dave Danforth helped round out the staff.

The 1922 Browns lost the pennant on three counts: lack of depth in the pitching staff, inability to beat the Yankees, and the midseason purchase of Joe Dugan and Elmer Smith by the Yankees from Boston. They lost their New York series, fourteen to eight. Oddly enough the last-place Red Sox, with a bunch of Yankee cast-offs, defeated New York on the year, thirteen to nine. The Browns, on the other hand, made hay with Boston, winning their series, fifteen to seven.

After the lead changed frequently in the early months, the Browns led continuously from June 16 to July 28. It was during this July period that the Yankees snared Joe Dugan, then the loop's best third baseman, and Elmer Smith, a slugging outfielder, from the ever willing-to-sell Harry Frazee of Boston. Before acquiring Dugan, Huggins had employed a slow and fading Frank Baker and the light-hitting Mike McNally at the hot corner; the acquisition of Jumping Joe gave the Yankees an immediate lift both at bat and in the field. St. Louis shouted its indignation to the high heavens; the Chamber of Commerce, civic, business and other groups drew up critical resolutions which they sent to baseball Commissioner Judge Landis and Ban Johnson. St. Louis' newspapers denounced the deal in their most pungent language. However, the deal then was legal, but out of it grew legislation, sponsored by Landis, that no player could be disposed of after June 15, except for the waiver price.

Though the Browns lost their 1922 series to New York, they won one of the unforgettable games in baseball, pulling out a late May victory in New York, 7 to 2, after Umpire Ollie Chill had called the last Brownie out in the ninth with the Yanks ahead, 2 to 1. Truly, it was one of the "believe it or not" games of baseball. It was the first game played by the Yankees after Babe Ruth and Bob Meusel had finished 70-day suspensions, and a crowd of 49,152 crammed into the Polo

Grounds, where the Yankees still were tenants. As usual, it was the hard-working Shocker who handled this one for St. Louis and a two-run homer by Aaron Ward had given New York the one-run edge it enjoyed in the ninth. Sam Jones, Shocker's opponent, got two out in the ninth, when two pinch-hitters, Chick Shorten and Pat Collins, stung him for singles. Fleet-footed Johnny Tobin tapped to first baseman Wallie Pipp, who tossed to Jones, covering first base, and the base umpire, Chill, waved Tobin out. The Yankee players ran to the clubhouse and the great crowd swarmed out on the field.

However, Fohl, coaching at first, had noticed that Jones had slightly juggled the ball before holding it securely, and at that moment the fast Tobin had crossed first base. Lee took it up with Brick Owens, the plate umpire, who told Chill in his opinion Tobin was safe. In the meantime, the tying Brown run had scored. The umpires ordered play resumed; the crowd had to be shooed back into the stands, and some of the un-believing Yanks had to be dragged from the showers and put back in their monkey suits. When the game was continued after a twenty minute delay, Jones had lost his stuff, as the Browns flogged him for five additional runs, four scoring on a grand slam homer by Bill Jacobson. Jones, who later was to pitch for the Browns, was so disturbed by this upheaval that he lost his next nine games.

An amusing sidelight of this game was that Willis Johnson, Brown road secretary, was paid a check for $12,079, the largest sum the St. Louis club ever had received for a road game. He wired what he believed was the good news to Phil Ball. Instead of receiving the expected congratulatory phone call or wire, Ball sent him an insulting letter, "never bother me again with such unimportant details as the club's finances."

The Browns led for the last time, September 7, but they were only a few points out of first place when New York came to St. Louis for a vital three-game series later in the month. Thousands of fans stood in line at 10 o'clock in the morning for the first game, scheduled for 3 o'clock that Saturday afternoon. They saw the valiant Shocker lose to Bob Shawkey, 2 to 1, and "Whitey" Witt, Yankee center fielder, carried off the field when a pop bottle split his head. After the incident, Ban Johnson ordered that no more outfield standees be permitted for the remainder of the series.

The second game, played before a large enthusiastic Sunday crowd, saw young Pruett down the famous New Yorkers, 5 to 1. The one Yankee run was a Babe Ruth homer, but this came after Pruett had stopped Ruth seventeen straight times, fifteen on strike-outs.

Every one conceded the pennant hinged on the Monday game with Dixie Davis opposing Joe Bush. The Browns led, 2 to 1, going into the ninth, and even today some older St. Louis fans criticize Lee Fohl's pitching moves on that eventful day. Wallie Schang opened New York's ninth with an infield single that squirted out of Davis' glove. Elmer Smith, a tough left-handed hitter, batted for Ward, and when the first pitch bounded out of Severeid's glove, Schang sprinted to second.

Then came a lengthy conference on the mound between Fohl, Davis, and the Brown infielders. Davis had given up only six hits, only two of which reached the outfield, but he was replaced by Hub Pruett, the previous day's winner. Huggins then pulled back Smith, and sent Mike McNally, a right-handed hitter, to bat. On Mike's bunt, Severeid threw too late to third to get Schang. That unsettled Pruett, who walked Scott on four straight pitches. Fohl then summoned the hardworked ace, Shocker. Urban induced his pitching rival, Bush, to force Schang at the plate, bringing up the little lead-off man, Witt, his head bandaged from the cut of the first game. "Whitey" avenged himself on the bottle-thrower and all St. Louis by singling over Shocker's head into short center, scoring McNally and Scott with the runs that gave New York the key victory, 3 to 2. St. Louis fans were so infuriated at the loss of the game—and as they rightly assumed, the pennant—that they tried to let out their frustrations by shying their leather seat cushions at the big New York press delegation as

198

it was typing and dictating news of the victory back to the nation's metropolis.

Sisler had been out of action with the shoulder injury just before the big series. He played before he was ready, never was the real Sisler, and with a promising rally underway he hit into a double play to end the first game.

The race still had over a week to go, and while the Browns clung on, sweeping their final three-game series with Chicago while the Yanks lost two out of three to Boston in the final days, the Browns still trailed by six points when the final standing was posted.

Following this fine season, Phil Ball double-decked Sportsman's Park, increasing its capacity to 34,000 for a possible 1923 World Series, but when a World Series finally was played there it was the Cardinals against the Yankees in 1926. That was a further vexation for Ball. "This is a hell of a note," he bawled. "They charge me $6.60 to get inside my own ball park."

After the Browns reached the zenith of their affluence, two bad breaks sent them back to mediocrity in 1923. The first was the total incapacity of George Sisler, their star of stars. A sinus malady severely affected his vision and one eye became badly crossed. It took long and patient treatment; George was out for the entire 1923 season and never regained his former keen eyesight. The second was the departure of the capable Bob Quinn to Boston. He left Ball's organization for an ill-fated venture as president and part owner of the Red Sox, using his 1922 St. Louis bonus as part of the purchase money.

Without Sisler, the Browns were just a ball club in 1923, and the near champions of 1922 slumped to fifth place. Shocker was good for another 20-12 season, and Danforth showed considerable ability, winning sixteen and losing fourteen. But Daring Dan was in constant hot water with Ban Johnson and his umpires for allegedly doctoring the ball. After being publicly rebuked by the league, some of the leading Brown players got up a petition defending Danforth. Lee Fohl declined to sign it, and a week later, Fohl, the Quinn man, was out of a job, as Jimmy Austin again served as fill-in manager.

Sisler was ready to resume play in 1924. In addition to trying to play with impaired vision, Sisler also was asked to assume the management of the club. Star playing managers then were all the vogue, Cobb in Detroit, Speaker in Cleveland, Eddie Collins in Chicago, Bucky Harris in Washington, and Hornsby on the rival St. Louis team. It helped absorb the star's high salary by charging part of it to the managerial account. Sisler never was meant to be a playing manager; he wasn't tough, lacked the aggressiveness of a Cobb or Speaker, the drive of a Hornsby, or the boyish enthusiasm of a Harris. Nevertheless, George had two first-division clubs, a fourth in 1924 and a third in 1925 before he wound up his managerial career with a seventh placer in 1926. From the super-star before the eye ailment, Sisler was just another good player, hitting .305, .345, and .289 in his three managerial seasons.

Dan Howley came in 1927. He was a good manager and a shrewd baseball man. During Jack Dunn's heyday in Baltimore, his toughest opposition came from Howley's Toronto Maple Leafs. Dan started in St. Louis with another seventh-place club in 1927, the year the Brownies lost 21 straight to the Yankees before winning the twenty-second, but before long Dan got a pretty good ball club together, finishing third in 1928 and fourth in 1929.

Except for the latter World War II years, when most of the game's top stars were in service, Howley's teams of 1928-29 marked the last time St. Louis was a real power in the American League. Sisler was let go to the Washington Senators, who soon sold him to the Boston Braves, but Howley came up with a flashy first baseman in Lu Blue. Heinie Manush, slugging outfielder, hit .378 in 1928, just a point behind Goose Goslin, the league batting champ. Red Kress was a hard-hitting rangey shortstop until he put on weight. Frank McGowan, later a distinguished Oriole, hit .347. Howley had the two former catching stars, Wallie Schang and Steve O'Neill, and in no time had a formidable pitching staff. In 1928, he had Alvin Crowder (21-5); Sam Gray (20-12); Johnny Ogden, Dunn's old standby (15-16); and George Blaeholder, a good pitcher despite his 10-15 finish. After winning only one game from the Yankees in 1927, a year later the inspired Browns almost fought Huggins' sixth championship team to an even break, losing the year's series, ten to twelve. But the Browns didn't know when they were well off, and Howley allegedly was unhappy over front office interference. At the end of the 1929 season, Dan was quoted as saying he wouldn't be back in 1930, remarking: "I would decline the job if it were offered to me."

When Ball was asked about it, he said curtly, "Well, if Dan has discharged himself, there is nothing else I can do."

The departure of Howley was followed by another dreary twelve-year sojourn in the second division as Bill Killefer, Rogers Hornsby, Jim Bottomley, Gabby Street, and Fred Haney tumbled over each other.

As the Browns waned, the Cardinals, helped by the farm system of Branch Rickey, the old Brown catcher, came more and more to the fore. Where St. Louis had been a red-hot American League town around 1920-1922, the Cardinals now got most of the city's depression baseball business.

Harry Sinclair, Ball's old Federal League associate, once chided Ball, "Phil, how much money did you lose last season?"

"Oh, I guess about $200,000," replied Philip deCatesby.

"You must be crazy," said the oil millionaire. "Why don't you stick to a business you know something about, building cold-storage plants?"

"Harry, how much did you lose last season with those slow-footed apologies for race horses you own?" asked Ball.

"About $300,000," admitted Sinclair.

"Well, you're $100,000 crazier than I am; why don't you stick to the oil business?"

Phil stopped putting money into the Browns after the 1933 season. He died that October, after his club finished deep in the cellar. His last move was to fire Killefer in midseason, and put Hornsby in charge.

Following Ball's death, Phil's estate ran the club for several years. It was under the direction of the executors, Louis B. von Weise, who became Brown president, and included Lew Carle McEvoy and Walter Fritsch. Von Weise had been associated with Ball in business, Fritsch was an old personal friend, and McEvoy was a former Texas oil man. McEvoy now is in charge of the American League's radio and television interests. At a conference with his new bosses on the 1934 training trip, Hornsby told them: "If you gentlemen stick with me, and listen to me, we'll carry this club through to success. We've got to do this in respect to Mr. Ball's memory."

But there was little success. The best Hornsby could do in three full seasons and parts of two others was sixth. The Brown just couldn't do anything right. On September 18, 1934, the colorful Bobo Newsom, now a popular Baltimore sportscaster, pitched no-hit ball for nine innings against the Red Sox only to lose the game in the tenth inning on two walks and a single. The defeated Browns made ten hits.

After the 1936 Browns, directed by McEvoy, attracted an unbelievable low of 80,500 fans, the club changed hands again. It came about largely through the friendship of Margaret Holekamp, then engaged to marry Bill DeWitt, bright young Cardinal treasurer, and Anita Barnes, daughter of Don Barnes, president of the American Investment Co. of Illinois, and other small loan companies. So anxious was von Weise to get the Ball estate out of baseball that he offered $25,000 to any one who would find a purchaser. That interested Branch Rickey and his young protégé, DeWitt. Miss Barnes invited Miss Holekamp and her nice young man to the Barnes country show place in St. Louis County. Naturally Anita's father, Don, wanted to talk baseball with DeWitt. Bill says Don brought it up himself, but the end product of their conversation was Barnes agreeing to head a syndicate to buy the Browns.

At first Barnes had some of St. Louis' wealthiest men associated with him in the venture, but a number of them soon dropped out. The Ball estate retained Sportsman's Park, which it leased to the rival St. Louis clubs. Bill DeWitt shifted over from the Cardinals to the Browns, taking over as general manager.

In Barnes' first year as president, he fired Hornsby, Ball's last manager, on July 21, 1937. Hornsby had purchased a piece of Brown stock, supposedly from horse track winnings.

"I don't like you to be using that kind of money to buy baseball stock," said Barnes, reproachfully.

Forthright but tactless Hornsby shot back, "I didn't ask you the kind of money you used in buying yours." Shortly after that, Jim Bottomley, Hornsby's first baseman on the 1926 Cardinal World's Champions, was named Brown manager.

CHAPTER XIX

Browns Win Lone Flag

THE EARLY PART of the Barnes-Bill DeWitt combination was anything but a joyous one. In 1939, under the management of Fred Haney, the Browns plummeted to the deepest pit of their 52-year career, 43 victories and 111 defeats and a percentage of .279. It inured Fred for some of his later years in Pittsburgh.

Just before Pearl Harbor in December, 1941, Barnes and DeWitt had things all rigged to shift the Browns to Los Angeles. The minor league conventions were held that year in Jacksonville in the first week of December. Practically all of the big league owners attend these minor league get-to-gethers, and the busy Brownies sounded out their associates on the deal. They claimed to have come to an understanding with Phil Wrigley, owner of the Cubs, Los Angeles Angels, and the Los Angeles ball park, whereby the Browns would move to Los Angeles and take over L. A.'s Wrigley Field and Wrigley would move his minor league club to Long Beach, California. Barnes had an air transportation company draw up a tentative American League schedule with Los Angeles as one of the loop's Western clubs, with costs of all flights to the Coast. With American League owners still recalling the Browns' 80,500 attendance of 1936, and subsequent years not too much better, the feeling was all in favor of the shift.

The big leaguers left Jacksonville on Saturday, December 6, for Chicago, where their annual meetings were to start on Monday, December 8. On Sunday, the Japs dropped their

204

bombs on Pearl Harbor and our Pacific fleet. They also blew Barnes' plan for a Los Angeles shift out of the window. By the time the big leaguers convened, the nation was at war, and that was no time for shifting franchises. Don still insists that but for the sneak attack, he would have been in L. A. for the opening of the 1942 season. He says Sam Breadon of the Cardinals would have paid him $250,000 to have St. Louis all to himself.

In midseason of 1941, Fred Haney had gone the way of many Brown managers when Barnes engaged handsome, personable Luke Sewell as his team boss. Luke had been a crack American League catcher in Cleveland, Washington, and Chicago and a successful coach in Cleveland. Sewell immediately improved conditions, for the 1941 Browns won 27 more games than the miserable 1939 outfit and 13 more than the 1940 team.

After the first year of war, things in the Brown camp were pretty black. There really was occasion for singing the "St. Louis Blues." Barnes issued a report to the stockholders stating that the club had used the last dollar of its original $600,000 capitalization. He recommended rigid economy and fired all the team's scouts, even faithful old Jack Fournier. It was necessary to float a loan with the American League. Individual stockholders helped by tossing currency into the empty pot.

Yet, despite the scoutless club, Bill DeWitt assembled a good war team, and Luke Sewell, the new manager, did a splendid job in directing it. Luke wrought some kind of a minor miracle by advancing the 1942 club to third place with a percentage of .536. It was the club's first appearance above the .500 mark since Howley's 1929 team. The Brownies were beset by injuries and bad breaks in 1943, and looked more natural when they finished back in the rut—in seventh place.

By 1944, Uncle Sam had taken a heavy toll on the better American League teams, especially the Yankees, Red Sox, Tigers, and Cleveland. Somehow, the Browns escaped the nation's draft boards better than their rivals. They also had a number of men rejected for military service because of spine and ankle injuries, amputated fingers, etc., such as first baseman George McQuinn, shortstop Vern Stephens, center fielder Mike Kreevich, and pitcher Bob Muncrief. Several others, pitchers Sig Jackucki and Jack Kramer and catcher Frank Mancuso, had been in service but had been discharged for one reason or another. Others, pitcher Denny Galehouse, outfielder Chet Laabs, and third baseman Mark Christman got themselves jobs in defense plants and played baseball in their off moments.

This 1944 Brownie team of 4-F's, rejects, those who were too young and too old, gave some sign of what it had in mind by winning its first nine games; that started the pennant bee buzzing. They never were far from the front and as the Browns reached the home stretch they were in a desperate battle with the Detroit Tigers and what was left of the old powerful Yankees. Sewell really did a magnificent job of managing when all the chips were down, and got the last ounce out of his team. If the spring winning streak gave the Browns their early momentum, they finally snagged their only pennant by winning ten of their last eleven games. Oddly enough, the one game they lost was one they would not have had to play. It was a home contest with the Red Sox, which was twice postponed, and then played on Sewell's insistence on a sodden field on a cold drizzly night. Boston won it, 4 to 1, and it well could have meant the pennant.

Reaching their final four-game series with the Yankees, the Browns trailed the Tigers by a game. St. Louis seemed an awfully long shot, with all the cards stacked against it. Third-place New York still had a mathematical chance for the pennant, whereas Detroit was closing with four games with last place Washington. Practically the only hope for the Browns was to sweep their New York series and pray for a little hope from the Senator tailenders.

The series with McCarthy's team was the brightest hour of the Browns' half-century stay in St. Louis. In a twi-night

206

double-header on Friday, September 29, they swept a double-header, 4-1 and 1-0, as pitchers Kramer and Nelson Potter turned in brilliant efforts. Potter beat Hank Borowy, even though the New Yorker served up a two-hitter. Washington obligingly held Detroit to an even split in its double-header the same day, and the race was all tied up again. It remained that way on Saturday, as both clubs won their games, Galehouse winning a 2-0 shutout for St. Louis.

If both contenders had won their games on the final Sunday, October 1, the league had decreed a post-season pennant play-off in Detroit the following Monday. But, with the valiant help of Emil "Dutch" Leonard, Washington knuckle ball pitcher, no play-off was necessary. On the morning of the game, an anonymous voice, perhaps that of a crackpot, contacted Leonard on the telephone, telling him it would be worth $10,000 to him if he blew the game. Dutch reported the incident to his superiors, tried all the harder, pitched a four-hitter against Dizzy Trout, and with the aid of a homer by Stan Spence won by a 4-1 score.

The greatest crowd in Brown history, 34,625, attended the final battle with the Yankees. It was necessary to close the gates an hour before game time, and police estimated an additional 15,000 persons were turned away. Owing to the difference in time between St. Louis and Detroit, the Browns—and the crowd—knew by the third inning that the Tigers had lost and that a St. Louis victory would mean the pennant. With Sig Jackucki opposing Mel Queen, a good Yankee war pitcher, the Yanks got off to an early 2-0 lead. But that scoreboard brought a lot of inspiration. In the fourth inning, Mike Kreevich singled and Chet Laabs tied the score with a homer into the left field stands. This act made such a hit with the crowd that Kreevich and Laabs dittoed in the fifth, another single by Mike and second homer by Chet making it 4 to 2. And, for an insurance run, Vern Stephens hit a third homer, giving the game to the Browns, 5 to 2. So, after 42 years of trying, and the spending of millions, the Browns won their first pennant with a club that didn't employ a scout.

It was a great victory for both Luke Sewell and Bill DeWitt, who had gathered the team together: Mark Christman, third base; Vern Stephens, shortstop; Don Gutteridge, second base; George McQuinn, first base; Chet Laabs and Al Zarilla, left field; Mike Kreevich, center field; Gene Moore, right field; Red Hayworth and Frank Mancuso, catchers; and Nelson Potter (19-7), Jack Kramer (17-13), Bob Muncrief (13-8), Sig Jackucki (13-9), and Denny Galehouse (9-10), pitchers. George Caster did a grand job in relief.

The Cardinals won their third straight pennant that year with practically no opposition, winning by 15½ games. It enabled the Browns to outdraw their more famous rivals, 508,644 to 486,851. Bill DeWitt got a big bang out of that. It generally was believed that Billy Southworth's Redbirds would easily dispose of Sewell's 4-F's in the all-St. Louis World Series. The Cardinals also had held on to most of their better players, Stan Musial, Marty Marion, Mort and Walker Cooper, Max Lanier, Harry Brecheen, Whitey Kurowski, but the Browns put up a sturdy fight, and with the aid of a break here and there, might have romped off with the big checks.

They actually got an early two game to one jump on the favored Redbirds, before the Cardinals swept the last three games. Though the Browns got only two hits off Mort Cooper in the opener, they won, 2 to 1, behind Denny Galehouse when the American Leaguers bunched a single by Moore with George McQuinn's fourth-inning homer. The Browns had several good opportunities to win the second game for Nels Potter, but finally were stopped by Blix Donnelly's fine relief pitching, losing in the eleventh inning, 3 to 2. Kramer pitched superbly to win the third game, 6 to 2, but then the luck of the Brownies turned, and they dropped the last three games, 5-1, 2-0 and 3-1. McQuinn was outstanding for the Browns, hitting .438, while Southworth's weak-hitting second baseman, Emil Verban, contributed heavily to the Cardinal victory by hitting .412.

208

Don Barnes was entitled to a big assist in Verban's phenomenal hitting. He didn't know Emil was a vengeful Serb. In the third game, in which the Browns were the home club, Mrs. Verban's seats were behind a post. Calling at Barnes' office the next morning, Emil reported to Don, "My wife's tickets are behind a post; is there any way of changing them?"

"Your wife's seats are behind a post! Haw! Haw!" laughed Barnes, who seemed to think the incident quite funny.

From then on, Emil went berserk with his bat. After the final game, in which Verban went "3 for 3," he dashed in front of Barnes' box and yelled, "Now, you sit behind a post, you meathead!"

Barnes didn't wait long to dispose of his American League championship team. On August 10, 1945, as World War II drew to a close, he sold out to Richard Muckerman, the largest minority stockholder, announcing: "Now that the Browns have won their first American League pennant and the company is in a favorable financial position, I feel the purpose for which I entered baseball is accomplished."

Muckerman, who rooted for the Browns in the Sisler era, was a man of means, executive vice-president of the City Ice and Fuel Co. and other enterprises. He started with a lot of enthusiasm, saying: "I never believed in pinching nickels and pennies, and always felt you had to spend one dollar to make two dollars."

The 1945 club, with a one-armed center fielder, Pete Gray, finished third, St. Louis' twelfth and last first-division club in the American League. With the war stars, Ted Williams, Joe DiMaggio, Tommy Henrich, Bob Feller, back in 1946, the magic of the 4-F's ran out. The club slipped quietly back to seventh. They thought Luke Sewell was to blame, bought up his contract in late season, and installed the old catcher, Zack Taylor, as temporary manager.

By 1947, Muckerman really began spending. He purchased Sportsman's Park from the Ball estate for $500,000. The park had been badly run down, with a leaky roof, broken chairs, and club houses that were a disgrace. The amiable Mucker-man gave orders "to fix everything that needed to be fixed." It was expensive fixing; he started to spend a half-million but it ran into $750,000 before he was through. In San Antonio, where the club had a valuable minor league farm, the team became homeless. Muckerman ordered the DeWitts—Bill and his brother, Charley—to handle the situation locally. It was handled by buying property and building a new park, which, with lights, cost another $750,000.

"Muddy" Ruel, former big league catching great, was engaged as manager. Muddy, a gentlemanly, native-born St. Louisan, who was educated in the law, had been working as assistant to Commissioner Happy Chandler. Muckerman told Bill DeWitt to "sign the players without bickering," and to get the best training site available. So the Browns went from a poor man's camp at Anaheim, California, to swank Miami.

Following the lead of Brooklyn's Branch Rickey, who had signed Jackie Robinson, the Browns engaged two Negro players, second baseman Hank Thompson, now playing good ball for the New York Giants, and outfielder Willard Jesse Brown. But, while St. Louis' negroes flocked to Sportsman's Park to see the Dodgers' Jackie, they showed little interest in Thompson and Brown, and the pair soon was released.

The season of 1947 was one of the lush years in baseball. Everybody was drawing the crowds and making money. That is, everybody but the poor Browns, who tumbled back into the cellar and drew a mediocre 320,000. Perhaps, it was the most disappointing tailender in Brown history, as the club still retained many valuable players, and Muckerman and the DeWitt brothers started the season firmly convinced they had a contender.

By the start of the 1948 season, Richard Muckerman was a very disillusioned club owner. He had his fill of not stinting the club; creditors were pressing, and the Browns again needed money. For the time being they found a real angel in Tom

210

Yawkey, multimillionaire owner of the Red Sox. On November 17, 1947, shortstop Vernon Stephens and pitcher Jack Kramer were traded to the Red Sox for $310,000, catchers Roy Partee and Don Palmer, infielder Eddie Pellagrini, outfielder Pete Layden, and pitchers Jim Wilson, Al Widmar, and Joe Ostrowski. The following day, in another big deal, pitcher Ellis Kinder and infielder Billy Hitchcock went to Boston for $65,000, infielders Sam Dente and Bill Sommers, and pitcher Clem Dreisewerd. Stephens, Kramer, and Kinder almost boosted the Red Sox to two pennants; Boston lost to Cleveland in a post-season play-off in 1948 and to the Yankees on the final day of the 1949 season.

Having begun to unload, the Browns really did a thriving business, for in the next year the diligent Bill DeWitt made a succession of deals that startled baseball. It was financial wizardry that outranked the deals made by Jack Dunn and George Weiss in Baltimore. Second baseman Gerald Priddy went to the Detroit Tigers for $125,000; outfielder Al Zarilla to the Red Sox for $125,000; pitcher Sam Zoldak to Cleveland for $100,000; catcher Les Moss to the Red Sox for $75,000; pitcher Fred Sanford to the Yankees for $100,000; third baseman Bob Dillinger and outfielder Paul Lehner to the Athletics for $100,000; pitcher Bob Muncrief and outfielder Walter Judnich to Cleveland for $60,000; pitchers Joe Ostrowski and Tom Ferrick to the Yankees for $60,000; infielder Johnny Berardino to Cleveland for $50,000; outfielder Jeff Heath to the Boston Braves for $25,000; pitcher Stubby Overmire to the Yankees for $30,000; infielder Snuffy Stirnweiss to Cleveland for $35,000. In addition, DeWitt peddled the Browns' run down Class AAA farm in Toledo to the Detroit club for $200,000.

Even though Muddy Ruel had a holdover contract for 1948, he was released at the end of the unhappy 1947 season and the team again was turned over to Zack Taylor. With the numerous cast-offs tossed into DeWitt's deals, the 1948 Browns advanced to sixth place. It induced Gene Kessler,

Chicago Sun-Times sports editor to remark: "Everybody pans Bill DeWitt for wrecking the Browns, but he sells a million dollars' worth of ball players and advances two positions in the standing. That's genius."

By the winter of 1948-49, Dick Muckerman decided he wasn't cut out for baseball. He felt he had enough. There were nibbles for the club from Baltimore, Los Angeles, Milwaukee, and Dallas, but when the club changed hands again, February 2, 1954, it was to the DeWitt brothers, Bill and Charley, both of whom had started their baseball careers as peanut and soda pop venders at Sportsman's Park. Muckerman was so pleased with the way Bill had gotten back much of his money through the sale of players that he thought the DeWitt boys were entitled to first crack. The sale of the Muckerman interests, 156,-226 of the corporation's 275,000 shares, was done almost entirely with notes. Bill DeWitt borrowed $300,000 from the American League as a down payment; the rest was in notes due February 2, 1954. Club stock was put up as collateral.

Bill DeWitt was proud to take his place among the major league club presidents. He and brother Charley, both St. Louisans, did their best to sell themselves and their club to their old home town. Bill launched a ticket selling campaign, organized a "Boost the Browns" club, and even engaged a psychologist to try to find what was wrong with the Browns and to get the players out of their defeatist complex. But, seventh placers in 1949 and 1950 chilled the ardor of the fans and voided the work of the club's tub thumpers. The 1949 Browns drew a poor 270,000 and in 1950 sagged still lower—to 247,131. The DeWitts again saved on all corners, and met pressing obligations by the old device of selling players.

It was a vicious circle: St. Louis fans wouldn't patronize the club because it was down and sold players; unable to get money at the gate, the Browns sold more players to meet notes and expenses; the fans grew more apathetic, and Brown teams became more abject.

212

CHAPTER XX

Bill Veeck Was No Moses

MANY OLD Brown fans, who went back to the 1908 contender, the near champion of 1922 and Dan Howley's fine teams, thought that in Bill Veeck the club had acquired a Moses who would lead the team out of the wilderness of defeats, deficits, and mediocrity. Bill Veeck was bizarre, individualistic, publicity-minded—the Barnum of big league club presidents. After some prolonged negotiations, Veeck gained control of the club on July 5, 1951. Some Brown fans, who later frothed at the very mention of Bill Veeck's name, actually thought the day was the Browns' Independence Day.

A Pacific war casualty, who suffered several leg amputations, Veeck wrote interesting chapters into post-World War II baseball history. Son of the first Bill Veeck, a Chicago baseball writer who became president of the Chicago Cubs, the second Bill Veeck bubbled forth with ideas like Old Faithful of Yellowstone Park spouts out the earth's entrails. Though his promotion schemes were shocking to old baseball conservatives, Veeck had scored sensational successes with the Milwaukee American Association club and later with the Cleveland Indians. He proved a promotional genius with the latter club when the Indians set the American League attendance record of 2,620,627 in 1948, including the loop's greatest crowd for a league game prior to 1954—82,781. In that same year, young Veeck, by a series of shrewd deals, had directed Cleveland to its second pennant and World's Championship two years after he had acquired a depressed 750,000-

213

drawing sixth-place club. Success seemed to follow the man like a tail follows a hound.

Veeck used the profits he made when the Cleveland club was sold in 1949 to take his 1951 flyer in the Browns. With the Browns crashing into the cellar in the spring of that year, the DeWitts decided that their home-town franchise was a very hot potato, too hot for them to handle.

Fred Miller, wealthy Milwaukee brewer, sent word he was interested, and diligent Rodger Pippin was trying to stir up interest in behalf of Baltimore. However, the DeWitts, still loyal to their home town, said that if possible they would sell the club to some one who would keep the team in St. Louis. Veeck, with a very straight face, said he was just that guy. He got an option to buy the club June 21, but announced he wasn't interested unless he could round up most of the club's outstanding stock.

In May, 1951, Mark Steinberg, a Brown-minded St. Louisan, purchased the note which the DeWitts gave Richard Muckerman in 1948, for a reported $500,000. Steinberg allegedly bought the note to make sure the club would remain in St. Louis. On Veeck's assurance that he would operate in St. Louis, Steinberg gave him first chance at the note, which was secured by 56 per cent of Brownie stock. By taking over the old Muckerman interest, buying some 5,000 shares the DeWitts had owned outright, and by picking up additional stock at $7 a share, Veeck had between 80 and 85 percent of the club's stock by July 3. Two days later, Bill Veeck took over Bill DeWitt's presidental chair in the Brownie offices, while DeWitt remained in the organization as vice-president.

Associated with Veeck in the purchase of the Browns were Sidney Salomon, Jr., a St. Louis insurance broker; most of the Chicago backers who had financed Bill's venture in Cleveland; Lester Armour and Phil Swift, packing company officials; Phil Clarke, Newt Frye, and Arthur Allen, bankers and investment brokers; and attorney Sid Schiff.

Almost immediately things began to happen. Yes, Bill had
214

acquired a last-place team, but he promised St. Louis it would be the most interesting tailender in the annals of baseball. Will Harridge, American League president, soon learned that to be strictly true. When the American League celebrated its Golden Anniversary in St. Louis, August 19, 1951, Veeck had a giant birthday cake wheeled to the center of the diamond. Out of the cake popped a Chicago midget, Eddie Gaedel, wearing a Brown uniform, with a number "⅛" sewed on the back.

However, Veeck had thought up an even more dramatic role for 3 foot, 7 inch Gaedel. In the first inning of the second game of a Brown-Tiger double-header, Eddie strode to the plate, with a toothpick bat, and told Umpire Ed Hurley, "I'm batting for Frank Saucier."

"You're batting for who?" asked the skeptical Hurley.

"That's right, I'm batting for Saucier," the midget insisted.

Manager Zack Taylor then strode to the plate and showed Hurley a legitimate Brown contract that Gaedel had signed that day. The umpire rubbed his head and permitted Eddie to bat. As the crowd guffawed with laughter, pitcher "Sugar" Cain of the Tigers pitched four straight balls to little Gaedel as the Detroit catcher, Bob Swift, an old Brownie, vainly tried to hold his mitt in the very limited strike zone. A pinch-runner ran for Gaedel, but the next day Veeck received a stiff telegram from Will Harridge, warning against any repetition of such a farce. But it made the nation's headlines as had no Brown story in years.

But Veeck wasn't through. He had a grandstand managers' night, in which the fans dictated strategy by flashing "Yes" and "No" signs to side line coaches. Connie Mack, the old patriarch of the Athletics, entered into the spirit of the occasion by sitting with the grandstand managers. The Sport Shirt shot off fireworks, provided ice cream and cake for his fans, nylon hose for the ladies, hired crooner Vic Damone, put on a dance after one game and an exhibition basketball game by the Harlem Globetrotters before another. He engaged two of the characters who had been with him in Cleveland, contor-

215

tionist coach Max Patkin, and the venerable Negro pitcher, Satchel Paige. He provided a contour chair, complete with a canopy, for old "Satchmo" in the bull pen. By putting on the pressure, Veeck boosted Brown attendance for 1951 to 293,-790, an increase of 46,659 over 1950. On the playing side, the feature of the 1951 season was pitcher Ned Garver winning 20 games with a tailender that won only 52 contests.

Many St. Louis fans remained suspicious, and felt that Veeck and his associates purchased the club only to shift it to Milwaukee or some other spot at the first favorable opportunity. But Bill insisted he was in St. Louis to stay, and had every intention of building up the Browns as he previously had built up the Cleveland Indians. As proof of his intent to remain in St. Louis, he had an apartment built for himself and the second Mrs. Veeck in Sportsman's Park. His lady made frequent radio appeals to the women fans of St. Louis to rally behind the Browns.

Another supposedly long-term move was the signing of Rogers Hornsby to a three-year managerial contract in 1952. From the first, it was an odd association, as Veeck's father, 1932 Cub president, had fired Hornsby as manager in mid-season of that Chicago pennant-winning year. However, old Rog had been on the comeback trail since Don Barnes let him out in 1937 and had turned in splendid managerial jobs in Beaumont and Seattle. At first Veeck was enthusiastic about Hornsby, and said he was "just the kind of manager to put the Browns back on the baseball map." Veeck even arranged a big deal with the Chicago White Sox so that Hornsby might have his favorite ball player, the controversial Puerto Rican outfielder, Jim Rivera, who had starred for Rog in Seattle. Veeck also signed Marty Marion, the Cardinals' former "Mr. Shortstop," as player-coach, after Fred Saigh had dismissed Marty as Cardinal manager.

The 1952 season started with the Browns moving along in high. For a fortnight or better, they were the sensation of the race. With Hornsby being lauded as a new wonder man, Ameri-

216

can League fans flocked back to the Browns. In the early spring games, they outdrew the Cardinals. Then, the inherent weakness of the club pulled it down. The Browns came down fast and settled in seventh place. As the team cascaded through the standings, the temperaments of the blunt, plain-spoken Hornsby and the exotic Veeck were bound to clash. After Hornsby had fulfilled only three months of his three-year contract, he was fired June 10, when the managerial reins were turned over to Marion. Veeck, and his successors, the 1954 Orioles, were saddled with this contract to the end of the 1954 season.

Veeck said his players were in open revolt against Hornsby's strong-handed, whip-cracking methods. There was no love by the Browns for their brusque, unsympathetic manager, but when a committee of Brown players handed Bill Veeck an "emancipation" loving cup for "freeing them from Hornsby's slavery," there was little doubt in any sports reporter's mind that it was another of Bill Veeck's stunts. The cup presentation was, of course, accompanied by photos and news reel shots, but it backfired on Veeck. The general feeling was that he had a right to fire his manager, even though it was an expensive move for an impoverished club, but that Bill had no right to attempt to humiliate a man who had been one of the game's foremost players.

Despite the Browns' seventh-place finish in 1952, Veeck's stunts and "monkeyshines" were a big factor in practically doubling the 1951 attendance. The Brownie home gate went up to 518,796. With the exception of the Brown pennant winner of 1944, that was the best Brownie home attendance in over two decades. The city thought it was doing "all right" by Veeck, and but for Fred Saigh's exit from the St. Louis picture, the Sport Shirt no doubt would have made another effort to cut in on the Cardinals' attendance in St. Louis. But when Gussie Busch and the Anheuser-Busch Brewery bought the Redbirds, Bill Veeck was ready to take it on the lam.

How Veeck tried vainly to move into Milwaukee, and next to Baltimore, during the 1953 training season, was told in an earlier chapter. Many St. Louisans aver that if Mark Steinberg, the man who sold Veeck the big note, had lived, Bill never would have dared to attempt these moves. With Veeck forced to remain in St. Louis in 1953 against his wishes, there was a paradoxical situation among St. Louis' "last stand" batch of American League fans. They hated Veeck's guts, saying, "that so-and-so will never get another nickel of my money," but they couldn't stay away entirely, hoping against hope that some little patronage might save the franchise for St. Louis. Despite one agonizing stretch, in which the Browns lost twenty successive games before their home fans, their last tailender in St. Louis drew 297,238. Many of them came to boo and belittle Veeck's unfortunate hirelings.

At the start of the season, Bill said he knew he was "dead" as far as operating in St. Louis was concerned. He even went out of his way to make himself unpopular. He snubbed a preseason luncheon of the St. Louis Advertising Club and gave out interviews which had the entire town boiling.

In Cleveland, he gave an interview to Herman Goldstein of the *Cleveland News* in which he said: "That town, St. Louis: They want one of two things. A—They want somebody to run the club and lose a million dollars. Or B—They want you to sell off your good players, finish in last place every year, but they'd still have the club in St. Louis."

Back in St. Louis, Bill said of Goldstein's interview: "Those were exactly correct quotations."

The previous fall, when Veeck still was thinking in terms of St. Louis, he had purchased Bill Hunter of Fort Worth, one of the crack young shortstops of the Brooklyn organization. The sum was given as $90,000, and a trio of fair-to-middlin' ball players, outfielder Ray Coleman, shortstop Stan Rojek, and pitcher Bob Mahoney. Bill was a good rangey shortstop, but hit only .219 in his first big league season. The cash payment Veeck owed the Dodgers was difficult to raise. So, he traded pitcher Virgil Trucks, acquired in a smart deal with the

218

Tigers, and third baseman Bob Elliott to the White Sox for pitcher Lou Kretlow, catcher Darrell Johnson, and a sum said to have been $75,000. That tided Veeck over one period, and the acquisition of Trucks made the White Sox contenders in 1953 and 1954.

Even though it was a final dismal season, it had its spots. One was a chilly drizzly night, May 6, when a sparse crowd of 2,473 came out for a game with the lowly Athletics. By the fourth inning, a feeling of compassion for the faithful 2,473 came over Veeck. He had his publicity man, Bob Fishel, announce that because of the bad night, the game would be on the house and that the fans' rain checks would be good for any later game.

It turned out that the 2,473 fans saw, for free, one of the most unusual pitching feats in baseball: a rookie pitcher, Gary Lee "Bobo" Holloman, pitch a no-hitter in his first start as a major leaguer. Holloman pitched the Browns to a 6-0 victory over the A's. Unfortunately, it was too good to last. It was poor Bobo's only complete game with the Browns, and after a record of three victories and seven defeats, he was shunted to Toronto. By 1954, Bobo, suffering with a lame arm, had difficulty in winning for Class B St. Petersburg.

Then, on June 16, the league's longest 1953 winning streak, 18 straight by the Yankees, clashed with the season's longest losing streak, 14 straight by the Browns, at Yankee Stadium. But, with the American League record only one game away and Casey Stengel talking of possibly passing the old 1916 Giant winning streak of 26, the lowly Brownies topped the proud New Yorkers, 3 to 1, as Vic Wertz slammed two home runs and Duane Pillette, a Yankee cast-off, and old Satchel Paige tamed the Yankee bats.

For a spell, games between the front-running Yankees and bottom-rolling Browns were real warfare. The Browns' pugnacious, spectacled catcher, Clint Courtney, known as "Scrap Iron" and the "Toy Bulldog," had declared a personal vendetta against Casey Stengel and his team ever since the Yankees

219

traded him to St. Louis for pitcher Jim McDonald after the 1951 season. Courtney had figured in earlier outbreaks with the Yankees, including a historic fist fight with Billy Martin at Yankee Stadium in July, 1952. But, even this paled into insignificance compared to the big mob scene at Busch Stadium which followed Courtney's high slide and spiking of little Phil Rizzuto, the Yankees' Scooter, in a tenth-inning play at second base. Both benches erupted on the field and soon players were swinging all over the place. Courtney, the Toy Bulldog, was pretty well mauled by more powerful Yanks, and even Umpire John Stephens suffered a shoulder dislocation while trying to break up the fight.

The brawl enriched the American League treasury by $850, as Will Harridge fined Courtney $250 and Billy Hunter, Brown shortstop, and Billy Martin, Yankee infielder, each $150. Fines of $100 each were slapped on Yankees Allie Reynolds, Joe Collins, and Gil McDougald. Harridge picked out Clint Courtney as the prime culprit, castigating the catcher for "violating all rules of sportsmanship by going extremely high into Rizzuto," and issued a sharp warning to the Toy Bulldog to play saner, if not less aggressive, baseball.

There was a little late season excitement when Veeck unveiled pitcher Bob Turley in the late season. After young Turley won 20 games and lost only 8 for the Browns' San Antonio farm in 1951, Bob put in the next two years in military service. While he won only two games out of eight, he showed a booming fast ball and struck out 61 batters in 60 innings. Anyone with half an eye could tell that he was a real comer. Bill DeWitt picked him up for practically nothing in 1948. The kid with the $100,000 arm signed with the Browns because he wanted to be near his home town, East St. Louis.

The sad season ran its course with the Browns closing at home with a three-game series with the White Sox. At the night game of September 25, a group of fans vented their feelings against Veeck by hanging him in effigy at Busch Stadium, erstwhile Sportsman's Park. A large dummy, wearing a

220

sport shirt, labelled "Bill Wreck" on one side and "Traitor's End" on the other, was suspended from the upper deck of the right field grandstand. Veeck wasn't present, having left for the American League meeting in New York. It was a pathetic St. Louis farewell party for the stunt man who in 1951 was expected to be the Moses who would lead the Browns to the land of milk and honey.

Two days later, 3,174 fans sat in on the "Wake of the Browns" on the final Sunday of the season, September 27, the same Sunday that the American League rejected Bill Veeck's second request for permission to move his Browns to Baltimore. The Browns went down to their one hundredth 1953 defeat losing a 12-inning struggle to the White Sox, 2 to 1. It ended on an especially drab note. When the game ran into overtime, and plate Umpire Art Passarella called for a fresh supply of baseballs, he was advised the supply was exhausted. It looked as though the game might have to be called "on account of lack of baseballs," but Passarella went over the scuffed balls that previously had been thrown out, and picked out the least damaged ones. When outfielder Bill Wilson of the White Sox caught the last ball of the game, it had a gash in it from seam to seam. Thus ended the proud 1902 dream of Ban Johnson when he moved his Milwaukee franchise to St. Louis, then the fourth city in the land, "to add strength and balance to the league."

CHAPTER XXI

A Million Fans See 1954 Oriole Seventh Placer

BALTIMORE took over Bill Veeck's "Rear Guard" team of 1953. At first, the city didn't mind. The proud Chesapeake town was so happy to be back in the big leagues again that such things as the 1953 finish of the Brownies didn't really matter. Anyway, people were saying that the 1954 Orioles weren't nearly as bad as that 1953 Brown record of 54 victories and 100 defeats seemed to indicate. It generally was agreed that disgruntled St. Louis fans depressed the morale of the club, as indicated by those 20 successive defeats at Sportsman's Park before their jeering home fans. Playing in front of Baltimore's appreciative fans, things were expected to be different.

Baltimore fans also had before them the picture of the amazing upswing of the 1953 Milwaukee Brewers. A seventh-place club in Boston in 1952, the Braves zoomed to second place and a contending position in 1953, as all Milwaukee rallied around the team. "It showed what the enthusiasm of a city can do for a team; the players catch some of it," argued many, including some smart baseball men. Anyway, it was felt all around, in Baltimore as well as elsewhere, that the new Birds would fare much better than the 1953 Browns. The club had two promising young pitchers in Bob Turley and Don Larsen, a good young second-base combination in Baltimore's Bob Young and Bill Hunter, and Vic Wertz, Vernon Stephens, and Dick Kryhoski were supposed to supply the new Oriole

222

punch. In one of Bill Veeck's last moves in St. Louis, he regained the services of Stephens, the former Brown shortstop that Bill DeWitt had sold to Boston for a king's ransom, from the Chicago White Sox. But Vern, who drove in 159 runs for the 1949 Red Sox, was now 35 years old and subject to back, knee, and other ailments. Vic Wertz, who had driven in 256 runs for the Tigers in the seasons of 1948 and 1949, was much younger, 29, and was expected to make a strong comeback with the cheers of Baltimore's enthusiastic fans to urge him on.

Following the arrival of Art Ehlers and Jimmy Dykes from the Athletics, the Orioles took on a still more Athletic look. For coaches, Dykes engaged Tom Oliver, one of his coaches in Philadelphia, and Frankie Skaff, who in 1952 and 1953 managed the Athletic farm team in Ottawa. The latter was the same Frank "Deacon" Skaff, who was third baseman on the Oriole's last International League champions, the war team of 1944. Other Athletic acquisitions were publicity man Dick Armstrong, catcher Ray Murray, a $25,000 purchase, and pitchers Joe Coleman and Frank Fanovich.

It led to a good-natured quip in Baltimore that "the Orioles should get less Athletics, and more athletes." As a matter of fact, the acquisition of Coleman was the best deal Ehlers made. Coleman, once good enough to pitch in an All-Star game, had suffered from a sore arm for four seasons, and from 1950 to 1953 had produced only four Athletic victories. Ehlers gave up pitcher Bob "Sugar" Cain for Coleman and Fanovich. Late in the 1953 season, Dykes had observed that Coleman gradually was regaining the old strength in his arm, also his former confidence. Joe developed into Baltimore's most consistent 1954 pitcher. Cain, on the other hand, flopped badly in Philadelphia and was released in the early season. He later caught on with his first major league team, the Chicago White Sox.

Unfortunately all of Ehlers' pre-season deals were not so successful. Taking over a tailend team, Art felt it was necessary to change faces. Two outfielders he took over from the

Browns, Roy Sievers and Johnny Groth, were swapped away. Sievers, 1949 American League rookie of the year, who had experienced throwing difficulty after a shoulder separation, was traded for outfielder Gil Coan, who had had an erratic career in the neighboring capital city. Groth and shortstop Lipon went to the White Sox for outfielder Sam Mele and Neil Berry, a second string infielder. "Groth is a better fielder," admitted Ehlers, "but I think Mele will give us more of what we need—a fellow who can hit a long ball."

Both Coan and Mele disappointed, and the latter was sold to the Red Sox in July. He did pretty well there and belted 12 home runs. As for Groth, he played regularly on the White Sox contending team, and Sievers set a new home run record for a Washington player with 24 home runs. Sievers also drove in 102 runs, far ahead of any 1954 Oriole.

In his efforts to strengthen the club, Ehlers also purchased Eddie Waitkus, the first baseman who was shot by a mad young woman in 1949, from the Phillies. Eddie immediately was pressed into service, as the former Brown first baseman, Kryhoski, suffered a severe wrist injury on the 1954 training jaunt. Art also reached into the National League for two pitchers, southpaw Dave Koslo of the Giants and Vern Bickford of Milwaukee. Bickford cost $10,000 and Charley White, a promising young catcher on the San Antonio farm, who became Milwaukee's second string catcher. Harry Brecheen, the crafty old Cardinal southpaw ace, came with the Browns as a pitching coach.

Before the 1954 training season, Ehlers showed a preference for a Florida training site, with a liking for Fort Lauderdale, but Bill Veeck had made commitments with Yuma, Arizona, and the new Orioles conditioned for the 1954 pennant grind in the cactus country. Furthermore, nothing in Yuma was too good for them. If they had been Casey Stengel's 1953 World's Champions, Yuma couldn't have done more. And the early news from Yuma was good—very good. The Orioles won their first five exhibition games with major league

224

teams, in which they scored 46 runs. Baltimore was impressed by the scores: Orioles, 13; Cubs, 5. Orioles, 8; Cubs, 6. Orioles, 13; Giants, 8. Orioles, 10; Giants, 9. Orioles, 2; Cleveland, 1. People in Baltimore were talking of "Oriole power." The Birds tapered off somewhat after that, but they had the best training record of any major league club, eighteen victories against twelve defeats. The Orioles won the mythical Grape Fruit League title and in midseason, 1954, a Yuma delegation visited Memorial Stadium to present the Birds with the Cactus Cup, symbolic of their spring Arizona championship over the Cleveland Indians and New York Giants, the two clubs that met in the 1954 World Series. The Birds' ended their 1954 exhibition season with a 5 to 3 victory over their former St. Louis neighbors, the Cardinals, in Busch Stadium before 15,710 St. Louisans, who saw Bob Turley strike out six and Joe Coleman five.

Playing their first American League game in 52 years, the new Orioles opened their 1954 season in Detroit, April 13, before 46,994 fans, who saw Don Larsen lose a well-pitched 3-0 game to Steve Gromek. But the very next day, Duane Pillette pitched the Orioles back to the .500 mark with a 3 to 2 victory over the Tigers. That was most encouraging for Oriole fans and whetted Baltimore's appetite for the city's greatest baseball day, April 15, when the new Orioles were welcomed royally back to Baltimore.

No conquering heroes could have been lauded, and cheered, more than the city's new big league representatives. People forgot, or no one cared to remember, the players were the 1953 St. Louis tailenders. The slogan of the day was: "Let's back up them Birds." The welcome mat was out for "them Birds" in the form of a carpet of flowers. From the crack of dawn to sunset, April 15 was a memorable, never-to-be-forgotten date in baseball annals. The day's game with the Chicago White Sox was preceded by a mammoth baseball parade, unquestionably the biggest athletic parade ever held in the State of Maryland. It was a spectacle of Mardi Gras proportions with twenty-five bands and thirty-two floats depicting the past and present history of Baltimore baseball. In one of the floats were ten uniformed figures, depicting the ten Orioles who were elected to the Hall of Fame—Cummings, McGraw, Robinson, Keeler, Jennings, Brouthers, McGinnity, Bresnahan, Ruth, and Grove. Another float showed downtrodden Yankee players in their dugout as a big scoreboard showed the Orioles routing New York, 10 to 0. Hundreds of Baltimore's prettiest girls, made up as orioles and baseballs, marched with mustached gladiators, representing the glorious Orioles of Ned Hanlon.

Despite ominous clouds, and occasional spatters of rain, the enthusiasm of the crowd was undampened. Baltimore's schools were closed for the day and city employes granted a half-day. Many business places closed, or did functional business, as over a half-million persons lined the three and a half mile parade route. It took the parade an hour and a half to pass any point. The parade, starting at 10:30 A.M., proceeded south on Charles Street to Madison Street, west on Madison to Howard, south on Howard to Baltimore, east on Baltimore to appropriately named Holliday Street, where it disbanded in front of City Hall Plaza. Unfortunately, Mayor D'Alesandro was too ill to be present at the welcoming home parade or the afternoon's ball game.

Streamers, "Good luck Orioles," "Welcome home Orioles," and other greetings were proudly displayed in the parade streets. Orange and black Oriole pennants and balloons were everywhere in evidence. Vice-President Richard Nixon came from Washington to ride in the parade and later to throw out the first ball. American League president Will Harridge rode in the parade, as did Ban Johnson fifty-three years before when he helped usher in McGraw's Baltimore American League season of 1901. Two of the managers of that early period, Connie Mack, grand old patriarch of Philadelphia, and Clark Griffith, Washington club owner and 1901 Chicago

226

White Sox manager, were accorded thunderous ovations, as were the two living members of Hanlon's champion Orioles, Jack Doyle, veteran Cub scout, and Bill "Boileryard" Clarke, Uncle Robbie's catching assistant of the nineties.

But the loudest cheers were for the new Orioles. Manager Jimmy Dykes, in uniform and waving greetings, and smiling general manager Art Ehlers, led this section of the parade. Then came the players, riding two or three to the car, in top-down convertibles. The players, who a year before frequently had been booed and derided in St. Louis, were in for a new experience. They were bombarded with miniature orchids, supplied by the parade committee, and showered with confetti. The players, in turn, threw plastic baseballs back to their cheering admirers. There even was a Negro Oriole among the heroes, pitcher Jehosie Heard. The parade made the nation's newsreels, *Life* magazine, the *New York Times* Sunday magazine section, and other national periodicals.

Workers at Memorial Stadium still were fastening down seats and attending to last minute chores on the morning of the game. The contractors had been handicapped by various delays, but they had the Stadium ready to take care of 48,000 fans, of which 46,354 were clocked as official attendance. In the enthusiastic crowd was Mrs. John J. McGraw, widow of the man who led the Orioles of 1901 and 1902. With Baltimore's opening-day crowd in Detroit two days before, it gave the new Birds the proud distinction of playing to the best combined home and road opening attendances of any of the sixteen major league clubs, 93,348.

What's more, the big day ended on a high note. With young Bob Turley pitching an effective seven-hitter and striking out nine, and Vern Stephens and Clint Courtney banging out homers, the club licked Virgil Trucks and Paul Richards' Go-go White Sox, 3 to 1. Waitkus whacked out three hits. In the ninth inning, Turley had a sudden streak of wildness, walking Carrasquel and Fox, but Bob induced Bob Boyd to hit weakly to the box for the final out. The cheers which

227

greeted Turley shook the new Stadium to the foundations of its newly poured concrete. Baltimore was immensely pleased. Not only did the city again have big league ball, but it felt it had a real team.

The Saturday game of April 17 saw Joe Coleman go down before Ned Garver of the Tigers in a tight 1-0 pitching duel, and 20,057 Easter Sunday fans had a rough afternoon as the Tigers batted out Larsen to win, 8 to 3. There was a two-day lull in the schedule, and on the 21st Baltimore suffered a real heartbreaker when Bob Turley blew both a no-hitter and the ball game with one out in the ninth. It was Baltimore's first major league night game, and a 43,383 crowd sat entranced as Turley set down the Indians inning after inning. For an opponent, Bob caught the Indian ace, Bob Lemon, but Turley went into the ninth inning, leading by 1 to 0.

The East St. Louis boy struck out pinch-hitter Dave Pope, first batsman in the ninth, for his fourteenth strike-out and twenty-fifth putout of the game. The great crowd hung on each pitch with a hush of expectancy as Al Rosen, 1953 most valuable American League player, strode to the plate. The no-hitter crashed when Al rifled the second pitch between third base and shortstop for Cleveland's first hit, bringing up Larry Doby, who twice had fanned. The Negro slugger lifted a ball to right field that at first looked like just an ordinary fly that could easily be handled by Vic Wertz. But the spring wind got hold of the ball and eventually carried it into the right field stands, 360 feet away, for a home run. It cost the brilliant young Turley the ball game, 2 to 1.

The next afternoon, Pillette avenged the defeat when he set back the Indians, 4 to 1. Alas, it was to be only one of three victories Baltimore was destined to score against the 1954 Cleveland champions all year. The first five games at Memorial Stadium drew 130,528, and president Miles and Baltimore sports writers began to figure on the possibility of the Orioles passing the 1,826,397 with which Milwaukee greeted the new 1953 Braves.

228

The Orioles were showing a conspicuous lack of punch, especially in the home-run department, but they still were winning their share of games on May 16, when 46,798 packed the Stadium for a Sunday double header with the Yankees. And they again thrilled at a near Oriole no-hitter. After Dave Koslo lost the opener to Allie Reynolds, 2 to 0, Larsen won the second game handily from Bob Kuzava, 6 to 2. Don had his no-hitter until two were out in the eighth, and lost his shutout when Cerv hit a two-run pinch homer in the ninth. Baltimore early adopted a "Hate New York" campaign, partly the result of the earlier Yankee votes to keep Baltimore out of the American League. The feeling was intensified when a 2,000 Baltimore crowd invaded Yankee Stadium, and the New York management compelled them to keep their placards and cowbells outside the big Bronx arena.

In the early season, enthusiastic Baltimoreans followed their team to New York, Washington, and Philadelphia. But some of the enthusiasm curdled when the club went on a ten-game losing streak from May 21 to 29, inclusive. This soon was followed by another nine-game string of defeats, between June 13 and 22. On the 22nd, young Turley held the Red Sox to one run for eleven innings, but lost in the twelfth, 3 to 1. Despite this run of reverses, a crowd of 24,843 saw the streak broken, June 23, as the Birds batted out an 8 to 7 victory against Boston. As defeats piled up, Dykes continued to get reasonably good pitching from Coleman, Turley, Pillette, and Larsen, but the offense became more and more futile. Those opening game home runs by Stephens and Courtney proved a snare and delusion. It soon became evident the Baltimore stands were out of the reach of ordinary hitters, and there were no Babe Ruths or Jimmie Foxxes on the new Orioles.

President Miles, Art Ehlers, and Jimmy Dykes didn't rest on their armpits. They made changes, tried to do anything that might help. Jim Brideweser, an infielder long in the Yankee chain, was purchased from New York. In an inter-league deal, outfielder Cal Abrams was obtained from Pittsburgh for

229

pitcher Dick Littlefield. Cal developed into a fine lead-off man, and Baltimore's most consistent hitter. Pitchers Bickford and Koslo, the two National League pick-ups, were released; Coan, Mele, and Hunter were temporarily benched; outfielder Don Lenhardt was sold to Boston and outfielder Jim Fridley recalled from Richmond.

The club made a good deal with Cleveland in getting veteran outfielder-third baseman Bob Kennedy for outfielder Jim Dyck. Not so good was Ehler's other transaction with Cleveland's Hank Greenberg—Vic Wertz for the Indian pitching second-stringer, Bob Chakales. Despite Vic's former extra-base power in Detroit, and to a lesser degree in St. Louis, his extra-base hits in Baltimore were practically nill. Wertz was hitting a puny .202 when traded, as Ehlers remarked: "I got so tired of seeing him hit those long caught flys to the outfield, I couldn't stand it any longer." However, the deal looked bad to Oriole fans, when Manager Lopez put Wertz on first base, and with Vic batting in one of the clean-up batting spots, the Indians went on to smash the Yankees' pennant trust. Wertz eventually brought his batting average up to .256, hit 15 homers, and drove in 62 runs. Vic then "busted out" with a .500 average in the 1954 World Series.

To make matters worse, Bob Turley lost all sense of direction around midseason. He was as fast as ever, but just couldn't find the plate. It was around the time of the All-Star game, when Bob was the only Oriole representative to Stengel's American League All-Stars. The kid, who looked like a Bob Feller in the spring, had the questionable distinction of being the only one of Stengel's eight pitchers who was not called into service in the American League's 9 to 7 victory in Cleveland.

In July came another dreary stretch in which the Orioles dropped fourteen out of sixteen games. Many Oriole fans had become most critical of Dykes. On the night of July 20, some 500 fans journeyed over to Washington and chanted, "Down

230

with Dykes," as the Orioles were being soundly drubbed, 7 to 1.

It was around this same time that reports of dissension, petty bickering, and clannishness came out of the Oriole camp. It was said to be hurting the team's performance. On July 18, at the request of some of the players, Bobby Young, the Orioles' player representative, held a meeting of the players in Boston from which Manager Dykes and Coaches Oliver and Skaff were excluded.

"Some of the boys came to me as player representative and said they'd like a meeting without Dykes and the coaches," said Young. "Dykes graciously consented, and we all agreed we were losing because we were playing poorly and that we'd have to try just a bit harder. The idea of the boys was that Manager Dykes was doing everything in his power to help us win and that it was our fault we were losing. I believe we came out of the meeting better men than when we went in and closer than ever. But, let me emphasize there never was any dissension among the players."

Billy Hunter, the shortstop, was even more emphatic, saying: "I never played on a team, winner or loser, where the guys were pulling harder for each other. The idea of a meeting was the players' idea of how we could help the team. There was no bickering or bitterness; everything was harmonious."

On May 29, Dykes had left his old third-base coaching box, turning the coaching duties over to Tom Oliver and Frank Skaff, remarking, "I think I can benefit the club more by sitting on the bench and observing things." But many Baltimore fans got the idea Jimmy was ducking the barbs of the fans in the comparative security of the bench.

One of the most dramatic moments of the season then came when Jimmy returned to coaching duty in a homecoming game, July 27, after the Birds had compiled a miserable road record of three victories and nineteen defeats. Despite this wretched showing, a crowd of 13,787 was on hand to "welcome home" the spring heroes. With no advance notice,

231

Dykes came loping out of his dugout as the Orioles went to bat in the first inning and took his former place in the third-base coacher's box. At first there was an awkward silence, and then the fans arose in their seats to cheer the chunky little pilot to an echo. Many who had taken part in earlier cat-calls joined in the cheers as Dykes received the best ovation of the season. "I'll never forget that applause," said Jimmy, after the game. "Frankly, I didn't expect it. But it was a warming experience, one of my greatest thrills in baseball." With Dykes directing traffic at third base, the Orioles batted out a 7 to 5 victory over Washington, and the next day the board of directors, at its monthly meeting, gave a vote of confidence to Dykes and Ehlers, as president Miles announced "there will be no change in the management."

The club went a little better for a spell and on July 30, the legend on a float in the April 15 welcome home parade, a 10 to 0 victory over the Yankees, happily came true. A crowd of 27,385 gloated as the Birds spoiled Casey Stengel's sixty-fourth birthday and snapped Allie Reynolds' ten-game winning streak. Larsen pitched the 10-0 shutout; he remained effective against New York, even if he could beat no one else.

Early in August, Ehlers purchased left-handed pitcher Bob Kuzava, a former Yankee World Series hero, from George Weiss. Bob had been with the International Orioles in 1947 and 1948 when the Cleveland Indians had a working agreement with young Jack Dunn. The club drifted along, winning a game here and there and bobbing in and out of seventh and eighth places with the lowly Athletics. Then came a barren stretch in which the Birds really descended to the depths, a fourteen straight losing streak, to match the longest losing streak of the 1953 Browns. It started in Chicago, August 11, when Bob Kuzava lost a 1 to 0 decision to Virgil Trucks. Seven of the defeats were suffered at home to the two Western contenders, four to the White Sox and three to Cleveland. Perhaps the cruelest defeat of the streak come in Cleveland, August 14, when the home-runless Birds erupted for three

232

homers in one inning, and still couldn't win. The unlucky Larsen battled Early Wynn of the Indians to a scoreless tie for seven innings, when in the eighth Cal Abrams hit his first homer of the season over the right field fence. It gave Bobbie Young an idea; he followed with his third 1954 four-bagger and Vern Stephens got into the act by hitting his seventh. And all for naught! In the Cleveland half, Bobbie Avilla cancelled the three Baltimore blows with one three-run homer of his own, and Cleveland won in the eleventh, 4 to 3, when Naragon, second string catcher, hit Bob Chakales for a two-out run-producing single.

Bob Turley, who under the tutelage of the old Cardinal Cat, Harry Brecheen, gradually had regained his earlier effectiveness, eventually stopped this long losing streak in Boston, August 26, with a 5 to 3 win over Boston. But the long string of defeats, plus the earlier reverses, brought dismay, disappointment, and dissatisfaction to some of the wealthy men who backed the club. Some of the trades rankled. The directors knew the Orioles had inherited a tailender, but they weren't satisfied with the progress made to improve it. The club was sure of drawing 1,000,000 fans, but early estimates of an 1,800,000 attendance several times had to be revised downward.

On the very day that the streak was broken in Baltimore, August 26, president Miles called the Baltimore writers to his hotel suite in Boston. He didn't mince words, saying there would be "drastic changes made in the Oriole organization for 1955, changes that may produce a contending club." Pressed on whether the changes would include general manager Art Ehlers and team manager Jimmy Dykes, Miles replied: "Draw your own conclusions, but the changes could include anybody. Furthermore, no one with the club has a contract for more than a year, so that 'anybody' still goes."

"We must fulfill our obligation to the loyal fans who have supported us," the Oriole prexy added. "We still owe the

233

NBC of St. Louis $1,000,000 in full payment for the franchise, but we have no worry about meeting it, and we have ample funds to open and operate next season."

The statement was bitter medicine for Dykes and Ehlers, the men who took the plaudits of Baltimore fans in the big opening day parade only four and a half months before. Dykes didn't mask his anger at stories that both he and Ehlers would be relieved of their posts. "Let's get it over with," he exploded. "If there are going to be wholesale changes in the direction of the club, including the manager, I want to know about it now. This is like waiting in the deathhouse for somebody to pull the switch."

"The guy I really feel sorry for is Ehlers. He's down in Texas scouting for players and he's got to read all of this in the papers down there, just as I had to read about what's going to happen to me in the Boston papers. Art worked hard to improve the club, giving it his all. This is a fine thank-you."

In Baltimore, there even were reports that Clarence Miles would go in the big impending shake-up. However, the lawyer-president received a vote of confidence in a three-hour meeting of the Oriole board of directors, September 1, when it issued a statement: "The board has unanimously reaffirmed its complete confidence in the administration of Clarence Miles as president of the Orioles, who recently was re-elected to serve until the end of 1956." Significant in the statement was that it made no mention of Ehlers and Dykes.

The board also squashed all rumors that it was ready to sell to another Baltimore group, saying: "No consideration has been given at any time to a change of ownership." However, while Miles' administration was upheld, several directors stood up in the meeting and not only demanded full voice in the future direction of the club but insisted on being advised of all steps as they came up.

Soon reports came out of Chicago that Paul Richards, the magnetic livewire of the White Sox, would come to Baltimore.

Frank Lane, Chicago's general manager, admitted Miles had made overtures to Richards and that he contemplated filing tampering charges against Baltimore but withheld action when he learned Miles' offer was for Paul to serve as Oriole general manager.

The full story burst on September 14, when Richards formally retired as manger of the White Sox "to run the whole show" in Baltimore, general manager as well as field manager, though Miles announced, "Richards will be relieved of the administrative functions usually undertaken by a general manager in order that his entire time, energy and talents may be concentrated on the task of rebuilding the Orioles and directing the team on the field." Oddly enough, Richards' Chicago managerial successor, was Marty Marion, the manager the Orioles inherited from the 1953 Browns and who was paid for not managing the Birds in 1954.

Richards' contract was for three years at a reported $45,000 per season, though his contract had a bonus attachment based on a nickel per admission on all attendance over 800,000. But the Texas scrapper said that the financial gain over his Chicago contract was not a prime factor. "Not many times does a man have a chance such as this," he said. "I simply could not allow it to pass."

It generally was admitted that Miles and the Orioles had made a ten-strike in engaging Richards. At the age of forty-six, Paul is one of the most forceful, magnetic personalities in the game and a managerial natural. As a catcher he played in the major leagues with Brooklyn, the Giants, Athletics, and Tigers, and his smart handling of Hal Newhouser and Dizzy Trout was a big factor in Detroit's pennant and World's Championship in 1945. However, even before Richards made a playing comeback with the Tigers during the war, he already had managed brilliantly in Atlanta, where Earl Mann, Atlanta owner, still regards him as the greatest of all Cracker managers. The White Sox had a long succession of second division clubs before the fiery Richards was hired in 1951. He lifted the club to fourth place that season and then finished third in each of the next three seasons. Gradually he and Frank Lane had built the White Sox into a formidable contender, and Chicago fans were loathe to see the "Go-go" man go.

The future of Ehlers and Dykes was left up to the new general manager-manager. Richards immediately announced that there was a place in the organization for Ehlers, to serve as his assistant with especial stress on the Orioles' farm club organization. Paul felt that was Art's strong suit. Dykes was invited to stay in the Orioles' scouting department but declined. Richards brought his Chicago coach, Luman Harris, to Baltimore, hired another former minor league associate, Al Vincent, and announced Brecheen's retention as pitching coach. Paul termed the rebuilding of the Orioles a "tremendous job," and said he would rip the Orioles apart from top to bottom. He was willing to trade any one but young Bob Turley, whom he termed the pitcher with the greatest possibilities in major league baseball. He had a $250,000 fund available for new players.

The Birds apparently thrived on all of the early September talk of unrest and the Orioles' subsequent new deal. While some of the players felt the new deal had been a tough deal for Dykes, they acted more relaxed and September was the team's best month. By winning eleven games and losing ten, they finally drew away from the lowly Athletics and finished in seventh place, a gain of one position. Oddly enough, the Orioles hit the record of the 1953 Browns right on the nose, 54 victories and 100 defeats. But, where Marion's St. Louis tailenders were 46½ games off the pace, the 1954 Baltimore seventh-place team trailed the champion Indians by 57 games.

The high spot of the Orioles' September campaign was a one-hitter hurled by Joe Coleman over the fading Yankees at Memorial Stadium, September 8. The lone New York hit, made by the veteran, Country Slaughter, in the eighth inning was a gift from the gods. Enos' grounder rolled straight at second baseman Bobby Young, when at the last moment it

236

took a sudden high hop and went over Young's outstretched gloved hand for a single. Coleman nosed out the New York youngster, Tom Morgan, 1 to 0, as Clint Courtney, a refugee from the Yankee farm system, knocked in the game's only run. The victory was especially palatable to Baltimore fans, as it came at a time when New York still was in the thick of the pennant battle. Another pleasant occasion was a night for Jimmy Dykes, September 15. While Baltimore knew the personable Philadelphian wouldn't be back as skipper, it tried to show its appreciation for a game guy who had done his best with the material handed him.

While Ehlers still was in charge, he called up three players from the Orioles' San Antonio farm, outfielder Joe Durham, first baseman Frank Kellert, and pitcher Rinold Duren. Both Durham and Kellert were employed in the September campaign, and Durham, a sturdy Negro playing his second year in pro baseball, showed much promise. A September casualty was Eddie Weidner, Oriole trainer for 32 years, who suffered a fractured skull in a locker room scuffle with a janitor.

If the 1954 Orioles had their ups and downs, the business office experienced some remarkable schedule breaks. Not a single game at Memorial Stadium was rained out or postponed. The club went over the million mark on September 14, the very day announcement was made that Paul Richards would be the Birds' new all-around boss. A crowd of 13,045 that night saw the redoubtable Coleman set back the Red Sox, 3 to 1, and boost the attendance to 1,004,750. It eventually closed at 1,060,910 for 67 dates, not as much as was expected when the Brown franchise changed hands but a remarkable showing for a team with a .351 percentage.

The final averages, especially in the scoring, home run, and runs-batted-in departments, showed why the Orioles lost so many close games and vexed some of their wealthy directors. Their punch was so futile. While the Birds finished sixth in club batting, ahead of Washington and the Athletics, they scored the least runs of any of the sixteen major league clubs, a poor 483. The club also was far down in homers with 51 against 81 for Washington, the next lowest club. Cal Abrams was the club's No. 1 hitter, with .293, but top man in runs batted in was Vern Stephens with a bare 46. Vern also led in Oriole homers with eight, though a bad back, twisted ankle, and other ailments limited his play to 101 games. No wonder Dykes yipped at one stage of the race, "I've got half a dozen lead-off men, but nobody to drive in runs for me."

The pitching staff fared much better in the statistics, and young Turley led both leagues in strike-outs with 185 and bases on balls with 181. His record was 14 and 15, against Coleman's 13 and 17. Pillette had a satisfactory 10-14 season. Lou Kretlow was effective in spots and closed with 6-11, .353, practically the same as the Orioles .351 finishing percentage. The real green pea of the staff was Don Larsen, with a record of only three victories against an incredible twenty-one defeats. A year before as a Brown freshman, he had a 7-12 record with the 1953 St. Louis tailenders. The twenty-one defeats enabled Larsen to tie Joe McGinnity of the 1901 Orioles for most Baltimore American League defeats, but alas the hard-working iron man bracketed twenty-six victories for McGraw that year. In justice to Don, it must be said he didn't pitch badly, but except when working against the Yankees he had abominable luck.

As the 1954 season closed on its .351 note and the Orioles were looking forward to the 1955 campaign, every one in the organization realized the need of enticing some power hitters into Baltimore uniforms. That was first in the minds of president Miles, the directors, and the new general manager, Richards. Everything else was secondary. Richards expressed his willingness to make any sacrifice in players and cash to obtain at least one player with a real sock. Before Art Ehlers relinquished the post of general manager, he already had plans for increased home run production in 1955, a wire fence stretched across center field, from bleacher to

238

bleacher, something on the line of the set-up in Cleveland's big stadium.

If the season of 1954 brought its disappointments and a re-shuffle of the Oriole deck, the club felt it had learned from past mistakes. While Baltimore directors, and fans, now realized fully that pennant winners are not constructed over-night, there still was the fine object lesson of the new Milwaukee club of the National League. Young pitchers, without the in-herent ability of a Turley, a few youngsters who came through, and a veteran added here and there, made the seventh place Boston Braves of 1952 a strong contender in the next two seasons.

CHAPTER XXII

The Million Dollar Deal

AFTER Paul Richards took full charge of the Birds following the 1954 World Series, he introduced a new Oriole theme song, "There'll be some changes made." "No one stands pat on a club that has lost 200 ball games in two years," he insisted. Yet, few Oriole fans or sports writers suspected the scope of the changes that the firm-jawed man from Waxahachie would bring about before the start of the 1955 training season.

Before Paul started on his wholesale swapping, president Clarence Miles gave a most glowing financial report for the 1954 season—a tidy profit of $942,153.29, after taxes. That was made possible by a real Santa Claus tax break, a $600,000 loss sustained by the company in its former operation of the Browns in St. Louis. Actually, Bill Veeck's losses for the seasons of 1952-53 were $707,000. With nearly a million in the till as 1954 profit, there were reports of big cash expenditures for new talent. But, the days for acquiring Ruths, Groves and Earnshaws by rolling out fat wads of folding money belong pretty well to the past.

When Richards felt it necessary to refurbish the Birds from top to bottom, he went into the game's trading marts, major and minor. Paul started with some smaller deals, trading the Orioles' Negro pitcher, Jehosie Heard, to the Portland Pacific Coast League club for right-handed pitcher Robert S. Alexander, who had a 10-12 record with the 1954 Beaver tailenders. Vinc Garcia, 1954 Mexican utility infielder, went to the Dodgers for Pitcher Ray Moore, a Brooklyn Bum in 1952 and 1953 and a Dodger farm-hand in St. Paul in 1954. Charley

240

Maxwell, an outfielder, was picked up from the Red Sox, closing the Mele deal Art Ehlers made with that club the preceding summer. Freddy Hofmann came back from a scouting trip to Germany, where he signed two service infield standouts, John Robert Davies and Jesse Jones, the latter a Negro. Both boys, with stratospheric Army batting averages, were sent to Oriole farms.

Then, while the 1954 football season still was on, Richards, the Waxahachie swapper, and Yankee George Weiss, the ex-general manager of Mrs. Dunn's International Orioles, pulled one of the biggest deals ever made on the big league chess board. They termed it "the million dollar deal," and as the huge swap involved eighteen players before it was finished, the million dollar price tag was no exaggeration.

It can't be said that the deal aroused many hosannas around Charles, St. Paul and Light streets and Maryland Avenue after enterprising Joe Reichler of the A.P. first broke the story in one of the biggest sports beats in years. For some twenty-four hours after the deal officially was announced on November 18, Oriole fans booed so loudly you could hear them as far as Washington. At first Baltimore sports columnists Paul Menton, Rodger Pippin and Jesse Linthicum were inclined to join in the Bronx cheers. But, after the loyal writers and fans took more time to digest the big deal, they concluded Richards was nobody's fool. His first business was to raise the Birds in the standing, and he had to give to get. In the first deal with the Yankees, and a secondary big trade with Chicago, he sacrificed three of Baltimore's most valuable chattels, pitcher Bob Turley, shortstop Billy Hunter and catcher Clint Courtney, for a raft of lesser players. It was a trade of quality for quantity, but quantity which Richards confidentially hoped would lift him into the first division in 1955.

In the first phase of the big deal with New York, the Orioles gave up pitchers Bob Turley and Don Larsen and shortstop Billy Hunter for pitchers Harry Byrd and Jim McDonald, outfielder Gene Woodling, Cuban shortstop Willie Miranda, and two highly touted catchers out on option by the Yanks, Gus Triandos and Hal Smith. Triandos also had played first base, and Richards considered him in that capacity. Smith was the American Association batting champion at Columbus, Ohio with an average of .350; the catcher and Gene Woodling were the players Richards particularly was after. It also was reported in New York that the Orioles received $200,000, but this was denied by both clubs, who insisted it was an all player deal.

In the second phase of the deal, involving mostly secondary players, the Birds received infielder Kal Segrist of Kansas City, who had several Yankee trials; another promising Yankee infield farm-hand, Don Leppert, who played in 1954 with Birmingham; and Pitcher Bill Miller, once considered one of the best rookies in the Yankee organization. Baltimore gave up six men, first baseman Dick Kryhoski, who broke into the majors as a Yankee in 1947; pitcher Mike Blyzka; outfielder Jim Fridley; catcher Darrell Johnson, a Richmond farm-hand; center fielder Ted Del Guericio, a .321 hitter obtained from Wichita; and a sixth player not named when the deal was closed. Most of these switched Orioles were destined for Yankee farm clubs, particularly the Yankees' new Denver affiliate.

Baltimore's resentment against the deal was largely on the trading of Bob Turley, and to a lesser degree of shortstop Billy Hunter. In their first reaction, the fans termed the deal crazy, rotten, a steal and a stinker. "It's like trading skilled mechanics for laborers," said one annoyed rooter. Newspapers polling the fan reaction found it to be ten to one against the deal. In Baltimore's impotent 1954 season, Turley had become the darling of the city's fans. The strike-out leader of both major leagues, Turley was credited with having the fastest ball since Bob Feller was in his prime. During the 1954 season, Bob had won an automobile, $1,000 in cash, and other gifts in popular player awards. After the deal, one disgruntled Baltimore fan wrote on Bob's car, "Damn Yankee."

Larsen was less successful than Turley—and also extremely unlucky—but every one admitted he had much natural ability

242

and always was at his best against New York. Baltimore fans also had become quite fond of Billy Hunter, a hustling youngster raised in the Brooklyn chain; he could make the most impossible stops, even if he booted some of the easy ones. In one of Bill Veeck's spending moments, he had purchased Billy for $95,000. "Now that Rizzuto is through, we make the Yankees a present of our fine shortstop," was the sad lament of one Baltimore fan.

Richards took the first abuse without flinching, and eventually won most of the fans to his reasoning. "I knew every one's reaction would be a shock," he admitted. "It was a shock to me, too. When you trade a pitcher such as Turley, who could be a really great pitcher, you have misgivings. But frankly, you can't win a pennant, or get into the first division, with one player, even a Turley. At best, he can work only every fourth day. I've got to have ball players of ability who can produce for me every day."

Four of the players who came from the Yankees, outfielder Gene Woodling and pitchers Byrd, McDonald and Miller were bothered with injuries and other ailments in 1954. Woodling, who was a valuable member on Stengel's five straight World's Champions of 1949-53, had an especially poor year, playing in only 97 games and hitting .250. But Richards said he knew what he was getting. "Yes, Woodling had a mediocre year in 1954—due largely to injuries," Paul said, "but he is a great clutch player and I'm planning to use him as my clean-up hitter. I'll venture to say right now that Byrd and McDonald will bring in more victories than the seventeen which were contributed by Turley and Larsen in 1954. Fans also overlook the youngsters we've picked up. They don't know that the Yankees turned down a $200,000 bid by the Cardinals for Hal Smith. I expect Smith to take his place among the game's great catchers. As for Gus Triandos, I'm counting on him to develop into our clouting first baseman. Baltimore's 1954 season proved pitching isn't enough; you've got to have somebody to drive in those runs.

"Getting down to Willie Miranda, he'll show Baltimore fans that he is even a better shortstop than Hunter, and more reliable. And Willie should hit as well. The main thing to consider is that the Baltimore club, inheriting the old Brown organization, had little of a farm system. By this deal, we've advanced three to four years from the progress we could have made relying solely on our farm players."

After the acquisition of Hal Smith, it generally was expected that Clint Courtney, the Toy Bulldog, would be the next to go. Richards knew the little battler represented real trading value, and held out for the best bargain he could make. Courtney eventually went to the White Sox in a seven-player deal in which Paul matched wits with his old Chicago boss, Frank Lane, at the major league meetings in New York.

Courtney, Bob Chakales, the pitcher Ehlers obtained from Cleveland in the Vic Wertz swap, and Jim Brideweser, the 1954 Yankee infield acquisition, went to the White Sox for pitchers Don Johnson and Don Ferrarse, catcher Matt Batts and infielder Freddy Marsh. Paul was especially sweet on Don Johnson, an ex-Yankee, who had an 8-7 record with his 1954 White Sox, and said he had heard fine things of little Ferrarse, a 5-foot 9-inch southpaw, who hung up a mess of strike-outs while compiling an 18-15 record with the 1954 Oakland, California team.

After Paul Richards completed his White Sox deal, he next tried to strengthen himself at first base when he purchased third baseman Billy Cox and left-handed pitcher Preacher Roe from the Brooklyn Dodgers for $55,000 and two rookies, pitcher John Jancse and second baseman Harry Schwegman, who in 1954 played with the Orioles' San Antonio farm team. While the 35-year-old Cox participated in only 77 games with the 1954 Dodgers, prior to that year he was regarded as the best defensive third baseman in the National League. Roe, 36-year-old former Dodger ace with a 22-3 showing in 1951, had a modest 3-4 record for 1954, but Richards figured his

244

slow stuff would be new in the American League, and that the Preacher might help him for several seasons.

By this time, survivors of the 1953 Browns on the Baltimore roster had been reduced to a corporal's guard. The players bombarded with flowers, streamers and confetti during the big parade of April 15, 1954 had been scattered to all points of the compass. Richards said he wasn't through trading, if any new opportunities presented themselves. But he expressed satisfaction with what had been done. "We've no longer got Turley, but I know I have a far better team than I had when they engaged me to take charge of the Orioles in September, 1953. I've been in this league now four years; I know its strength and weakness, and fourth place isn't too far from seventh. We're definitely in a battle for a first division berth in 1955. And, except in rare instances, you've got to be in the first division before you can start shooting for a pennant."

"The first division" was the watchword at the Orioles' 1955 training camp at Daytona Springs, Florida. One of Art Ehlers' last moves as general manager was to shift the training camp from Arizona to Florida. The players had caught some of the new manager's unbridled enthusiasm. Richards promised to have the same kind of a running team which he had in Chicago, and there was the fond hope that some of the "Go-go" of the White Sox of recent years would be injected into the 1955 Birds. And that when Baltimore's sports voices, Ernie Harwell and good-natured Bobo Newsom, discussed the deeds of the made-over Birds, there would be a cheerier story to tell. For back of Baltimore's new team remains the magic word, Orioles, which in the past has stood for some of the greatest teams in baseball, and which again must stand for the best in the future. Didn't Ned Hanlon jump his earlier Birds from an eighth place finish in a twelve-club league in 1893 to a glorious pennant in 1894? Even in an era of slugging baseball, Richards likes to play Foxy Ned's inside baseball and to direct a base-running attack. Perhaps, as the aggressive Paul develops, and acts on his own authority, he will acquire the old Hanlon knack of finding nuggets in the raw and trading off battered veterans for the Hugh Jenningses, Willie Keelers, and Joe Kelleys of tomorrow. And the 1,060,910 loyal fans, who paid their money at the Memorial Stadium ticket windows in 1954, and the enthusiastic thousands who lined the Baltimore streets for the "Welcome back, Orioles" parade of April 15, 1954, will unite in a nightly prayer that Richards will be the new Hanlon who will lead the Orioles back to the seats of the mighty.

Index

John E. Spalding of the Society for American Baseball Research prepared this index.

248

Fanovich, Frank, 223
Farrell, Duke, 48, 122
Farrell, Frank, 109, 115, 118, 120
Feller, Bob, 16, 185, 209, 230, 242
Ferrarese, Don, 244
Ferrick, Tom, 211
Ferris, Albert "Hobe," 99
Fewster, Wilson "Chick," 146
Fink, Harold I., 181
Fishel, Bob, 219
Fisher, Charles "Cherokee," 8
Fisher, Ray, 193
Flack, Max, 139
Fletcher, Art, 30
Flick, Elmer, 106
Fohl, Lee, 194–95, 197–98, 200
Ford, Russ, 139
Foreman, Francis Isaiah, 19, 95, 102
Foster, Eddie "Kid," 142–43, 195
Fournier, Jack, 205
Foutz, Dave, 44, 97–99
Fox, Howard, 171
Fox, Nellie, 227
Foxx, Jimmy, 229
Frank, Harry, 150, 152
Frank, Sidney, 94, 98, 105, 111, 116, 118, 123, 147
Fraser, Chick, 106
Frazee, Harry, 196
Freedman, Andrew, 60, 88, 104–5, 109–10, 113–15, 119
Freeman, John "Buck," 99
Frick, Ford, 176–77
Fridley, Jim, 230, 242
Fritsch, Frank, 31
Fritsch, Walter, 202
Frye, Newt, 214
Fullerton, Hugh, 76–77, 115, 119
Fultz, Dave, 86

Gaedel, Eddie, 215
Gaffney, John, 69
Galehouse, Denny, 206, 208
Garcia, Vince, 240
Garver, Ned, 216, 228
Gedeon, Joe, 193
Gehrig, Lou, 149, 189

Gerber, Wally, 195
Gibbs, C. M. "Abe," 170
Gilbert, Billy, 106, 113
Gilbert, Pete, 23
Gill, Johnny, 163
Gilmore; James A., 137–38
Gleason, Bill, 50
Gleason, William "Kid," 26, 49–50, 54, 56, 59, 71, 81
Goldman, Harry S., 93–94, 111, 116, 118, 137, 147
Goldstein, Herman, 218
Goliat, Mike, 171
Gordon, Joe, 149
Gorman, Arthur Pue, 5–7, 10
Goslin, Leon "Goose," 200
Graham, Frank, 28, 31
Gray, Pete, 209
Gray, Sam, 201
Greenberg, Hank, 175, 230
Greenwood, Billy, 18
Greenwood, Bob, 171
Griffin, Mike, 17
Griffin, Steve, 125
Griffith, Clark, 95, 101–3, 106, 118, 121, 161, 166, 178, 226
Gromek, Steve, 225
Groom, Bob, 192
Groth, Johnny, 224
Grove, Robert "Lefty," 149, 151–55, 158–60, 163, 226, 240
Gutteridge, Don, 208

Haddix (misspelled *Hendrix*), Harvey, 184
Hall, George, 8, 11
Haney, Fred, 201, 204–5
Hanlon, Ned, 34–37, 38–45, 47, 49–50, 52–54, 56, 58–60, 62–65, 71–74, 79–80, 83–89, 94–96, 105–6, 122–24, 126–28, 130, 138, 142, 156, 168, 172, 226–27, 245
Hanna, Bill, 119
Hargrave, William "Pinky," 163
Harley, Dick, 107–9
Harper, Jack, 184
Harridge, William, 175–77, 215, 220, 226
Harris, Luman, 236

251

254

Other Books in the Writing Baseball Series

The Best Seat in Baseball, But You Have to Stand!
  The Game as Umpires See It
  LEE GUTKIND
  Foreword by Eric Rolfe Greenberg

Line Drives: 100 Contemporary Baseball Poems
  EDITED BY BROOKE HORVATH AND TIM WILES
  Foreword by Elinor Nauen

Full Count: Inside Cuban Baseball
  MILTON H. JAMAIL
  Foreword by Larry Dierker

Owning a Piece of the Minors
  JERRY KLINKOWITZ
  Foreword by Mike Veeck

The Boston Red Sox
  FREDERICK G. LIEB
  Foreword by Al Silverman

The Pittsburgh Pirates
  FREDERICK G. LIEB
  Foreword by Richard "Pete" Peterson

The St. Louis Cardinals: The Story of a Great Baseball Club
  FREDERICK G. LIEB
  Foreword by Bob Broeg

Bottom of the Ninth: Great Contemporary Baseball Short Stories
  EDITED BY JOHN McNALLY
  Foreword by Richard Russo

The National Game
  ALFRED H. SPINK
  Foreword by Steven P. Gietschier

Dead Balls and Double Curves: An Anthology of Early Baseball Fiction
  EDITED BY TREY STRECKER
  Foreword by Arnold Hano

Baseball's Natural: The Story of Eddie Waitkus
  JOHN THEODORE
  Foreword by Ira Berkow